Packet Guide to Core Network Protocols

Bruce Hartpence

Beijing · Cambridge · Farnham · Köln · Sebastopol · Tokyo

Packet Guide to Core Network Protocols

by Bruce Hartpence

Copyright © 2011 Bruce Hartpence. All rights reserved.

Printed in the United States of America.

Published by O'Reilly Media, Inc., 1005 Gravenstein Highway North, Sebastopol, CA 95472.

O'Reilly books may be purchased for educational, business, or sales promotional use. Online editions are also available for most titles (*http://my.safaribooksonline.com*). For more information, contact our corporate/institutional sales department: (800) 998-9938 or *corporate@oreilly.com*.

Editor: Mike Hendrickson	**Cover Designer:** Karen Montgomery
Production Editor: Jasmine Perez	**Interior Designer:** David Futato
Copyeditor: Amy Thomson	**Illustrator:** Robert Romano
Proofreader: Jasmine Perez	

June 2011:   First Edition

Revision History for the First Edition:

2011-06-15:   First release

2012-09-28:   Second release

2014-05-21:   Third release

See *http://oreilly.com/catalog/errata.csp?isbn=9781449306533* for release details.

ISBN: 978-1-449-30653-3

[LSI]

To my wonderful wife, Christina, and our three great kids, Brooke, Nick, and Sydney. A husband couldn't be happier or a dad more proud.

Table of Contents

Preface

Trying to find the perfect networking resource or textbook can be a real challenge. Sometimes they are extremely focused on one technology and thus miss the mark, or they are extremely broad, covering every networking idea known to man. Networks have a few basic building blocks: routers, switches, access points, and hosts. These building blocks use a particular set of rules when forwarding bits of information from one place to another, and these rules are organized into protocols. This book is about something that all networks have in common—the core protocols. A very fair question might be how I came to develop my list of core network protocols. It is quite simple—I looked. As proof, I offer the following brief examination of a pair of computers.

For this introduction, traffic on a small network was captured as computers went through the boot process. Examining real-world traffic will be a common approach throughout the book. First up is the Windows 7 machine seen on the left in Figure P-1. Computers running variations of the Windows operating system are quite chatty, but node configuration (DHCP, file sharing, etc.) can make a big difference in the amount of traffic generated. This computer issued hundreds of packets just starting up. After it was started, I accessed a single web page. We can see that 100% of the packets used an Ethernet frame. This is because the packets came from the Ethernet network interface card (NIC) on the computer. We will explore Ethernet in Chapter 2. More than 90% of the packets (and 98% of the bytes) generated by this computer also used the Internet Protocol version 4 (IPv4) packet type. Almost all of the transmissions seen on networks today continue to be of this type, although use of IPv6 is growing. IPv6 packets represent about 2% of this network traffic. We will spend Chapter 3 talking about IPv4 and Chapter 8 discussing IPv6.

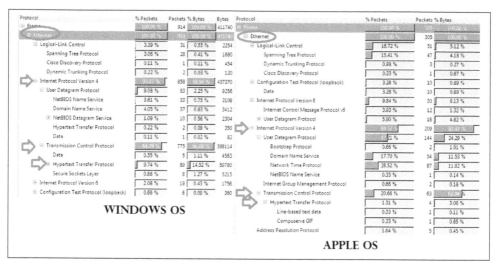

Figure P-1. Protocol distribution comparison

Now let's compare this to the startup traffic generated from an Apple computer running OS X version 10.5 and accessing the same web page. We can see that while the total number of packets making use of a particular protocol might be different, the protocols in use are the same. Some of the protocols seen in this image are not generated by the computers in the topology, but by devices on the surrounding network. For example, the Spanning Tree Protocol (STP) used by switches is a management protocol designed to prevent loops. Many of these other protocols are covered in the *Packet Guide to Routing and Switching*, also from O'Reilly. Note that the list is also indented, with Ethernet located at the far left. Moving to the right, protocols such as Hypertext Transfer Protocol (HTTP) are listed. This is an indication of *layering* or *encapsulation*. Lower-layer protocols encapsulate, or contain, upper-layer protocols. Ethernet encapsulates IP, which encapsulates TCP (or UDP), which is followed by the application. With all of that, it is clear that the lion's share of the traffic from these nodes was from a small collection of *core network protocols*.

Given this information, it is reasonable to say that if we are to understand how networks really operate by understanding the protocols, these will be the protocols to study. Not enough? OK—let's take a look at network communication from another point of view: applications that we use on a regular basis.

On the left in Figure P-2 we see the distribution of packets that were generated when playing a game. In this case, I tried my luck on a field of battle known as *StarCraft II*. Guess what—we see the exact same collection of protocols. On the right there is another distribution, but this collection is from a Voice over IP (VoIP) conversation. And yes, we again see the same suite of protocols.

Protocol	% Packets		Protocol	% Packets
⊟ Frame	100.00 %		⊟ Frame	100.00 %
⊟ Ethernet	100.00 %		⊟ Ethernet	100.00 %
Address Resolution Protocol	0.52 %		⊞ Logical-Link Control	2.63 %
⊞ Logical-Link Control	1.03 %		Address Resolution Protocol	3.24 %
⊟ Internet Protocol Version 4	98.12 %		⊟ Internet Protocol Version 4	93.51 %
⊞ User Datagram Protocol	69.45 %		⊞ User Datagram Protocol	90.27 %
⊞ Transmission Control Protocol	3.29 %		⊞ Transmission Control Protocol	2.94 %
Internet Group Management Protocol	0.38 %		Internet Control Message Protocol	0.31 %
⊞ Configuration Test Protocol (loopback)	0.20 %		⊞ Configuration Test Protocol (loopback)	0.53 %
⊟ Internet Protocol Version 6	0.13 %		802.1X Authentication	0.08 %
⊞ User Datagram Protocol	0.10 %			
Internet Control Message Protocol v6	0.03 %			
GAME			VOIP	

Figure P-2. Applications and the protocols they use

When bits are transmitted across a network, they are wrapped up in a neat little package called a *packet*. Packets have many qualities, but one thing they never do is lie. If a packet is present, it is there because some device or network host put it there. By looking at the packets running on a network and understanding the forces (sometimes good, sometimes evil) that put them there, we can gain a deep understanding of how networks operate and what is happening at a given moment. This book provides the structure (a.k.a. model) used to formulate network transmissions and then dives into the major protocols populating almost every single network today: Ethernet, the Internet Protocol (IP), the Address Resolution Protocol (ARP), the Internet Control Message Protocol (ICMP), the Transmission Control Protocol (TCP), and finally the User Datagram Protocol (UDP). But this is not simply a description of the foundation protocols. In each chapter, the protocols are analyzed by examining topologies and the packets generated on actual networks. Wireshark is the tool of choice. It is not only powerful, but the folks at Wireshark (*http://wireshark.org*) continue to provide it free of charge. An example of a packet can be seen in Figure P-3. Some of the headers have been expanded to show the fields used to make decisions.

```
⊕ Ethernet II, Src: Vmware_b3:e4:e7 (00:0c:29:b3:e4:e7), Dst: Vmware_e7:20:44 (00:50:56:e7:20:44)
⊟ Internet Protocol Version 4, Src: 192.168.172.137 (192.168.172.137), Dst: 129.21.21.1 (129.21.21.1)
    Version: 4
    Header length: 20 bytes
  ⊕ Differentiated Services Field: 0x00 (DSCP 0x00: Default; ECN: 0x00: Not-ECT (Not ECN-Capable Transport))
    Total Length: 60
    Identification: 0x878a (34698)
  ⊕ Flags: 0x00
    Fragment offset: 0
  ⊕ Time to live: 1
    Protocol: UDP (17)
  ⊕ Header checksum: 0x2edf [correct]
    Source: 192.168.172.137 (192.168.172.137)
    Destination: 129.21.21.1 (129.21.21.1)
    [Source GeoIP: Unknown]
    [Destination GeoIP: Unknown]
⊟ User Datagram Protocol, Src Port: 31415 (31415), Dst Port: 43436 (43436)
    Source port: 31415 (31415)
    Destination port: 43436 (43436)
    Length: 40
  ⊕ Checksum: 0x3f4d [validation disabled]
⊕ Data (32 bytes)
```

Figure P-3. UDP packet

These fields indicate some of the complexity and operations that might take place at any given time. By the time you are done reading this book, you will have a handle on the inner workings of any network.

But packets and protocols are only a part of the picture. Almost all network devices and hosts use *tables* to make decisions. The packets are on the network because a table, like the routing table seen in Figure P-4, was consulted.

```
IPv4 Route Table
===========================================================================
Active Routes:
Network Destination        Netmask          Gateway       Interface  Metric
        127.0.0.0        255.0.0.0         On-link        127.0.0.1    306
        127.0.0.1  255.255.255.255         On-link        127.0.0.1    306
  127.255.255.255  255.255.255.255         On-link        127.0.0.1    306
      169.254.0.0      255.255.0.0         On-link   169.254.123.38    276
   169.254.123.38  255.255.255.255         On-link   169.254.123.38    276
  169.254.255.255  255.255.255.255         On-link   169.254.123.38    276
    192.168.172.0    255.255.255.0         On-link    192.168.172.1    276
    192.168.172.1  255.255.255.255         On-link    192.168.172.1    276
  192.168.172.255  255.255.255.255         On-link    192.168.172.1    276
        224.0.0.0        240.0.0.0         On-link        127.0.0.1    306
        224.0.0.0        240.0.0.0         On-link   169.254.123.38    276
        224.0.0.0        240.0.0.0         On-link    192.168.172.1    276
  255.255.255.255  255.255.255.255         On-link        127.0.0.1    306
  255.255.255.255  255.255.255.255         On-link   169.254.123.38    276
  255.255.255.255  255.255.255.255         On-link    192.168.172.1    276
===========================================================================
```

Figure P-4. Host routing table

The table contents indicate how a transmission is to be handled, and the packets are the end result. Inside these pages you will find discussion and examples of ARP tables, routing tables, and source address tables. Tying it all together will be step-by-step descriptions of the processes used so that you will be able to completely trace and understand the content of the packets and the events within the communications architecture.

Other key topics in this book include addressing and equipment operation. Since lists of addresses are not much use to someone wishing to understand actual behavior, each chapter describes variations and application of these addresses. A chapter on masks (Chapter 7) has also been included because masking is such an integral part of every single network. Just for fun, there is a section on cabling too (in Chapter 2) to provide an explanation of why we connect things the way we do.

The sources used in this book are the actual standards as described by the Institute of Electrical and Electronics Engineers (IEEE) and the Telecommunication Standardization Sector of the International Telecommunications Union (ITU-T). Wherever possible, Requests for Comments (RFCs) are directly referenced. So, if you see it here, it came from either the original source or an operational network.

In a nutshell, this book will describe the core protocols, tables, and equipment used on contemporary networks. Each chapter will take topologies and packets from actual networks and explain why the packets were generated and the purpose of the content found in each. The goal is to provide an in-depth understanding of these components, including security concerns and their operation.

Audience

For those not familiar with O'Reilly books, they commonly do two things: provide lots of solid information and help with the real world. I've tried to do the same thing here, making this book an excellent resource for anyone trying to understand networks for the first time and anyone who works with them on a regular basis.

If you have never run packet capture or analysis software, the first time is always an eye-opener—all those packets whizzing around the network, and each one chock-full of arcane information. With this book as a guide, you will be able to interpret what you see and understand why it is there.

For the professional out there, well, we forget things and sometimes get lost in the weeds. When that happens, or if you need a refresher, this book is a great reference, not only for the chapter content but for the decomposition of the standards as well. The expert in the field will also find many details not explained elsewhere.

Supporting Materials

At the end of each chapter in this book, you'll find a set of lab activities. Simple networking experiences can be accomplished on almost any topology. However, it is not always possible to obtain the resources necessary to build and study networks. So, the lab activities in this book will have companion capture files posted on the book's website (*http://bit.ly/RIjCIJ*). For additional background, there is also a YouTube channel (*http://www.youtube.com/brucehartpence*) with videos for each chapter. I've also included a collection of How To videos.

Contents of This Book

Here's a summary of what you'll find in this book. Chapters 9 and 10, new to this addition, were added to provide coverage up through Layer 4 transport protocols:

Chapter 1, *Networking Models*

Many networking texts start with models, but this is models with a twist. This book focuses on the TCP/IP model. This chapter gives models a place in the universe and describes components actually deployed. Backed up with captures and standards, the models are populated with protocols, equipment, and addresses.

Chapter 2, *Ethernet*

Ethernet provides the basis for a very large percentage of the networks deployed today. This chapter discusses the choices of the network administrator while providing significant details about operation and configuration. Topologies and cabling are two other focal points providing further details about actual networking practice.

Chapter 3, *Internet Protocol*

Leaving Layer 2, we arrive at Layer 3 and the domain of IP. This chapter takes us through the structure and operation of IP, backed up by packet captures, of course. Every field is given an example. Particular attention is paid to addressing and how it is deployed, including the entries standard to the host routing table.

Chapter 4, *Address Resolution Protocol*

ARP is arguably the simplest protocol on a network, but it is also a very neat troubleshooting tool and a point of attack for the bad guys. This chapter discusses the operation and particular addressing associated with ARP. It also covers storage of learned information and network behavior.

Chapter 5, *Network Equipment*

It is easy to outline network device responsibilities and assign them to the various layers of the networking model. This chapter goes a step further to include tables used in making forwarding decisions and guides the reader through a series of step-by-step examples.

Chapter 6, *Internet Control Message Protocol*

This protocol defines a large collection of error and informational message types. However, contemporary networks utilize a subset of this collection. For every one of these practical message types, a topology is provided and sample packet captures analyzed to give the reader a complete understanding of the situations resulting in their transmission.

Chapter 7, *Subnetting and Other Masking Acrobatics*

A network cannot be built without using network masks. This chapter describes the subnetting and supernetting procedures and provides two methods for arriving at the correct answer when dividing up address space. Several examples are provided and explained completely.

Chapter 8, *Internet Protocol Version 6*

Limitations in IPv4 address space, IPv6 Day, and the US government are working together to bring about change at Layer 3. IPv6 is the replacement for IPv4, and this chapter discusses the protocol, including IPv6 addressing and operation. ICMPv6 is added for good measure.

Chapter 9, *Transmission Control Protocol*

It is difficult to imagine what life would be like without web pages and web services. The majority of traffic heading for web or other services is wrapped up in TCP for transport. This chapter covers connection and teardown handshakes, operation, and all the flags that have made port scans so popular.

Chapter 10, *User Datagram Protocol*

The "other" transport protocol, UDP, handles all of the transmissions that TCP does not. UDP is the protocol of choice for many of our infrastructure operations, such as DNS and DHCP. UDP is also used to handle real-time transport of voice and game data. This chapter not only covers the operation of UDP, but also the basics of both DHCP and DNS.

Conventions Used in This Book

The following typographical conventions are used in this book:

Plain text

Indicates menu titles, menu options, menu buttons, and keyboard accelerators (such as Alt and Ctrl).

Italic

Indicates new terms, URLs, email addresses, filenames, file extensions, pathnames, directories, and Unix utilities.

`Constant width`

Indicates commands, options, switches, variables, attributes, keys, functions, types, classes, namespaces, methods, modules, properties, parameters, values, objects, events, event handlers, XML tags, HTML tags, macros, the contents of files, or the output from commands.

`Constant width bold`

Shows commands or other text that should be typed literally by the user.

`Constant width italic`

Shows text that should be replaced with user-supplied values.

This icon signifies a tip, suggestion, or general note.

 This icon indicates a warning or caution.

Using Code Examples

This book is here to help you get your job done. In general, you may use the code in this book in your programs and documentation. You do not need to contact us for permission unless you're reproducing a significant portion of the code. For example, writing a program that uses several chunks of code from this book does not require permission. Selling or distributing a CD-ROM of examples from O'Reilly books does require permission. Answering a question by citing this book and quoting example code does not require permission. Incorporating a significant amount of example code from this book into your product's documentation does require permission.

We appreciate, but do not require, attribution. An attribution usually includes the title, author, publisher, and ISBN. For example: "*Packet Guide to Core Network Protocols* by Bruce Hartpence (O'Reilly). Copyright 2011 Bruce Hartpence, 978-1-449-30653-3."

If you feel your use of code examples falls outside fair use or the permission given above, feel free to contact us at *permissions@oreilly.com*.

Safari® Books Online

 Safari Books Online is an on-demand digital library that lets you easily search over 7,500 technology and creative reference books and videos to find the answers you need quickly.

With a subscription, you can read any page and watch any video from our library online. Read books on your cell phone and mobile devices. Access new titles before they are available for print, and get exclusive access to manuscripts in development and post feedback for the authors. Copy and paste code samples, organize your favorites, download chapters, bookmark key sections, create notes, print out pages, and benefit from tons of other time-saving features.

O'Reilly Media has uploaded this book to the Safari Books Online service. To have full digital access to this book and others on similar topics from O'Reilly and other publishers, sign up for free at *http://my.safaribooksonline.com*.

How to Contact Us

Please address comments and questions concerning this book to the publisher:

O'Reilly Media, Inc.
1005 Gravenstein Highway North
Sebastopol, CA 95472
800-998-9938 (in the United States or Canada)
707-829-0515 (international or local)
707-829-0104 (fax)

We have a web page for this book, where we list errata, examples, and any additional information. You can access this page at:

http://www.oreilly.com/catalog/0636920020516

To comment or ask technical questions about this book, send email to:

bookquestions@oreilly.com

For more information about our books, courses, conferences, and news, see our website at *http://www.oreilly.com*.

Find us on Facebook: *http://facebook.com/oreilly*

Follow us on Twitter: *http://twitter.com/oreillymedia*

Watch us on YouTube: *http://www.youtube.com/oreillymedia*

Content Updates

September 28, 2012

- Modified Figure 7-4.
- Added a new Chapter 8 on IPv6.

May 21, 2014

- Modified the Preface.
- Added a new Chapter 9 on TCP.
- Added a new Chapter 10 on UDP.

Acknowledgments

When networking, I live for packets. While I would have used any packet analysis tool available, the folks at Wireshark sure make it easy with a terrific tool and a nice set of resources.

Thanks to all of my students, who, after realizing the coolness and importance of understanding packets, reaffirmed my own belief in those magical little packages. Thanks also to my colleagues for the kind words of encouragement—especially those of you who helped me get started in the early days. Ten Hungry Writers and Bill Stallings—you know who you are. Special thanks to Jim Leone, who not only followed my style changes, but kept up with the editing when I needed it—and all for the price of a burrito. By the way Jim—e4.

In writing the updates for the book, I was fortunate to have a couple of guys who share my passion for understanding how things work and what is happening on the network. They also happen to be really good at what they do. For IPv6 and general networking, I could not ask for a better resource than Jonathan S. Weissman of FLCC. For transport protocols and all things DNS and DHCP, I have the good fortune of having access to Bill Stackpole of RIT. Many thanks to this highly knowledgeable and wonderfully energetic pair.

CHAPTER 1

Networking Models

*Mod-el: noun: 1–structural design, 2–a miniature
representation, 3–an example for emulation or imitation*

—The Merriam-Webster Dictionary

Basic network architecture and construction is a good starting point when trying to understand how communication systems function, even though the topic is a bit dull. Architectures are typically based on a model showing how protocols and functions fit together. Historically, there have been many models used for this purpose, including, but not limited to, Systems Network Architecture (SNA-IBM), AppleTalk, Novell Netware (IPX/SPX), and the Open System Interconnection (OSI) model. Most of these have gone the way of the dodo due to the popularity of TCP/IP. TCP/IP stands for *Transmission Control Protocol/Internet Protocol* and represents a suite of protocols used on almost all modern communication systems. As the name suggests, this is the language of the Internet. This chapter focuses on the practical TCP/IP model, using the OSI model as a reference point.

What Is a Model?

A *model* is a way to organize a system's functions and features to define its structural design. A design can help us understand how a communication system accomplishes tasks to form a protocol suite. To help us wrap our heads around models, communication systems are often compared to the postal system (Figure 1-1). Imagine writing a letter and taking it to the post office. At some point, the mail is sorted and then delivered via some transport system to another post office. From there, it is sorted and given to a mail carrier for delivery to the destination. The letter is handled at several points along the way. Each part of the system is trying to accomplish the same thing—delivering the mail. But each section has a particular set of rules to obey. While in transit, the truck follows the rules of the road as the letter is delivered to the next point for processing.

Inspectors and sorters ensure the mail is metered and safe, without much concern for traffic lights or turn signals.

Figure 1-1. Postal system

A communication system is not much different, since messages created on a computer are processed and delivered, with each piece of equipment involved performing some function and obeying certain rules for transmission. Figure 1-2 depicts a typical scenario in which two computers are connected by their network cards via a networking device. Two people are communicating using an application such as an instant messaging or email program. At some point, we have to decide exactly how to handle this communication. After all, when you mail that letter, you cannot address the envelope in some arbitrary language or ignore zip codes, just as the mail truck driver cannot drive on the wrong side of the road.

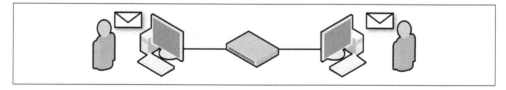

Figure 1-2. Small communication network

So, how is the job of each device or connection determined? An application at the user level should not be responsible for choosing the encoding sequence or the signal type used between the client and server. The letter doesn't decide to go by air or boat. Similarly, the network interface card (NIC) is not in the business of message header construction, just as the mail sorting system doesn't care if you use pen or pencil when writing a letter.

Models are routinely organized in a hierarchical or layered structure. Each layer has a set of functions to perform. Protocols are created to handle these functions, and therefore, protocols are also associated with each layer. The protocols are collectively referred to as a *protocol suite*. The lower layers are often linked with hardware, and the upper layers with software. For example, Ethernet operates at Layers 1 and 2, while the File Transfer Protocol (FTP) operates at the very top of the model. This is true for both the TCP/IP and OSI models. Network traffic can also be viewed in terms of these layers, many of which can actually be seen using a packet capture tool like Wireshark. In Figure 1-3, the major layers of the TCP/IP model are displayed in a message going to a web server.

```
Ethernet II, Src: WesternD_89:ba:fa (00:00:c0:89:ba:fa), Dst: Cisco_2c:0c:80 (00:11:21:2c:0c:80)
Internet Protocol, Src: 192.168.1.1 (192.168.1.1), Dst: 192.168.1.254 (192.168.1.254)
Transmission Control Protocol, Src Port: optima-vnet (1051), Dst Port: http (80), Seq: 1, Ack: 1, Len: 336
Hypertext Transfer Protocol
```

Figure 1-3. Packet showing layers

Why Use a Model?

Before we go too far, let's do a little reality check. A model describes the entire structure. At the beginning of the chapter, I stated that many networking models "have gone the way of the dodo." There may have been good ideas in each, but everyone ended up using one model in particular—TCP/IP. For example, both Apple and IBM initially developed their own protocol suites, but converted to TCP/IP due to its popularity. This section explains the historical use of models and provides a more modern viewpoint.

Even a simple communication system is a complicated environment in which thousands or even millions of transactions occur daily. Interconnected systems are considerably more complex. A single electrical disturbance or software configuration error can prevent completion of these transactions.

Models provide a starting point for determining what must be done to enable communication or to figure out how systems using different protocols might connect to each other. They also help in troubleshooting problems. For example, how would a Novell NetWare client running IPX/SPX communicate with an IBM AS/400 over a TCP/IP-based network? Figure 1-4 depicts a scenario in which several different platforms might be required to interact with each other. Windows nodes are based on the TCP/IP protocol suite but, if required, can run Novell NetWare client software for network authentication. Novell developed internetworking and transport protocols called IPX and SPX. At the other end of the network, the IBM mainframe communicates via the protocols used in the SNA model. Imagine the programming and extra effort required to maintain all of the transactions between these separate architectures.

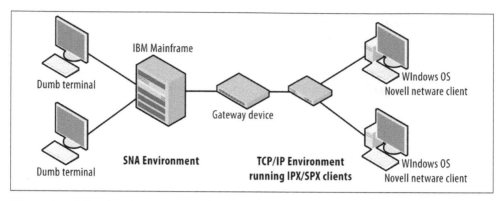

Figure 1-4. Mixed architecture topology

Another example is a network of Apple computers running AppleTalk while connecting to a network of Windows machines running TCP/IP.

As I've said, TCP/IP is the prevalent architecture today. The complexities of interplatform communication are dramatically reduced with TCP/IP. Protocol systems such as AppleTalk, NetWare, and SNA are considered legacy. However, understanding protocol layers on a particular communications device or how processes might interact on the network are still critically important ideas. When troubleshooting standard problems or potential security threats, the models and their associated layers offer logical reference points to begin the process. One would not start looking at the routing protocols if the link light was dark.

OSI Model

The OSI model is called a *reference model*. This means this particular model provides a method by which standards and protocols can be compared in order to assist in connectivity and consistency. Developers can use a reference model to understand how transmissions are framed and create methods to translate between systems.

The OSI basic model is standardized in ISO/IEC (International Standards Organization/ International Electrotechnical Commission) 7498, which includes most of the definitions used here. These two organizations have actually created a Joint Technical Committee (JTC) that handles the issues associated with information technology. This model was developed in collaboration with the ITU-T and has also been printed as ITU-T Recommendation X.200. The ITU-T is the International Telecommunications Union —Telecom sector. Now that we've had our fill of acronyms, on to the standard.

The first version of ISO/IEC 7498 was written in 1984. This was replaced in 1994 by version 2, with additional corrections after that date. ISO/IEC 7498 has four parts:

- Part 1—The Basic Model

- Part 2—Security Architecture
- Part 3—Naming and Addressing
- Part 4—Management Framework

This section examines the basic model, which is defined in Section 6 of 7498-1 as having seven layers: *Application, Presentation, Session, Transport, Network, Data Link,* and *Physical.* Figure 1-5 depicts these layers and the connection to a similarly structured *open* system. An open system is one that adheres to this architecture.

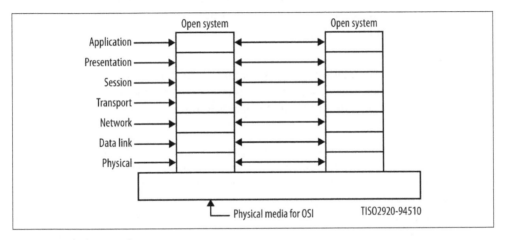

Figure 1-5. The OSI layers

Section 6 of the document also includes the guiding principles for layers, such as:

- Not creating so many as to make the engineering of the system difficult
- Reducing the number of interactions across a layer boundary
- Collecting similar functions and separating fundamentally different functions
- Identifying those that may receive a benefit by being based in hardware or software

Additionally, the OSI framework includes as its goals the improvement of current standards, flexibility, and the quality of being "open," which simply means that systems have mutually adopted accepted standards for the exchange of information. Each layer defined in 7498-1 includes details about the functions and processes occurring at that layer. It is worth noting that this ISO/IEC/ITU-T document specifically states:

> It is not the intent of this reference model to either serve as an implementation specification or to be a basis for appraising the conformance of actual implementations or to provide a sufficient level of detail to define precisely the services and protocols of the interconnection architecture.

So, the OSI model does not specify protocols, services, or rules to be used in a communication system, but it does detail the ideas and processes that may be required. Section 7 of 7498-1 provides some particulars for each of the layers, and these are summarized next (if you are driving heavy machinery, be careful!):

Application (Layer 7)

Provides the sole means for the application to access the OSI environment (OSIE) with no layer above it. The functions are divided into *connection mode* and *connectionless mode*. Connection mode facilities include quality of service (QoS), security, identification of the parties, error control, and mode of dialogue. Connectionless facilities are essentially a subset of those already mentioned, without error control and some security.

Presentation (Layer 6)

Handles the representation and preservation of the data provided by the Application Layer entities. Specifically, the Presentation Layer is focused on syntax that is acceptable to both ends and facilitates access to the layers above and below.

Session (Layer 5)

Specifies both full-duplex and half-duplex modes of operation. This layer provides the means (setup and teardown) for communicating nodes to synchronize and manage the data passed between them. A mapping is provided between the Transport Layer and Session Layer (session service access point) addresses. Support is present for many-to-one session-to-transport addresses. The bulk of the responsibilities at this layer involve connection-oriented transmissions, but connectionless transmissions are also supported.

Transport (Layer 4)

Protocols at this layer are end-to-end between communicating OSI nodes and deal primarily with low-cost and reliable transfer of data. A single Transport Layer address may be associated with many session addresses and provides the performance required by each session entity. Basic functions include transport connection establishment, release, data transfer, and QoS. While this layer is not responsible for routing, it does map to Network Layer addressing. All modes handle error control, but when running in connection-oriented mode, sequence control is required.

Network (Layer 3)

Provides the means for managing network connections between open systems. This layer is not responsible for negotiating QoS settings, but rather focuses on routing between networks and subnetworks. Network Layer addresses uniquely identify transport entities. The Network Layer is also responsible for error control, sequencing, and mapping to the data link addresses.

Data Link (Layer 2)

Responsible for the construction of the data link connection between Network Layer entities. The addresses used are unique within the open system set of devices. Like most of the OSI layers, connectionless and connection-oriented modes are utilized. In addition to interfacing with the Network Layer, the data link connection can be built upon one or more Physical Layer interfaces.

Physical (Layer 1)

As in most models, the OSI Physical Layer contains the electrical, mechanical, and functional means to establish physical connections between Layer 2 devices. The interface is largely determined by the medium, but the bit-level transmissions must be organized into their physical service data units.

OSI—Beyond the Layers

It is common to limit the discussion of the OSI reference model to the seven layer specifications. While these ideas have been discussed here, the OSI model also provides potentially valuable insight into the design and implementation of networking models and protocols. The architects of this model spent a lot of time thinking about and enumerating those items demanded at each layer and what is necessary for each to communicate with the layers immediately above and below it. As an example, Section 5 of 7498-1 includes discussion on the various aspects of layering. These include but are not limited to the following:

- Communication between peer entities, including the following:
  - Modes of communication (connection or connectionless)
  - Relationships between services provided at each adjacent layer boundary
  - Mode conversion functions (Transport and Network Layers, primarily)
- Identifiers such as N-address—unambiguous names used to identify a set of service access points at a particular layer
- Properties of service access points
- Definitions and descriptions of data units
- Elements of layer operation:
  - Connections to/from
  - Multiplexing
  - Flow control
  - Segmentation
  - Sequencing
  - Acknowledgment

— Protocol selection

— Negotiation mechanisms

— Connection establishment and release

— Quality of service

— Error detection

Along with these generalized aspects of communication within a layer model, further discussion regarding each individual layer is included where appropriate. For example, the section dedicated to the Transport Layer details connection establishment/release, data transfer, functions within the layer, addressing, multiplexing/splitting, and management. Where necessary (where a one-to-one mapping between services/addresses is not always present), a layer description will include details about the negotiation of the connections between the layers or even sublayers.

OSI/ITU-T Protocols

So far we've examined a layered model and outlined the responsibilities of each layer. What about the actual protocols? For every protocol used in the TCP/IP model, there is a corresponding (and perhaps more complex) version in the OSI/ITU-T architecture. For ease of access to the reference material, this section refers to the ITU-T X series of standards.

As stated previously, the model itself is described in ITU-T X.200. While the layers are also described, more-detailed specifications are contained within X.211–X.217bis. These additional documents are similar to RFCs for individual protocols in that they provide the rules and guidelines for those actually developing protocols, including state diagrams and primitive definitions. For both the Network and Transport Layers, special attention is paid to connectionless and connection-based communication. One of the major differences between these two forms of transmission is controlling the flow of information between endpoints. It is interesting that the two Layer 4 protocols used today—TCP and the User Datagram Protocol (UDP)—are differentiated from each other in the exact same way, with TCP characterized as connection-oriented while UDP is connectionless. TCP is very concerned with sequence numbers and ensuring that all packets arrive at the destination. UDP is not.

Figure 1-6 is from ITU-T X.220 and shows the protocols to be used. The original diagram is quite large, so only a portion of it is shown here. While a bit old (written in 1993), it does provide some insight into the structure of the model. Many of the protocols are outdated, but we can see the modularity of the protocol stack that aids in subsystem replacement. For example, at the lower layers, X.25 has been replaced by Frame Relay and ATM. These, in turn, have been replaced by the transmission standards we use today.

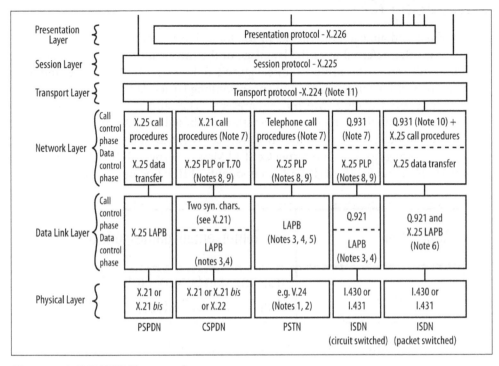

		X.25 call procedures	X.21 call procedures (Note 7)	Telephone call procedures (Note 7)	Q.931 (Note 7)	Q.931 (Note 10) + X.25 call procedures
Presentation Layer {		Presentation protocol - X.226				
Session Layer {		Session protocol - X.225				
Transport Layer {		Transport protocol -X.224 (Note 11)				
Network Layer {	Call control phase	X.25 call procedures	X.21 call procedures (Note 7)	Telephone call procedures (Note 7)	Q.931 (Note 7)	Q.931 (Note 10) + X.25 call procedures
	Data control phase	X.25 data transfer	X.25 PLP or T.70 (Notes 8, 9)	X.25 PLP (Notes 8, 9)	X.25 PLP (Notes 8, 9)	X.25 data transfer
Data Link Layer {	Call control phase	X.25 LAPB	Two syn. chars. (see X.21)	LAPB (Notes 3, 4, 5)	Q.921	Q.921 and X.25 LAPB (Note 6)
	Data control phase		LAPB (notes 3,4)		LAPB (Notes 3, 4)	
Physical Layer {		X.21 or X.21 *bis*	X.21 or X.21 *bis* or X.22	e.g. V.24 (Notes 1, 2)	I.430 or I.431	I.430 or I.431
		PSPDN	CSPDN	PSTN	ISDN (circuit switched)	ISDN (packet switched)

Figure 1-6. OSI/ITU-T protocols

As a practical matter, OSI/ITU-T protocols are not seen nearly as often as the protocols specified for use in the TCP/IP model, although there are exceptions. Some wide area network (WAN) connections continue to use these specifications, and, of course, we still have traditional telephony systems. Perhaps one of the best examples of an ITU-T standard that continues to survive even as more and more communications shift to TCP/IP is in the area of Voice over IP (VoIP). H.323, Q.931, and G.711 are still a big part of contemporary VoIP transmissions, as shown in Figure 1-7. H.225 is part of H.323.

No.	Source	Destination	Protocol	Time	Info
10	192.168.16.1	192.168.16.183	H.225.0	0.02190	CS: Facility OpenLogicalChannel

```
Frame 10: 151 bytes on wire (1208 bits), 151 bytes captured (1208 bits)
Ethernet II, Src: Avaya_e3:e3:d5 (00:04:0d:e3:e3:d5), Dst: Giantele_05:cb:12 (00:09:6e:05:cb:12)
Internet Protocol, Src: 192.168.16.1 (192.168.16.1), Dst: 192.168.16.183 (192.168.16.183)
Transmission Control Protocol, Src Port: h323hostcall (1720), Dst Port: ssql (3352), Seq: 169, Ack: 43, Len: 97
TPKT, Version: 3, Length: 97
Q.931
H.225.0 CS
```

Figure 1-7. ITU-T protocols used in VoIP

Introducing TCP/IP

The Internet and almost all networks in use today have standardized on the TCP/IP model. It is often referred to as the language of the Internet, because applications are typically built around this protocol suite. Figure 1-8 shows the TCP/IP model and some of the more well-known protocols and corresponding layers. At Layer 4 (the Transport Layer), there are actually two protocols present—TCP and UDP. While this model shares its name with the former, many operations are based on UDP, so Layer 4 is shared by the two protocols. Layers 1 and 2 are governed by the local area network protocol, but Layer 3 belongs to IP, with Internet Control Message Protocol (ICMP) and Internet Group Membership Protocol (IGMP) components of IP-based operations.

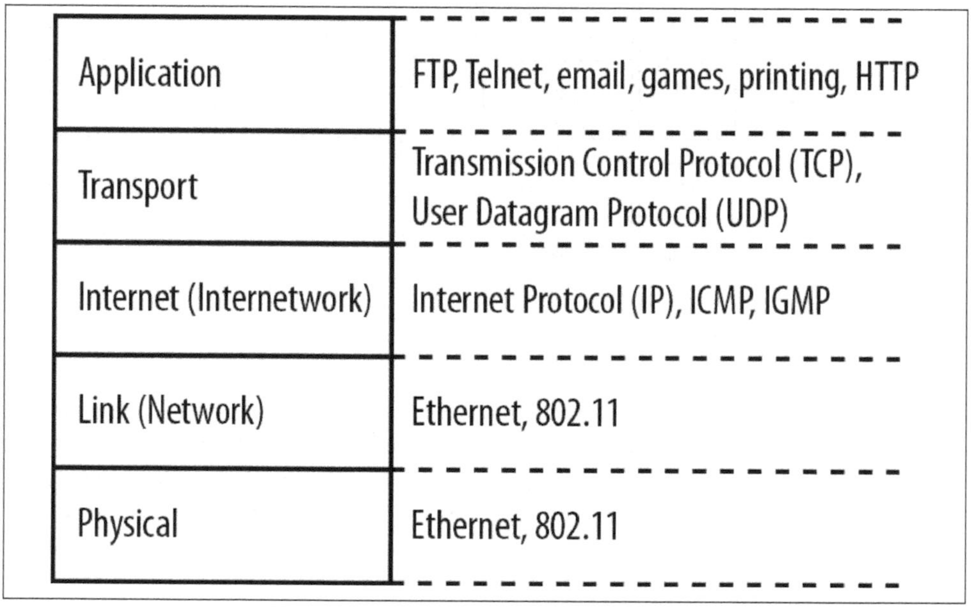

Application	FTP, Telnet, email, games, printing, HTTP
Transport	Transmission Control Protocol (TCP), User Datagram Protocol (UDP)
Internet (Internetwork)	Internet Protocol (IP), ICMP, IGMP
Link (Network)	Ethernet, 802.11
Physical	Ethernet, 802.11

Figure 1-8. The TCP/IP model and protocols

The TCP/IP model does not specify any particular protocol to be run at the lower (LAN) layers. Historically, networks have been built upon many technologies, including Fiber Distributed Data Interface (FDDI), LocalTalk, Token Ring, Ethernet, and wireless protocols from the 802.11 family of standards. Today, only Ethernet and 802.11 in their various forms survive, and even these have eliminated certain variations. For example, Ethernet based on coaxial cable and 802.11 frequency hopping are almost nonexistent.

In a typical network, most of the decisions regarding protocols—at least for Layers 1–4 —are made for you, and the real variation is in the applications you choose to deploy. This argument can even be made for advanced technologies such as voice communications, where traditional circuit-switched telephone systems are quickly being replaced by VoIP. The dominance of the TCP/IP model can be demonstrated using a tool within Wireshark. Examining the protocol distribution for a particular network segment reveals a picture (shown in Figure 1-9) of the protocols in use.

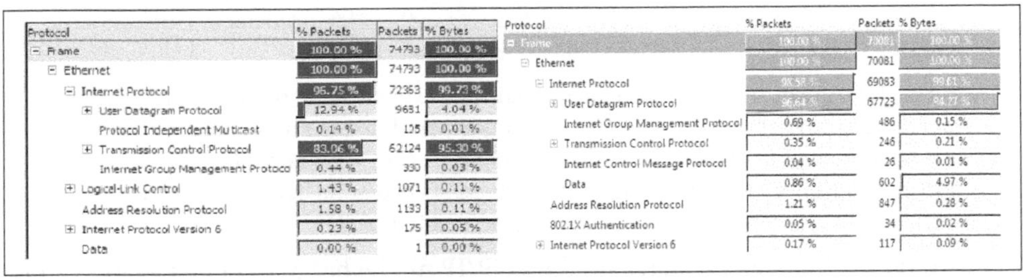

Figure 1-9. Windows and Mac OS protocol distribution

On the left is packet capture data from a Windows machine and on the right is data from a Mac OS platform. Nearly 100 percent of the Layer 3 traffic caught is IPv4, with a small amount of IPv6. At Layer 4, TCP and UDP dominate, with ARP and 802.1x contributing. *Missing from the data collected are protocols from any other model.*

Comparing the TCP/IP and OSI models, it can be said that the functions are the same but the structure is different. Figure 1-10 shows a side-by-side comparison of the OSI and TCP/IP model layers. Layers 5–7 of the OSI model map to Layer 5 of the TCP/IP model.

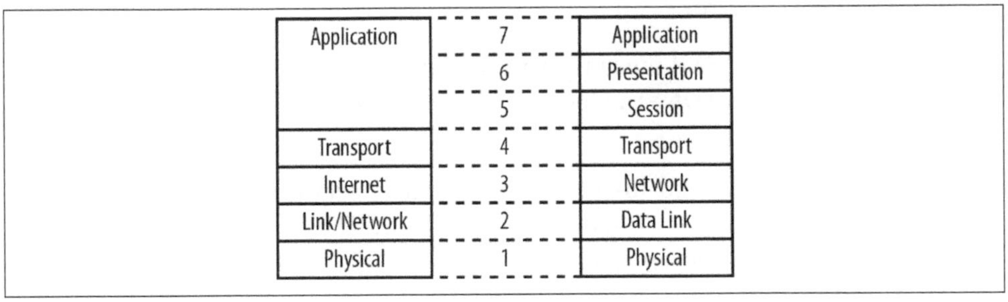

Application	7	Application
	6	Presentation
	5	Session
Transport	4	Transport
Internet	3	Network
Link/Network	2	Data Link
Physical	1	Physical

Figure 1-10. The TCP/IP and OSI networking models

TCP/IP and the RFCs

The TCP/IP model is presented in RFCs 1122 and 1123. These documents, released in 1989, provide the same level of detail encompassed in the ISO/IEC standard. An examination of the standard dates, historical deployments, and the difference in complexity between the two models provides insight into the adoption of TCP/IP over the OSI model. If you survived reading the earlier OSI section, you might be left with the impression that the OSI model is very complex in comparison to TCP/IP. A quick look at the "companion" RFCs that go along with RFCs 1122 and 1123 also reveals a significant level of complexity. To quote from RFC 1122:

> This RFC enumerates standard protocols that a host connected to the Internet must use, and it incorporates by reference the RFCs and other documents describing the current specifications for these protocols. It corrects errors in the referenced documents and adds additional discussion and guidance for an implementor.
>
> For each protocol, this document also contains an explicit set of requirements, recommendations, and options. The reader must understand that the list of requirements in this document is incomplete by itself; the complete set of requirements for an Internet host is primarily defined in the standard protocol specification documents, with the corrections, amendments, and supplements contained in this RFC.

As with the OSI model, each layer of the TCP/IP model has a particular set of responsibilities. While most of these are defined in RFC 1122, those for the Application Layer come from RFC 1123. One significant difference between the two models is that RFC 1122 does specify particular protocols at the various layers. What follows are some of the major requirements of what *must* occur at each layer:

Application

The top TCP/IP layer combines the OSI Application and Presentation Layers and includes user-based and support/management protocols. Items at this layer must do the following:

- Support flexibility (naming and length) in hostnames
- Map domain names appropriately
- Handle DNS errors

Telnet, FTP, Trivial FTP, the Simple Mail Transport Protocol (SMTP), and the Domain Name System (DNS) all have more specific additional requirements.

Transport

This layer provides end-to-end communication services based on either TCP (connection-oriented) or UDP (connectionless). TCP is much more concerned with sequence numbers and handshaking than UDP. Items at this layer must do the following:

- Pass IP options and Internet Control Message Protocol messages to the Application Layer
- Be able to handle and manipulate checksums
- Support IP addresses, including local and wildcard addresses, such as broadcast, multicast, and unicast destinations
- Treat window size as an unsigned number
- Manage window size effectively and allow 0 window size
- Support urgent data and a pointer to the last octet of the urgent data

- Support TCP options
- Gracefully handle opening of connections
- Silently discard improper connection requests
- Handle retransmissions per recommended algorithms
- Follow recommended procedures when generating ACKs (acknowledgments)
- Gracefully handle connection failures

Internet

The Internet Layer specifies the use of IP, ICMP, and the Internet Group Management Protocol. Operationally, this is a connectionless "best effort" protocol concerned with addressing, type of service (ToS), security, and fragmentation. It relies on upper-layer protocols for accurate delivery. Items in this layer must do the following:

- Handle remote multihoming
- Meet the appropriate gateway specification, if used
- Discard improper IP and ICMP packets
- Properly handle all forms of addressing, including subnets
- Maintain packet IDs
- Support ToS and reassembly
- Support source routing options

Link

This is the network interface, and includes framing and media access to communicate directly with the network to which it is attached. Items at this layer must:

- Clear the ARP cache
- Prevent ARP floods
- Send and receive RFC 894–encapsulated datagrams (should also support IEEE 802)
- Use ARP on Ethernet and IEEE 802 networks
- Report Link Layer broadcasts to the Internet Layer
- Receive IP ToS values

Physical

Typically, the network interface card or port defines the Physical Layer. Each LAN protocol has within its specification the electrical and mechanical characteristics for communication on the link. These include items such as voltage level, encoding, pin assignments, and the shape of the interface.

Not all of the requirements were actually implemented in protocol suites running on hosts and network equipment. For example, IP hosts were intended to be much more active in detecting gateway or next hop failures. The reality is that if a gateway fails, hosts simply can't communicate to destinations outside their networks.

The Practical Side of TCP/IP

The models discussed in this chapter are usually drawn from the top layer (Application) down. Wireshark displays them in reverse order, as shown in Figure 1-11, where the protocols corresponding to Layers 1–5 are identified. This packet happens to be from a VoIP conversation. Starting from the bottom of the model, we see Ethernet Type II (also called Ethernet Type 2 or Ethernet II). Ethernet as a protocol exists at Layers 1 and 2, with Layer 2 defining the frame (error control, addressing, etc.) and the Ethernet network interface defining the Physical Layer (Layer 1) characteristics.

```
Ethernet II, Src: Avaya_8e:da:79 (00:04:0d:8e:da:79), Dst: GiantEle_05:cb:12 (00:09:6e:05:cb:12)
Internet Protocol, Src: 192.168.16.4 (192.168.16.4), Dst: 192.168.16.183 (192.168.16.183)
User Datagram Protocol, Src Port: njenet-ssl (2252), Dst Port: slc-systemlog (2826)
Real-Time Transport Protocol
```

Figure 1-11. Real-time Transport Protocol (RTP) example showing TCP/IP protocols

In addition, Layer 2 LAN protocols can be split into two major areas: Logical Link Control (LLC) and Media Access Control (MAC). These become *sublayers* within the model. LLC functions include frame construction, error control, and addressing. The MAC layer defines line discipline and network transmission. Specifically, this includes a method for determining which node is in line to communicate and for how long. Figure 1-12 depicts these TCP/IP sublayers. Sublayers are also found in the OSI model.

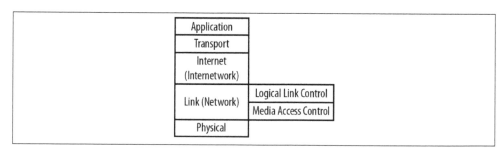

Figure 1-12. Layer 2 sublayers

Encapsulation

Encapsulation is the method by which the various layers interact and pass information up and down the protocol stack. A message generated by an application must be formatted for transmission. On the sending node, the upper layer places packaging around the message that describes the application used to generate the message. This is called the *header*. The package and header are then passed to the next layer down. Each layer completes its own required encapsulation operation, which includes a header.

By the time the message reaches the bottom of the protocol stack, it has several of these wrappers. This process is the encapsulation. For ease of processing, each header contains information regarding the contents. Thus, the Ethernet header provides some indication that it has encapsulated IP, the IP header indicates that it is carrying TCP, and so on. Basic encapsulation and the encapsulation specific to the packet in Figure 1-11 are shown in Figure 1-13.

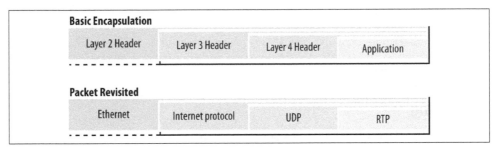

Figure 1-13. Encapsulation

At the receiving node, the same process occurs, but in reverse. Each layer, beginning with the lowest, processes the appropriate information and strips off the outermost wrapper before handing the message to the next layer up. This continues as the message travels up the stack until the last bit of packaging is removed. This process is called *de-encapsulation*.

The packet shown in Figure 1-14 has been expanded to reveal the headers. Each layer contains a code identifying the content of the encapsulated data. Ethernet uses the code 0800 to indicate that IP is encapsulated. At Layer 3, IP uses code 17 to show that it has encapsulated UDP. At Layer 4, UDP uses port numbers to direct the data to the proper process or application. The receiver uses this information to properly parse and de-encapsulate the data.

```
Ethernet II, Src: Ibm_43:49:97 (00:11:25:43:49:97), Dst: IPv4mcast_7f:ff:fa (01:00:5e:7f:ff:fa)
⊞ Destination: IPv4mcast_7f:ff:fa (01:00:5e:7f:ff:fa)
⊞ Source: Ibm_43:49:97 (00:11:25:43:49:97)
  Type: IP (0x0800)
Internet Protocol, Src: 192.168.1.1 (192.168.1.1), Dst: 239.255.255.250 (239.255.255.250)
  Version: 4
  Header length: 20 bytes
⊞ Differentiated Services Field: 0x00 (DSCP 0x00: Default; ECN: 0x00)
  Total Length: 125
  Identification: 0xb23a (45626)
⊞ Flags: 0x00
  Fragment offset: 0
  Time to live: 1
  Protocol: UDP (17)
⊞ Header checksum: 0x5592 [correct]
  Source: 192.168.1.1 (192.168.1.1)
  Destination: 239.255.255.250 (239.255.255.250)
User Datagram Protocol, Src Port: blockade-bpsp (2574), Dst Port: ssdp (1900)
  Source port: blockade-bpsp (2574)
  Destination port: ssdp (1900)
  Length: 105
⊞ Checksum: 0x0118 [validation disabled]
Hypertext Transfer Protocol
```

Figure 1-14. HTTP packet

Addressing

Addressing used within networked systems can also be tied to layers and equipment, as shown in Figure 1-14. Some protocols require addressing as part of their basic operation. For example, an Ethernet switch processes Layer 2 frames, which contain addresses called *hardware* or *MAC addresses*. For example, the source MAC address in Figure 1-14 is 00:11:25:43:49:97. The Internet Protocol uses IP addresses at Layer 3, and these are processed by routers. In this case, the source is 192.168.1.1 and the destination is 239.255.255.250. Both TCP and UDP communicate via port numbers at Layer 4. Thus, a TCP/UDP message possesses not only the port numbers necessary to communicate with an application, but also the IP and MAC addresses necessary to complete the transmission. Understanding relationships like these better prepares the network administrator to build, troubleshoot, or secure the infrastructure. For example, if the administrator is concerned about port scanning at Layer 4, it is unlikely that solutions will be found by working with the network switches down at Layer 2.

Equipment

Layering the model can also provide a picture of device responsibilities. Each device on a network is designed for a particular task. They have different levels of intelligence and process traffic in a variety of ways. Applying the layers to equipment makes the impact on traffic and the capabilities of the devices at a particular location easier to understand. Routers and switches form the building blocks of almost any network. While they have many individual features and can be configured for a variety of functions, they all provide the same basic services when you plug them in, regardless of the vendor. The relationship between devices, addressing, and the layers is outlined in Figure 1-15.

Layer	Device	Addressing
Application		
Transport	Gateway	TCP/UDP ports
Internet	Router	IP addresses
Link/Network	Switch	MAC addresses
Physical	Hub	Bits

Figure 1-15. Equipment and addressing layers

Switches operate at Layer 2 and forward LAN frames based upon the MAC addresses contained within those frames. They also perform error checking for each frame. Switches provide some measure of network segmentation, since the processing of MAC addresses will result in network traffic control. Switches have a variety of management features, such as support for SNMP and virtual local area networks (VLANs).

Routers operate at Layer 3 and process IP packets. They will read Layer 2 frames when their MAC addresses appear in the frames, but their main function is to get IP packets to the proper destination. In so doing, the router calculates the IP header checksum and can act on any QoS or fragmentation information the packet contains. Many routers also support advanced features such as firewalling, virtual private network (VPN) termination, authentication, and network address translation (NAT).

The term *gateway* has several meanings. Routers and network hosts are configured with a *default gateway*, but this is actually a router. It is called a default gateway because this is the network path to the rest of the world. The more traditional gateway existing at Layer 4 is a device used to convert between systems that do not share the same networking model. This type of environment is depicted in Figure 1-4, and requires protocol translation for network nodes to communicate. We might say this sort of thing is another legacy item, but with the emergence of VoIP, the gateway is making a comeback. The language of the public switched telephone network (PSTN) is Signaling System 7 (SS7). A gateway that understands both TCP/IP and SS7 is required if an IP-based VoIP phone is to communicate with a traditional telephone.

Not all devices fit neatly into boxes. An *access point* is sometimes referred to as a *wireless hub* because it broadcasts certain kinds of traffic everywhere. However, like an Ethernet switch, the access point not only is aware of MAC addresses but also uses them to make some forwarding decisions. More recently, the emergence of multilayer switching has blurred the line between processing frames at Layer 2 and some of the higher-level functions like routing. Figure 1-16 provides an example of how these devices and addresses interact within the confines of the protocol layers.

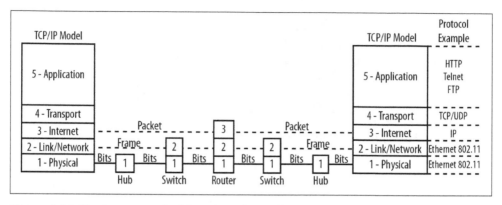

Figure 1-16. Equipment and addressing relationship

Summary

The OSI and TCP/IP models provide an architecture in which the functions and rules for communication, addressing, and equipment are organized. The OSI model is standardized in ITU-T X.200, and the companion documents X.211–X.217 and X.220 provide the specifications for the developers and protocols. The TCP/IP model is described in RFC 1122, which lists the required protocols for hosts that communicate on the network.

The OSI model, now primarily considered a reference model, is in limited use. The TCP/IP model is the language of the Internet. Adoption of IP-based communication in many systems, such as VoIP, will further marginalize the OSI model's use—a factor not lost on major companies like Apple and Novell, which have adopted the TCP/IP model.

Modern practitioners and researchers will be well served by an understanding of standards for communication requirements in widely varying conditions. These architectures help us to better understand the evolution of communication standards.

Additional Reading

- ISO/IEC 7498-1: "Information Technology—Open Systems Interconnection—Basic Reference Model: The Basic Model"
- ITU-T X.200: "Information Technology—Open Systems Interconnection—Basic Reference Model: The Basic Model"
- ITU-T X.220: "Use of X200-Series Protocols in CCITT Applications"
- RFC 1122: "Requirements for Internet Hosts—Communication Layers"
- RFC 1123: "Requirements for Internet Hosts—Application and Support"

Review Questions

1. What is the name of the process by which an upper-layer protocol is wrapped up in a lower-layer protocol?

2. Name four communication models.

3. What two documents specify the standardization of the OSI model?

4. How many layers are in the OSI and TCP/IP models, respectively?

5. Name the layers of the OSI model.

6. Name the layers of the TCP/IP model.

7. What two documents present and detail the use of the TCP/IP model?

8. There are two forms of communication described in both standards. These forms are predominantly part of Layers 3 and 4. What are they?

9. Network administrators typically have the ability to use whatever protocols they wish, regardless of the layer in question. True or false?

10. One big difference between the documentation of the TCP/IP and OSI standards is that the TCP/IP RFC specifies the protocols to be used and the OSI ITU-T model documentation does not. True or false?

11. For each address type or device, specify its proper layer (Layer 2, Layer 3, or Layer 4):

    a. Switch

    b. Router

    c. Gateway

    d. MAC address

    e. IP address

    f. Port number

Review Answers

1. Encapsulation

2. TCP/IP, OSI, SNA, AppleTalk, Novell (IPX/SPX)

3. ISO/IEC 7498 and ITU-T X.200

4. 7, 5

5. Application, Presentation, Session, Transport, Network, Data Link, Physical

6. Application, Transport, Internet, Data Link, Physical

7. RFCs 1122 and 1123

8. Connection-mode (oriented) and connectionless-mode

9. False

10. True

11. a) Layer 2, b) Layer 3, c) Layer 4, d) Layer 2, e) Layer 3, f) Layer 4

Lab Activities

Activity 1—Examining Encapsulation

Materials: Wireshark and a network connection

1. Start a capture.

2. Complete several different transactions from your computer.

3. Stop the capture and examine the individual packets.

4. Find examples of the following: ARP, ICMP, TCP, UDP, and IPv6.

5. Describe these packets in terms of their encapsulation or protocol stacks.

Activity 2—Protocol Distribution

Materials: Wireshark and a network connection

1. Start a capture and allow it to run for several minutes (the longer, the better).

2. Complete as many different transactions from your computer as possible.

3. From the Statistics menu in Wireshark, select Protocol Hierarchy.

4. Examine the distribution of protocols and attempt to determine the models used and the level of traffic specific to each protocol. What is the most common upper-layer protocol? What caused it to be generated?

Activity 3—Developing a Protocol/Architecture

Using the models discussed in this chapter as references, develop a series of rules or parameters that describe a conversation between two people who have never met. Considerations might include the mode of communication, language, nonverbal communication, access method, body language, expressions, speed, and parameter negotiation.

CHAPTER 2

Ethernet

Computers cabled together in a network are almost certainly going to be connected via Ethernet. *Ethernet* is a technology that describes the rules used for communication between LAN-based systems and is considered a Layer 2 protocol. This chapter discusses the structure and operation of the Ethernet protocol, the differences between Ethernet Type II and 802.3, cabling types, and deployment considerations.

A historical review of the current standards can be a little confusing. The story begins in the 1970s with Bob Metcalfe, who envisioned a cable-based network, which later evolved into Ethernet Type II. Shortly after Metcalfe's ideas were disseminated, the IEEE standards committee developed 802.3 Ethernet. Both versions are in use today and are described more fully below. For the information-hungry, some interesting documents to read include the following:

- "Ethernet: Distributed Packet Switching for Local Computer Networks" (Metcalfe and Boggs)
- "The Ethernet: A Local Area Network—Physical Layer and Data Link Layer Protocol Specifications" (DEC, Intel, and Xerox)
- "802.3-1985 IEEE Standard for Local and Metropolitan Area Networks: Carrier Sense Multiple Access with Collision Detection (Original 10Mb/s Standard)" (IEEE Standards Association)

The first paper, written by Bob Metcalfe and David Boggs, describes Ethernet as a LAN system with such characteristics as shared communication, broadcast packet switching (all nodes hear the transmission), extension via repeaters, distributed control for packet transmission, and controlled behavior in the presence of interference or collisions.

While their paper describes operation on a coaxial-based line, these properties have also been central to noncoaxial Ethernet systems. The 802.3 standard describes the communication on a network employing the carrier sense multiple access with collision detection (CSMA/CD) access method. It includes sections for aggregation, multiple speeds, and full/half-duplex operation.

There have been many versions of this ubiquitous protocol, including 10Base5, 10Base2, 10Base-FL, 10Base-T, 100Base-T, and 100Base-FX. Of these, 10Base-T, 100Base-T, and 1000Base-T (gigabit) are the most common and are the focus of this chapter. Network equipment is sometimes referred to as 10/100/1000 (or 10/100), Ethernet having the capability of running at 10, 100, or 1000 Mbps. The popularity of Ethernet as a LAN protocol has forced personal computer and laptop vendors to include Ethernet ports and/or auxiliary slots for Ethernet cards on all their products.

Remember the Models

Ethernet governs the two lowest layers (Physical and Network) of the TCP/IP model. Chapter 1 introduced RFC 1122, which requires nodes operating on a TCP/IP-based network to support the Ethernet encapsulation scheme described in RFC 894. Nodes on the network should also be able to receive frames described by RFC 1042 (IEEE 802.3 frames) and may support transmission of these frames. Today we see both types of frames coexisting on the network, but typically RFC 894 (Ethernet II) frames are generated by hosts. When an IEEE 802.3 frame appears, it is almost always from a network communication device such as a router, switch, or access point.

As previously stated, Ethernet resides at Layers 1 and 2 of the TCP/IP (or OSI) model. Layer 2 is further subdivided as shown in Figure 2-1.

OSI	TCP/IP	Ethernet	
7 Application	5 Application		
6 Presentation			
5 Session			
4 Transport	4 Transport		
3 Network	3 Internet	Logical Link Control (LLC)	
2 Data Link	2 Link/Network	Media Access Control (MAC)	
1 Physical	Physical	Physical	

Figure 2-1. Models and Ethernet

The two sublayers are called Logical Link Control (LLC) and Media Access Control (MAC). The LLC sublayer is where the Ethernet frame and its associated fields are assembled and is similar to the IEEE 802.2 structure. The MAC sublayer is responsible for what is called the *access method*. Discussed in detail later in this chapter, the MAC sublayer detects the carrier, transmits to and receives from the media, and passes frames to/from the LLC sublayer.

We know that encapsulation causes user data to be wrapped in headers from each layer in our networking model. As an example, a DHCP (BOOTP) packet is encapsulated first in UDP, followed by IP. This packet must then be placed in a LAN frame. This is true whether the network is wireless (802.11) or wired via Ethernet. Figure 2-2 shows the encapsulation concept, and Figure 2-3 shows an example of an actual Ethernet Type II frame carrying the information.

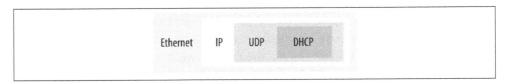

Figure 2-2. Encapsulation

```
⊟ Ethernet II, Src: Standard_44:12:65 (00:e0:29:44:12:65), Dst: Broadcast (ff:ff:ff:ff:ff:ff)
  ⊞ Destination: Broadcast (ff:ff:ff:ff:ff:ff)
  ⊞ Source: Standard_44:12:65 (00:e0:29:44:12:65)
    Type: IP (0x0800)
⊞ Internet Protocol, Src: 192.168.16.195 (192.168.16.195), Dst: 255.255.255.255 (255.255.255.255)
⊞ User Datagram Protocol, Src Port: bootpc (68), Dst Port: bootps (67)
⊞ Bootstrap Protocol
```

Figure 2-3. Ethernet frame encapsulating DHCP

Structure

The Ethernet frame (Layer 2) in Figure 2-3 is expanded in Figure 2-4 to show several fields used to control various aspects of the transmission. When you capture traffic using Wireshark, protocols above Layer 2 are shown in their entirety. However, several parts, or fields, of Layer 2 are not shown. Figure 2-4 shows a simple Ethernet frame as defined in the standard.

Preamble	Destination MAC addr	Source MAC addr	Control	Data	FCS
8 bytes	6 bytes	6 bytes	2 bytes	46-1500 bytes	4 bytes

Figure 2-4. Ethernet fields

Preamble

The preamble is a series of alternating 1s and 0s that provide timing for the receiving interface. The Ethernet II preamble is eight bytes in length, with each successive byte repeating the 1-0-1-0 sequence. The 802.3 frame has a seven-byte preamble with the alternating 1-0-1-0 pattern, but the eighth byte is slightly different (10101011) and is referred to as a *start frame delimiter*, or SFD. The preamble and the SFD are invisible to packet analyzers.

Source and Destination MAC Addresses

A MAC address (also known as the hardware, Ethernet, or physical address) is the six-byte address encoded into the network interface card (NIC) of a particular machine. The Ethernet frame has two addresses—destination and source—with the destination transmitted first. MAC addresses are used to send frames to the correct recipients on the LAN. MAC addresses have no significance beyond a computer's own network, so the MAC addresses of machines beyond the local network are unknown. When transmitting outside the network, the MAC address of the default gateway is placed in the destination field.

Control Field (Type)

This is a two-byte field that describes what is contained in the data field. Figure 2-3 shows a value of 0x0800 following the two MAC addresses. The "0x" means that it is a hexadecimal (hex) number. The hex decode of a Wireshark capture will show only "0800," leaving out the "0x." The value 0800 is the most common value for this field, indicating that an IP packet is encapsulated. Another common value for this field is 0806, which indicates an Address Resolution Protocol (ARP) message. This same two-byte field in an 802.3 frame indicates the length of the data field in bytes.

Data Field

All higher layers of the protocol stack are encapsulated in the data field, or *payload*. All of the traffic to be sent over the network must be encapsulated into the data field of an Ethernet frame. As indicated in Figure 2-4, the minimum payload is 46 bytes and the maximum is 1,500. These values are directly related to Ethernet operation. A payload of less than 46 bytes requires trailing zeros to be added to obtain the minimum of 46 bytes. An example of this is shown in Figure 2-5. However, the padding is not to be included in the length calculation for the IP packet. If the data chunk is greater than 1,500 bytes, it is split up into two or more frames to be sent across the network separately.

```
⊟ IEEE 802.3 Ethernet
  ⊞ Destination: Spanning-tree-(for-bridges)_00 (01:80:c2:00:00:00)
  ⊞ Source: Nortel_05:30:8a (00:15:9b:05:30:8a)
    Length: 38
    Trailer: 0000000000000000
  ⊞ Logical-Link Control
  ⊞ Spanning Tree Protocol
```

Figure 2-5. Use of trailing zeros

Frame Check Sequence

The frame check sequence (FCS) is the last field of the Ethernet frame and is used for error checking. A 32-bit cyclical redundancy check (CRC-32) algorithm is computed using the entire frame's binary sequence, excluding the FCS field itself. This algorithm does error detection, but not error correction. In fact, it checks only for single-bit errors. When a frame is created, the CRC calculation result is appended to the frame. Any node receiving or forwarding the frame will also calculate the CRC. The two values are compared, and if they are different, an error has occurred. By default, switches calculate the CRC of each frame. A CRC error will result in the switch discarding the frame. Typically, error repair is left to the upper layers of the protocol stack or model. When errored frames are dropped, the TCP conversation will be missing packets, as indicated by out-of-order sequence numbers. Clients will ask for retransmission of the missing data.

Bit error rate (BER) refers to the number of bits that we can expect to transmit without a problem. BERs can range from 1 in 10^9 bits to less than 1 in 10^{12} on today's high-performance networks. This means that for every 10^9 or 10^{12} bits transmitted, only 1 will be in error, causing a CRC test to fail. Even in the early Ethernet standards, the BERs were limited to 1 in 10^9.

Ethernet Type II Versus 802.3

As mentioned previously, Ethernet frames conform to two different formats. NICs and devices understand these variations, and they coexist. Ethernet Type II is the standard used for IP-based data packets. IEEE 802.3 is often used with management protocols such as Spanning Tree. Figure 2-6 depicts the two frame types for comparison.

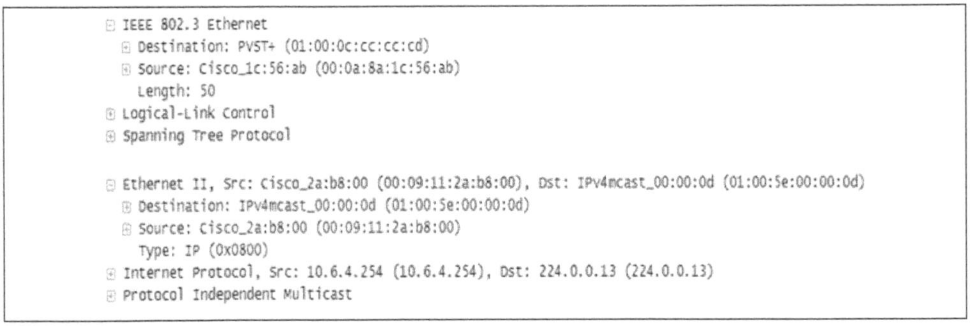

```
⊟ IEEE 802.3 Ethernet
  ⊞ Destination: PVST+ (01:00:0c:cc:cc:cd)
  ⊞ Source: Cisco_1c:56:ab (00:0a:8a:1c:56:ab)
    Length: 50
  ⊞ Logical-Link Control
  ⊞ Spanning Tree Protocol

⊟ Ethernet II, Src: Cisco_2a:b8:00 (00:09:11:2a:b8:00), Dst: IPv4mcast_00:00:0d (01:00:5e:00:00:0d)
  ⊞ Destination: IPv4mcast_00:00:0d (01:00:5e:00:00:0d)
  ⊞ Source: Cisco_2a:b8:00 (00:09:11:2a:b8:00)
    Type: IP (0x0800)
  ⊞ Internet Protocol, Src: 10.6.4.254 (10.6.4.254), Dst: 224.0.0.13 (224.0.0.13)
  ⊞ Protocol Independent Multicast
```

Figure 2-6. 802.3 vs. Ethernet Type II

The major difference between these two standards that can be seen with packet capture software is the two-byte control field. Ethernet Type II uses this as a type or protocol identifier, while 802.3 uses this field as a length value. All Ethertypes are greater than a base 10 value of 1536 (0x0600 in hexadecimal), and the most common of these are shown in Table 2-1.

Table 2-1. Control field values

Hex value	Base 10 value	Meaning
0x0800	2048	IP packet
0x0806	2054	ARP packet
0x86DD	35425	IPv6 packet

A complete list can be found at the IEEE Registration Authority (*http://bit.ly/RIjWY6*). If the base 10 value of the control field is 1500 or less, the frame is 802.3 and the control field is a length value, as shown in Figure 2-7.

 The standard actually considers any value below 1,536 (0600 in hex) to be a length. However, RFC 1122 tells us that the maximum size of an Ethernet data field is 1,500 and the maximum transmission unit (MTU) for 802.3 is 1,492 bytes.

```
⊞ IEEE 802.3 Ethernet
⊟ Logical-Link Control
    DSAP: Spanning Tree BPDU (0x42)
    IG Bit: Individual
    SSAP: Spanning Tree BPDU (0x42)
    CR Bit: Command
    ⊟ Control field: U, func=UI (0x03)
        000. 00.. = Command: Unnumbered Information (0x00)
        .... ..11 = Frame type: Unnumbered frame (0x03)
⊞ Spanning Tree Protocol
```

Figure 2-7. 802.2 LLC

While we're here, we might as well take a closer look at the header of an 802.3 frame. Expanded, the LLC header provides a little more detail about the frame's functionality. Ethernet Type II frames use the control field for this purpose, but 802.3 frames do not possess the same control field. Instead, they utilize a collection of fields defined in the IEEE 802.2 standard to indicate a frame's purpose.

The general form of an LLC packet includes four fields:

Destination Service Access Point (DSAP)
> This first byte indicates the ending point or target for this frame. This address includes the individual or group bit at the beginning. An address of all ones is reserved for the global address. All zeros is a null address. A value (DSAP or SSAP) often seen on networks is AA, referring to the Subnetwork Access Protocol (SNAP). SNAP provides support mechanisms for multiple protocols on the same Ethernet sublayer.

Source Service Access Point (SSAP)

The second byte indicates the starting point or reason for the frame. This address includes the command/response bit at the beginning. All zeros indicate a null address.

Control

These are values for the command and response functions, depending on the operation, as well as possible sequence numbers.

Information

This field contains the data carried by the frame. Figure 2-8 shows that the frame is carrying a Spanning Tree Protocol packet, and shows the general format for 802.3 frames with 802.2 LLC. Spanning Tree is a standard management protocol used on Ethernet networks.

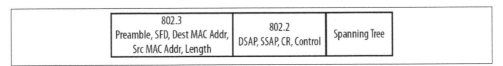

Figure 2-8. 802.3 frame with 802.2 header

MAC Addresses—Another Look

Before we get into Ethernet operation, it is worth spending some time on the various MAC addresses seen on a network. These addresses can drastically affect how frames are processed. Generally, MAC addresses are divided into two parts: a three-byte vendor code and a three-byte host ID. In the example shown in Figure 2-6, the Ethernet Type II source MAC address is 00:09:11:2a:b8:00. The vendor code is 00:09:11, which corresponds to Cisco. Wireshark can interpret this value for us because the value is registered, and a list of registered values and a handy lookup tool are publicly available at the IEEE site (*http://standards.ieee.org/develop/regauth/oui/public.html*). The unique value for the network node is 2a:ba:00. So, a single vendor code can have as many as 2^{24} possible host addresses. These values are almost always written in hexadecimal notation, though the frame is transmitted in binary.

There are three different types of MAC addresses on an Ethernet network: unicast, broadcast, and multicast. *Unicast* MAC addresses are those assigned to individual nodes, and their first byte is always 00. In an Ethernet frame, the source MAC address is always a unicast address. Figure 2-9 shows a unicast-to-unicast communication: the source and destination addresses both begin with 00 and correspond to individual machines. We call this a *unicast frame*. In the case of the destination, the vendor code is 00:19:55 and the unique node ID is 35:1a:d0.

```
⊟ Ethernet II
  ⊞ Destination: 00:19:55:35:1a:d0
  ⊞ Source: 00:11:25:43:49:97
    Type: IP (0x0800)
⊞ Internet Protocol
⊞ Internet Control Message Protocol
```

Figure 2-9. Unicast Ethernet frame

Broadcast frames are those sent by a single node (unicast address) to everyone on the local network, using a broadcast address. This special hexadecimal address (ff-ff-ff-ff-ff-ff) is used for several types of messages, but a couple of the most common are ARP and DHCP requests. A hexadecimal value of ff corresponds to a base 10 value of 255. Figure 2-10 shows a broadcast frame.

```
⊟ Ethernet II
  ⊞ Destination: Broadcast (ff:ff:ff:ff:ff:ff)
  ⊞ Source: D-Link_c4:40:7f (00:50:ba:c4:40:7f)
    Type: IP (0x0800)
⊞ Internet Protocol
```

Figure 2-10. Broadcast Ethernet frame

Broadcast frames are read by all nodes on a network. They are also forwarded everywhere by Layer 2 networking equipment. When a switch receives a broadcast frame, it is sent out every port except the one through which the frame arrived. Routers will not forward broadcast frames. Routers are said to be the boundary of the *broadcast domain*. In fact, routers generally do not forward Layer 2 frames to other networks. Stated another way, no network but your own will ever see the MAC addresses used on your network.

Multicast frames are created by a single host (unicast) but destined for a subset of the entire network. Multicast is important when a message must be sent to a particular process or group of nodes. One example might be the wireless equipment on a network. A controller or node might send out a multicast frame that reaches all devices with a particular vendor code. Another example is the Spanning Tree Protocol. Switches engaging in the Spanning Tree Protocol send and receive frames with a particular reserved multicast address. Nodes ignore this address. Multicast frames will have 01 as the first byte of the MAC address.

The example in Figure 2-11 is a Spanning Tree frame called a *bridge protocol data unit*. The source address is a unicast and the destination is 01:80:c2:00:00:00, which corresponds to the MAC address reserved for Spanning Tree. This is an 802.3 Ethernet frame rather than an Ethernet Type II frame.

```
⊟ IEEE 802.3 Ethernet
  ⊞ Destination: Spanning-tree-(for-bridges)_00 (01:80:c2:00:00:00)
  ⊞ Source: Nortel_05:30:8a (00:15:9b:05:30:8a)
    Length: 38
    Trailer: 0000000000000000
⊞ Logical-Link Control
⊞ Spanning Tree Protocol
```

Figure 2-11. Multicast Ethernet frame

Ethernet Operation

If you imagine yourself as a computer trying to communicate on a network fully populated with a large number of other computers, you might discover that there are a significant number of issues associated with trying to be understood. For example:

- How would you ensure that the correct destination received the transmission?

- How would you determine how fast or how slow you were supposed to send the
data?

- How would you decide which computers had permission to speak or transmit?

These issues are similar to those encountered when having a conversation with a group
of friends. Who is talking? For how long? Can we interrupt? Like many conversations
with our friends, some topologies are easier to manage than others. For these reasons,
every single LAN protocol has a set of rules.

As a protocol, Ethernet is pretty straightforward. As for the first issue, Ethernet uses
MAC addresses to uniquely identify the network nodes. When a frame is transmitted,
the recipient is specified in the Ethernet header. Moving to the second issue, data rate
is a function of the NIC. NICs are normally capable of two or three speeds, including
10 Mbps, 100 Mbps, and 1 Gbps. The NIC either negotiates an acceptable data rate with
the network or uses an incoming frame's preamble to help it sync up with the incoming
transmission.

The third issue is a little more complicated. Before a node can transmit, it must determine if the wire or medium is clear for transmission. This is handled via the access
method. Specifically, Ethernet uses CSMA/CD along with a truncated binary
exponential random backoff algorithm. It's quite a mouthful, but simpler than it sounds.
First, the node will listen for other transmissions. "Hearing" none, it will assume the
medium is clear and begin its own transmission. If the line is not clear (i.e., if a collision
is detected), the node waits for the transmission to complete and then sends its own
frame.

Shared Media

Early Ethernet operated on a bus topology, meaning every node on the network could hear what you transmitted, and vice versa. In fact, early generations such as 10Base5 and 10Base2 connected nodes via coaxial cables and tapped into the central shared conductor. The next generation was called 10Base-T: it dropped coaxial cable in favor of unshielded twisted pair (UTP) as the media, but it is still a bus. The naming convention (10Base-T) is described in 802.3 and indicates the speed (10, 100, or 1000 Mbps), the type of transmission (baseband or broadband), and the type of media or distance, with T indicating twisted pair. Earlier standards such as 10Base5 use the trailing number as a distance value to indicate the maximum network diameter. For example, 10Base5 has a maximum collision domain distance of 500 meters (m).

In a UTP-based bus topology, all of the transmissions use the same pair of wires. The transmission eventually winds up on the receive pair of wires for every single node. The central node is a hub or repeater. With bus topologies, if two separate transmissions are initiated at the same time, they will collide somewhere on the network, causing a spike in voltage or power (Figure 2-12). Just like vehicular collisions, Ethernet frame collisions are bad. In the event of a collision, the two nodes involved must back off from the transmission and try again later.

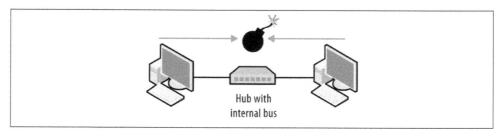

Figure 2-12. Collision on a hub-based topology

Network nodes can detect when a collision occurs because their NICs have transmit and receive wire pairs. If a signal is detected on your receive wires while you are transmitting, another node must be transmitting at the same time; the frames have collided with yours, and the collision now propagates to the receive pair. Normally, a frame from a single node will effectively "fill up" the entire network for the duration of the transmission, ensuring that all other network nodes will remain quiet.

To ensure that we can detect all possible collisions, regardless of when the transmission started, we have rules that must be obeyed regarding frame size, bit rate, and maximum network diameter. Ethernet frames must be a minimum of 64 bytes in length (recall that the data field can range in size from 46 to 1,500 bytes), measured from the destination MAC address field to the CRC field, as shown in Figure 2-13.

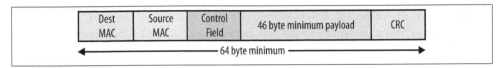

| Dest MAC | Source MAC | Control Field | 46 byte minimum payload | CRC |

← 64 byte minimum →

Figure 2-13. Ethernet minimum frame size

The minimum size restriction prevents the generation and transmission of very small frames. A 10Base-T network is limited to 500 m end to end. The goal is to prevent a node from transmitting the last bit of a frame before the first bit arrives at the destination. If we allowed the network size to exceed the limit, or if we transmitted really small frames, it would be possible for the entire frame to leave the NIC and then get destroyed in the network. Violation of these restrictions makes it possible for a transmitting node to finish putting a frame onto the network before the leading edge of the frame reaches its destination. Should a collision occur, the transmitting node will have no idea that its own frame was involved in the collision. At the other extreme, nodes with large frames may monopolize the network.

Any node capable of detecting a collision is a member of the same *collision domain*. A collision domain is the distance that collision electrical noise travels. Hubs will forward collisions, but switches and routers will not. More on these devices can be found in Chapter 5.

The Ethernet standard includes guidelines for the construction of shared (bus topology) Ethernet networks. A 10Base-T network should follow a 3-4-5 rule—three populated segments, four repeaters or hubs, and a maximum distance of five hundred meters (Figure 2-14). The rule imposes a maximum distance between any two Ethernet UTP endpoints of 100 meters.

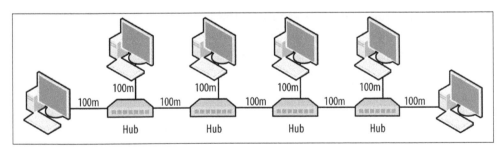

Figure 2-14. 3-4-5 rule for 10Base-T Ethernet

For 100Base-T (the 100 Mbps upgrade for 10Base-T), we use the 1-2 rule, which means that only one repeater or hub is allowed and the maximum network diameter is 200 meters. This rule allows either translational or nontranslational hubs. Nontranslational hubs do not convert between media types. An exception to the 1-2 rule is adding a second hub if it is nontranslational (Class II) and placed close by the other hub, as in a wiring closet. The Ethernet standard specifies that "It must be possible [for] any two DTEs [data terminal equipment] on that network to contend for the network at the same time."

Remember that these rules are for shared Ethernet, meaning hubs, bus topologies, and a broadcast system. The minute a device like a switch is used, these rules go out the window, because the network behavior changes. On a practical note, today's networks are usually built with switches, so these rules serve mainly as background. However, Ethernet default configuration settings are typically aligned with the shared network mentality.

We know that Ethernet has a minimum frame size of 64 bytes, or 512 bits. A frame of this size on a 10Base-T network (capable of transmitting 10 million bits per second) takes 51.2 µsec to transmit. This is referred to as the *slot time*. If a node has a frame to transmit, it must listen to the media for a short period of time, called the *interframe gap*. This minimum wait time prevents transmitting into a frame already on the network and allows the station a chance to reset. An interframe gap (time distance between two frames) of 96 bits (9.6 µsec) also prevents a node from transmitting one frame after another and monopolizing the media. For 100Base-T, the interframe gap is shortened to .96 µsec. The slot time is also shorter, based on the faster transmission time of each bit. Just for fun, 1000Base-T has a slot time of .096 µsec and a corresponding drop in slot time.

When the media is free and the wait is over, a frame may be sent via the transmit pair. If a spike in voltage or power (a collision) is detected on the receive pair while the frame is being transmitted, the stations involved in the collision know that their frames were destroyed, because they were obeying the minimum frame size rules. The transmitters now have two tasks—first, they issue a 32-bit jam signal to ensure all devices are aware of the collision, and then they back off and wait for another chance to transmit.

Here is where the truncated binary exponential backoff algorithm comes in. The backoff time is dependent upon the following formula, where r is a random integer between the two values and n is the number of transmission attempts:

$$(0 > r > 2^k) \times \text{slot time}$$
$$k = \min(n, 10)$$

If, after 16 attempts, a node does not manage a transmission, it stops trying.

Physical Layer

So far we've discussed the operation and framing of Ethernet from Layer 2 of the protocol stack. The Physical Layer specifies the electrical and mechanical properties, such as voltage levels, encoding schemes, and the connectors. On a practical note, users are given limited options when configuring a network. We no longer use NICs that have different types of connectors. Connectors are almost always RJ45 terminations for UTP. Before we look at the electrical details, it is worth spending some time on the cabling and connectors. It turns out that this is where we make many of our mistakes.

Cabling

UTP wiring is the most common network media type and is used for a wide variety of network types and devices. UTP describes the construction of the actual wiring: eight conductors, twisted into four pairs, with nothing but plastic protecting the copper from the environment. The conductor size is American Wire Gauge (AWG) 22-26. The RJ45 jack (male or female) has eight pins for these connections and a locking tab to keep it secure in the outlet.

Figure 2-15 shows both the male and female RJ45 jacks. On the male, pin 1 is at the top and is connected to the orange pair along with pin 2. In the female jack, pin 1 is on the right. UTP cabling is tested for performance and given a rating, or *category*, based on this performance. The standard categories and some of their performance ratings are given in Table 2-2.

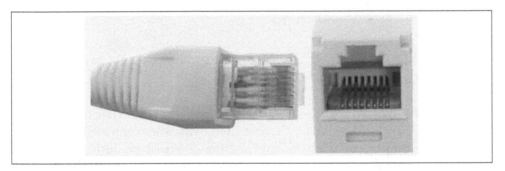

Figure 2-15. RJ45 male and female ends

Table 2-2. Cable specifications

	Attenuation (insertion loss)	Reflection	Near-end crosstalk	Max frequency
Category 5	22 dB	15.1 dB	32.3 dB	100 MHz
Category 5e	22 dB	20.1 dB	35.3 dB	100 MHz
Category 6	19.8 dB	20.1 dB	44.3 dB	250 MHz

Values given in Table 2-2 are for 100 MHz operation, and there are differences between cable types. Category 3 cables are not rated for performance at these frequencies.

As the category number increases, so does the range of frequencies that can be sent over the cable. This means a greater data rate and improved performance. These improvements are due largely to the changes in the construction of the cables. The biggest physical difference is in the number of twists per inch in each pair of conductors. The higher the number of twists, the better the cable is at avoiding crosstalk and interference problems. Figure 2-16 shows the differences between early Category 3 (Cat 3) cable through Category 5e (Cat 5e) to Category 6 (Cat 6).

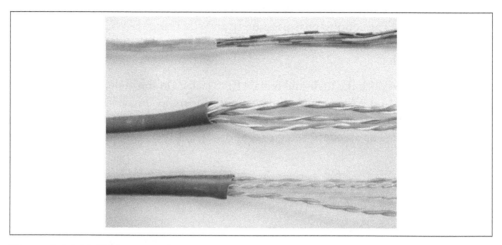

Figure 2-16. Cable construction comparison

A close look at Figure 2-16 reveals several interesting characteristics relating to the cable construction. First, Cat 3 cables (top) have very few twists when compared to the others. In fact, 3–5 twists per foot is the standard. Cat 5e has 3–5 twists per inch, and if we look closely, we can see that the individual pairs have different twist densities. Cat 6 cable (bottom) can have even more twists, but may add the plastic separator and bond the pairs together. This makes the cable an excellent transmission medium, although it makes life more difficult for the cable installer when terminating cables manually, as the pairs typically have to be separated.

In addition to categories, individual conductors can be manufactured differently. Permanent cabling (horizontal cabling) is installed in the wall connecting the female jack to the wiring closet distribution frame. This cabling is fabricated using solid copper for each of the eight individual conductors. Patch cables connect your computer to the wall jack and make connections in the data closet. Patch cables are constructed using stranded copper. If you were to take one of the eight conductors and strip off the insulation, you would see many small strands of copper rather than one thicker piece. This stranding makes the cable more flexible and therefore less likely to break than solid-core cable, but it increases the attenuation of the signal it carries. For this reason, we usually like to keep the patch cables as short as possible. These differences can be seen in Figure 2-17.

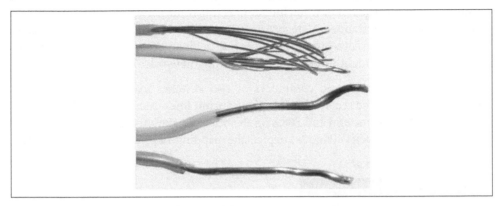

Figure 2-17. Stranded vs. solid-core cable

Both permanent cabling and patch cables are straight-through, which means that pin 1 on one end goes to pin 1 on the other, and so on. These connections follow the EIA/TIA 568 cabling standards. For data networks, we are actually concerned with EIA568B, while telecommunications networks generally employ EIA568A. A straight-through data cable is terminated on both ends using 568B.

At the Physical Layer, Ethernet uses only pins 1, 2, 3, and 6 for transmission and reception (Table 2-3).

Table 2-3. Ethernet pin usage

Pin	Purpose
1	Tx+
2	Tx−
3	Rx+
6	Rx−

Pins 4 and 5 can be used to handle traditional telephone connections, and the telephone jack (RJ11 style) fits right into the center of an RJ45 connector. In addition, modern communications often deploy Power over Ethernet, or PoE. This also runs over unused connectors. Power over Ethernet is standardized in IEEE 802.3af and 802.3at. These standards describe the method and electrical characteristics used to energize devices such as VoIP phones and access points over the unused pairs of the Ethernet cable. This is a much more convenient solution than installing power outlets everywhere.

In addition to categories and construction, another consideration is that there are several different nonpermanent cable types used on a network, including straight-through, crossover, and rollover. They all use the same stranded copper, but the pins don't always start and end in the same place. Standard straight-through patch cables are used to connect a computer to a hub or switch. However, they do not work when connecting computers directly together or when interconnecting some network devices. A standard patch cable is likely a stranded, Category 5e, straight-through (568B to 568B) data cable terminated with RJ45 jacks. But most people just call it an Ethernet cable, even though the exact same cable might be used for a Token Ring network or a VoIP phone.

A crossover cable allows two computers or two switches to be connected directly together by crossing the receive wires to the transmit lines. A crossover cable is terminated using 568B on one end and 568A on the other. To simplify things, we can look at the orange and green pairs. Table 2-4 depicts the mapping, or *pinouts*, of 568A and 568B.

Table 2-4. 568A and B pins

T568A for patch cable		T568B for patch cable	
Pin	Wire color	Pin	Wire color
1	White/green	1	White/orange
2	Green	2	Orange
3	White/orange	3	White/green
4	Blue	4	Blue
5	White/blue	5	White/blue
6	Orange	6	Green
7	White/brown	7	White/brown
8	Brown	8	Brown

This crossing is normally handled by the switch or hub.

When a network administrator configures a device such as a router, it is often accomplished via a *rollover cable* connected to a console port. A rollover cable maps pin 1 to pin 8, pin 2 to pin 7, pin 3 to pin 6, and pin 4 to pin 5. We use these cables to connect from a computer serial (COM) port to a switch/router console port, and EIA232 is used for communication. When connecting a DB9 serial port to a router console port, the rollover cable is connected to a terminal adapter that converts the RJ45 wiring to DB9. Often, these cables come premade with the conversion built in. Figure 2-18 shows networks utilizing the various cable types.

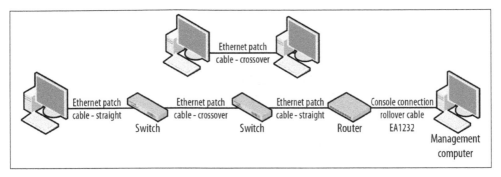

Figure 2-18. Connection and cable types

The top image in Figure 2-18 shows two computers directly connected to each other. The required cable is an Ethernet crossover. The same is true of the switch-to-switch connection if an uplink port is not present. The straight-through Ethernet patch cables are running between the computer and the switch. There is also a straight-through cable between the router and the switch. Finally, the management station is connected to the router console port via a rollover cable. Of course, ports on newer devices negotiate many of the cross-connections for us, but we're better off knowing how things work.

Encoding

Now that you understand framing and operation, and have connected the computer to the network, what is actually going on over the orange and green pairs? When a frame is sent, the NIC generates an electrical signal conveying the binary 1s and 0s (encoding) that are read by the receiver on the same network. The main electrical features of the Physical Layer, including encoding, are outlined in this section.

10Base-T

- Connector type and media—RJ45, UTP
- Encoding—Manchester

Manchester encoding specifies that a binary 1 is indicated when the voltage transitions from a low point to a high point in a single-bit interval, and a binary 0 is the exact opposite. This transition also aids in timing of the signal, and it means that when a series of 1s (or 0s) is transmitted, a single-bit interval may have two transitions. Examples are shown in Figure 2-19.

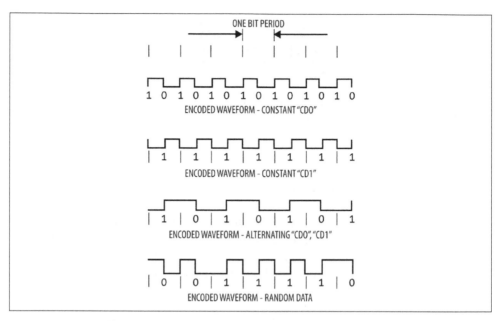

Figure 2-19. Manchester encoding (source: IEEE 802.3-2002)

100Base-T

- Connector type and media—RJ45, UTP
- Encoding—NRZI

For the most part, 100Base-T (also known as Fast Ethernet or 802.3u Ethernet) is functionally the same at Layer 2 as 10Base-T. However, when we move from the slower speeds to the increased data rates, we have shorter bit times or intervals, less time is used to transmit frames, and the rate at which bits are produced is faster. So the real changes are at the Physical Layer.

An interesting point is that 100Base-X (the general Fast Ethernet specification) imports the signaling used on Fiber Distributed Data Interface (FDDI) networks. Specifically, the signaling interface runs at 125 Mbps but exchanges four-bit (nibble) data chunks for five-bit patterns. This is called *4b/5b substitution*. This also means that even though the signaling is 125 Mbps, the effective throughput is 100 Mbps.

The actual signaling is called *nonreturn to zero inverted* (NRZI). With NRZI, a binary 1 is indicated by a polarity transition and a binary 0 is indicated by the absence of a transition (Figure 2-20). A basic problem with this encoding is that when a series of 0s is transmitted, synchronization can be lost. The 4b/5b substitution provides for additional transitions by ensuring that 1s are injected into the data stream.

Figure 2-20. NRZI encoding

1000Base-T

- Connector type and media—RJ45, UTP
- Encoding—4D, five-level Pulse Amplitude Modulation (PAM5)

With the move to 1 Gbps speed (1000Base-T), we have similar changes to the frame transmission rates. It turns out that supporting this data rate on Cat 5 copper is very difficult, so the standard calls for the use of additional wire pairs. Each pair actually transmits 250 Mbps, with the aggregate result of 1000 Mbps. The signaling rate is still 125 Mbaud. To manage these values, the encoding scheme is quite complex, utilizing what is called a four-dimensional symbol and five different voltage levels. While this complexity is a little beyond what we want to accomplish here, the important thing for us is that these symbols allow the receipt of data even while transmitting on the same pair, preserving full-duplex operation.

 All of the Ethernet standards discussed here have fiber transmission specifications. Fiber is typically used for high-speed uplinks or backbone transmissions. Fiber to the desktop, while certainly not unheard of, is rare due to the expense and the additional management requirements.

Other Types of Signaling

In addition to the Ethernet frame, a couple of signals are used to indicate the health/status of the line or the capabilities of the link. This form of signaling is considered out of band because it occurs between the frames flowing across the network cabling.

Link Pulse

What activates the link light? Answer: the link pulse. There are two types of link pulse signals—normal and fast. 10Base-T nodes support only the *normal link pulse* (NLP), which indicates link status. The NLP is simply a blip sent every 16 ±8 ms while the link is idle. Devices on either end of a link send each other these pulses to indicate that the link is up.

Autonegotiation

Autonegotiation uses the same NLP, but for a different purpose. In this chapter, we have discussed full- and half-duplex and 10/100/1000 Mbps systems. The question is, how do we determine the correct communication parameters? Autonegotiation replaces a single NLP blip with the *fast link pulse* (FLP) signal. There are 33 pulse positions in the time reserved for an NLP pulse, and these are divided into 17 odd and 16 even positions. The FLP blips are spaced every 62.5 ±7 μsec. The odd positions are for link pulse and the clock. The even positions are used for autonegotiation data. If a pulse is present, it indicates a binary 1; if not, the position is a binary 0.

The first 13 of the 16 data bits do most of the work. They are broken up into five-bit selector and eight-bit technology fields. The selector bits provide information on protocol type, which will almost always be set to 802.3.The technology bits provide details on Ethernet flavor (10Base-T, 100Base-T, etc.) and support for full-duplex operation. This list is prioritized so that the highest common denominator is chosen. The last three bits are the remote fault, acknowledge, and next page bits, set respectively to indicate detection of a link failure, successful receipt of the partner's link code word (LCW, or page), and that the partner intends to send another page. In the event that an NLP is received in response to the FLP, it is assumed that a 10Base-T node is on the other end.

Topologies

In the previous sections, we established that traditional Ethernet is a broadcast, shared media that uses a "listen then transmit" approach. In addition, if a node transmits without obeying the rules, it destroys any other transmission. These characteristics make Ethernet a *half-duplex* system. Hubs and repeaters have an internal bus, so while they work to extend the network, the half-duplex operation remains unchanged.

With the addition of a switch as the central node, or if Ethernet nodes are connected directly together, the devices may negotiate *full-duplex* operation. In these situations, the shared portion of the network is removed. This means that simultaneous transmissions can exist and a node can both transmit and receive at the same time.

Traditional Ethernet configurations such as 10Base5 are called *bus topologies*, based on their operation. We might go one step further and say that a network of this type is physically wired as a bus and logically acts like a bus. With the addition of a hub, the network still acts like a bus in that every node can "hear" all that is transmitted on the network, but the wiring looks like a star or tree. For this reason, we often call 10Base-T shared Ethernet a *star wired bus* (Figure 2-21).

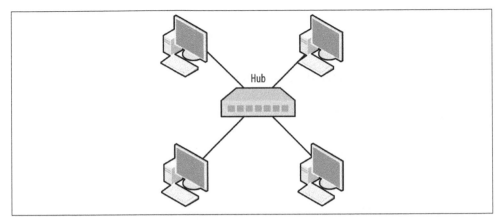

Figure 2-21. Star wired bus with a central hub

When we move to contemporary networks, it is far more common to have a switch as the central point. The network is no longer a bus topology, and collisions are almost a thing of the past. With a switch, the network is a physical star as well as a logical star. Capturing packets is a bit more difficult, as we must set up monitor sessions or mirrored ports on the switches.

Final Thoughts on Ethernet

Almost anyone can build an Ethernet network. The fact of the matter is that because of features like autonegotiation, and since we do not have much choice in the selection of signaling, most of the configuration options are handled without any interference from us. In many cases, network administrators can simply take a switch (no hubs, please) out of the box, plug it in, and presto, instant network. Today, many ports will even autoconfigure themselves if you plug in the wrong cable. Of course, we prefer not to test these features, especially if someone is watching.

The real work comes in trying to understand what is happening when things go wrong, optimizing performance, or improving security. It is then that knowledge of protocol structure and operation becomes critical. There are times when human interference is essential, and preferably it is informed interference.

Summary

Ethernet is by far the most used LAN standard for contemporary networks. Existing at Layers 1 and 2 of our networking models, Ethernet drives many of the decisions we make regarding network equipment. The signaling, physical characteristics, framing, low-level error checking, and operation of LANs are all determined by this protocol.

Historically, Ethernet has used several media types and topologies. Today, we consistently see the use of UTP for end nodes wired in switched star or tree configurations, with fiber typically reserved for network backbones.

Ethernet is standardized in the IEEE 802.3 series.

Additional Reading

- RFC 894: "A Standard for the Transmission of IP Datagrams over Ethernet Networks"
- RFC 895: "A Standard for the Transmission of IP Datagrams over Experimental Ethernet Networks"
- RFC 1042: "A Standard for the Transmission of IP Datagrams over IEEE 802 Networks"
- ISO 9314-3:1990: "Information Processing Systems—Fibre Distributed Data Interface (FDDI)—Part 3 Physical Layer Medium Dependent (PMD)"
- IEEE 802.3-2002: "Part 3: Carrier Sense Multiple Access with Collision Detection (CSMA/CD) Access Method and Physical Layer Specifications"
- IEEE 802.3u: "Supplement to CSMA/CD Access Method and Physical Layer Specifications—MAC Parameters, Physical Layer, MAU and Repeater for 100Mbps Operation"
- IEEE 802.3ab: "Supplement to CSMA/CD Access Method and Physical Layer Specifications—Physical Layer Parameters and Specifications for 1000Mbs Operation over 4-pair Category 5 Balanced Copper Cabling"
- IEEE Registration Authority (*http://bit.ly/RIjWY6*)
- For Ethertypes (*http://standards.ieee.org/develop/regauth/ethertype/eth.txt*)

Review Questions

1. What are the two sublayers for Ethernet at Layer 2?
2. What are the two main parts of a MAC address?
3. What are the three types of destination MAC address?
4. A collision domain ends at what device?
5. What are two differences between Ethernet II and 802.3 frames?
6. What is stranded UTP used for?
7. What are the names of the Ethernet access method and the "wait" algorithm?

8. Counting the preamble and the CRC, what is the maximum size for an Ethernet frame?

9. How many data bits are part of the autonegotiation fast link pulse?

10. Ethernet has error-detection capability, but not error-correction capability. True or false?

Review Answers

1. Logical Link Control (LLC) and Media Access Control (MAC)

2. Vendor code and unique node ID

3. Unicast, broadcast, multicast

4. A switch or router

5. Preamble (preamble and start frame delimiter) and control (length)

6. Patch cables

7. Carrier sense multiple access with collision detection (CSMA/CD), truncated binary exponential random backoff

8. 1,526 bytes

9. 16

10. True

Lab Activities

Activity 1—Basic Framing

Materials: Wireshark and a computer with an active connection

1. Open up a command shell and run `ipconfig /all`.

2. Identify the IP mask, default gateway, and DNS server.

3. Start Wireshark.

4. In the command shell, ping your default gateway (or other nodes on the network).

5. Within Wireshark, examine the packets that result from this command.

6. Identify the individual fields in the Ethernet header.

7. What are the values for each field? Does the value found in the control field match the payload?

8. What fields of the Ethernet frame are not displayed? Can you verify the addresses from step 2?

Activity 2—Control Field Values

Materials: Wireshark and a computer with an active connection

1. Capture packets continuously.
2. Examine the control field of the Ethernet frames until you identify at least one other control field type.
3. What type of frame is this?
4. Why does it have a different value from the previous frame?

Activity 3—Addressing

Materials: Wireshark and a computer with an active connection

1. Capture packets continuously.
2. Identify a frame sent by your computer by matching the MAC address found in the source address field.
3. What type of address is this?
4. What is the vendor code?
5. What is the unique ID?

Activity 4—Destination Addresses

Materials: Wireshark and a computer with an active connection

1. As you capture, start examining the destination MAC addresses in the frames you see.
2. What are the three types of destination address?
3. Collect frames matching each of these destination types.
4. Can you identify the purpose of these frames?

Activity 5—Logical Link Control

Materials: Wireshark and a computer with an active connection

1. Begin capturing with Wireshark.
2. Examine the captures until you find an Ethernet Type II frame.
3. Continuing capturing until you find an 802.3 frame.
4. What are the differences between these frame types? What does Wireshark show you?
5. What was the purpose of the 802.3 frame?
6. Decode the 802.2 header within the 802.3 frame. What do the subfields mean?

CHAPTER 3

Internet Protocol

"During my service in the United States Congress,
I took the initiative in creating the Internet."

—Al Gore

"He [Al Gore] is indeed due some thanks and
consideration for his early contributions."

—Vint Cerf

As stated in Chapter 2, the language of the Internet and of the networks connected to the Internet is TCP/IP. This chapter examines the later part of this protocol pair. The Internet Protocol (IP) exists at Layer 3, regardless of which model you are using as a reference. It is often referred to as a "best effort" protocol, which simply means that IP provides very little in the way of connection or error control. Communication networks rely on upper-layer protocols such as TCP and the associated applications to handle these issues. However, all applications and processes running on the network have one thing in common—they all use IP. So, it is critical that we understand the operation of this ubiquitous protocol. This chapter takes an in-depth look at the protocol fields and their uses, the protocol's operation, and the addressing used for networks today.

Protocol Description

IP has been around for more than three decades. Perhaps the easiest and best place to start is with RFC 791, titled "Internet Protocol DARPA Internet Protocol Specification." This RFC was written in 1981, and the following quote gives some indication of its roots and age:

> This document is based on six earlier editions of the ARPA Internet Protocol Specification, and the present text draws heavily from them.

This early document also describes IP as the protocol that "provides for transmitting blocks of data called datagrams from sources to destinations." Today, we use the terms *packets* and *datagrams* interchangeably, but the goal is the same. Every time a node connected to a network tries to communicate with another node, the transmission is broken up into these datagrams or packets. For example, the request to see a web page and the delivery of the web content returned to the desktop are accomplished via IP packets. The size and number of the packets depends on the amount of information. The device primarily responsible for getting these packets to the correct destination is a router. This also means that every single IP packet must contain all of the information necessary to be routed independently from all other packets.

Structure

IP packets are encapsulated in whatever Layer 2 protocol is running. Today, this would mostly commonly be either Ethernet or 802.11. IP packets have a payload field into which the upper-layer protocols and data are inserted, as shown in Figure 3-1.

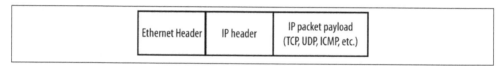

Figure 3-1. Basic IP encapsulation

Figure 3-2 shows the basic form of an IP packet and is taken directly from RFC 791. This is perhaps the most common image used to describe this structure, but it can be difficult to understand. The figure is read from left to right and is in rows of 4 bytes (32 bits) each. Counting begins at zero, so the scale at the top ranges from 0–31. Figure 3-3 depicts an actual IP packet. These two figures will help you gain an understanding of the fields used in IP packets.

```
          0              10            20            30
          0 1 2 3 4 5 6 7 8 9 0 1 2 3 4 5 6 7 8 9 0 1 2 3 4 5 6 7 8 9 0 1
         +-+-+-+-+-+-+-+-+-+-+-+-+-+-+-+-+-+-+-+-+-+-+-+-+-+-+-+-+-+-+-+-+
         |Version|  IHL  |Type of Service|          Total Length         |
         +-+-+-+-+-+-+-+-+-+-+-+-+-+-+-+-+-+-+-+-+-+-+-+-+-+-+-+-+-+-+-+-+
         |         Identification        |Flags|      Fragment Offset    |
         +-+-+-+-+-+-+-+-+-+-+-+-+-+-+-+-+-+-+-+-+-+-+-+-+-+-+-+-+-+-+-+-+
         |  Time to Live |    Protocol   |         Header Checksum        |
         +-+-+-+-+-+-+-+-+-+-+-+-+-+-+-+-+-+-+-+-+-+-+-+-+-+-+-+-+-+-+-+-+
         |                       Source Address                          |
         +-+-+-+-+-+-+-+-+-+-+-+-+-+-+-+-+-+-+-+-+-+-+-+-+-+-+-+-+-+-+-+-+
         |                    Destination Address                        |
         +-+-+-+-+-+-+-+-+-+-+-+-+-+-+-+-+-+-+-+-+-+-+-+-+-+-+-+-+-+-+-+-+
         |                    Options                    |    Padding    |
         +-+-+-+-+-+-+-+-+-+-+-+-+-+-+-+-+-+-+-+-+-+-+-+-+-+-+-+-+-+-+-+-+
```

Figure 3-2. RFC 791 IP packet format

Figure 3-3 shows this encapsulation for an ICMP packet. As you can see, the Layer 2 protocol is Ethernet and the IP header has been expanded. Whatever follows the IP header is actually considered to be in the IP packet payload.

```
⊞ Ethernet II, Src: HonHaiPr_90:d5:db (00:22:68:90:d5:db), Dst: Cisco-Li_7f:fb:9d (00:14:bf:7f:fb:9d)
⊟ Internet Protocol, Src: 192.168.15.103 (192.168.15.103), Dst: 192.168.15.1 (192.168.15.1)
    Version: 4
    Header length: 20 bytes
  ⊞ Differentiated Services Field: 0x00 (DSCP 0x00: Default; ECN: 0x00)
    Total Length: 60
    Identification: 0x066b (1643)
  ⊞ Flags: 0x00
    Fragment offset: 0
    Time to live: 128
    Protocol: ICMP (0x01)
  ⊞ Header checksum: 0x949d [correct]
    Source: 192.168.15.103 (192.168.15.103)
    Destination: 192.168.15.1 (192.168.15.1)
⊞ Internet Control Message Protocol

0000  00 14 bf 7f fb 9d 00 22  68 90 d5 db 08 00 45 00   ......." h.....E
0010  00 3c 06 6b 00 00 80 01  94 9d c0 a8 0f 67 c0 a8   .<.k.... .....g..
0020  0f 01 08 00 4d 42 00 01  00 19 61 62 63 64 65 66   ....MB.. ..abcdef
0030  67 68 69 6a 6b 6c 6d 6e  6f 70 71 72 73 74 75 76   ghijklmn opqrstuv
0040  77 61 62 63 64 65 66 67  68 69                     wabcdefg hi
```

Figure 3-3. IP header from packet capture

The IP packet begins with the highlighted "Internet Protocol" line. This line is not actually part of the datagram. It is important to start packet analysis at the correct point. For this reason, the hexadecimal values for the packet have been included. When a field or header is selected, the corresponding hexadecimal values are highlighted.

Here's a breakdown of what you'll find in the IP header:

Version

This is a straightforward indicator of the format currently in use. Today, the only variation would be IPv6, which would significantly change the structure of the packet. The Wireshark decode describes this, and since 4 in base 10 numbers is also 4 in base 16, the hexadecimal also shows the value of 4 in the first highlighted octet.

Header length

The Internet Header Length (IHL) is the number of four-byte "words" at the beginning of the IP packet. The RFC specifies that the minimum number of bytes will be 20 and therefore the smallest value in the header length field will be 5. The Wireshark decode indicates that the header is in fact 20 bytes long and the hex value is 5 ($5 \times 4 = 20$). It turns out that while the minimum number of bytes is 20, almost all IP packets are 20 bytes. In fact, if this is not the case, something very special or very wrong is going on. One special example is a packet that specifies the path to use for a particular packet. In that case, the header will be expanded to include IP addresses on routers along the intended path.

Type of Service (ToS)/Differentiated Services field

This eight-bit field indicates whether special or priority handling is to be used in the processing of a particular packet. The first two bits indicate the precedence, and the other parts of this field are single bits to be set for delay, throughput, and reliability, as shown in Table 3-1. While there is built-in capacity for varying degrees of quality of service (QoS), as indicated in the table, this field is almost never used. This means that this field typically has a value of 0, as is the case in Figure 3-3. In addition, when QoS is implemented, it is usually done without utilizing the precedence specified in the RFC.

Table 3-1. IP ToS bits

Bits 0–2: precedence	Bit 3: delay	Bit 4: throughput	Bit 5: reliability	Bits 6–7: reserved for future use
000—routine	0 = normal delay	0 = normal throughput	0 = normal reliability	Always 0
001—priority	1 = low delay	1 = high throughput	1 = high reliability	
010—immediate				
011—flash				
100—flash override				
101—CRITICAL/ECP				
110—internetwork control				
111—network control				

Today, when prioritization or quality of service configurations are desired, DiffServ Code Point (DSCP) values and the Differentiated Services architecture are used instead of ToS values to mark and handle IP-based network traffic. The definition of this field and the architecture can be found in RFCs 2474 and 2475. Network devices such as routers can read the DSCP values set in the IP header and provide resources based on configured policies. Table 3-2 depicts the DSCP bits. The first six bits are for the DSCP value; the last two are unused.

Table 3-2. IP DSCP bits

Per-hop behavior (PHB)	DSCP bit positions						Unused	
	0	1	2	3	4	5	6	7
Default	0	0	0	0	0	0	0	0
Class selector	x	x	x	0	0	0	0	0
Expedited forwarding	1	0	1	1	1	0	0	0
Assured forwarding	DSCP values vary with configuration (0, 8, 16, 24, 32, 48, etc.)							
ex. DSCP=8	0	0	1	0	0	0	0	0
	x = 0 or a 1							

There are four general per-hop behaviors (PHBs) defined for Differentiated Services, beginning with the default of all zeros (000000) and progressing through expedited and assured forwarding. For the latter configurations, higher numbers for the DSCP value (0, 8, 16, 24, 32, 48) typically mean a greater allocation of resources. Convert these values to binary to obtain some of the values seen in Table 3-2. The first three bits of the field, called the class selector bits, allow for some backward compatibility between IP ToS and DSCP values. As an example, a DSCP value of 8 would be converted as shown and have a class selector of 1. An IP packet that has been modified to include a DSCP value is shown in Figure 3-4.

```
⊟ Internet Protocol, Src: 192.168.16.253 (192.168.16.253), Dst: 192.168.16.2 (192.168.16.2)
    Version: 4
    Header length: 20 bytes
  ⊞ Differentiated Services Field: 0x20 (DSCP 0x08: Class Selector 1; ECN: 0x00)
    Total Length: 100
    Identification: 0x0087 (135)
  ⊞ Flags: 0x00
    Fragment offset: 0
    Time to live: 255
    Protocol: ICMP (0x01)
  ⊞ Header checksum: 0x18a2 [correct]
    Source: 192.168.16.253 (192.168.16.253)
    Destination: 192.168.16.2 (192.168.16.2)
⊞ Internet Control Message Protocol
```

Figure 3-4. IP header showing DSCP values

Total length

This two-byte field indicates the size of the data in bytes, including the header. In the case of the packet shown in Figure 3-4, the total length is 100 bytes. The maximum size of an IP packet is 65,535 bytes (2 bytes yields a range of 0–65,535), but most of the traffic seen on communication networks is made up of smaller packets. RFC 791 focuses on 576-byte packets (512-byte payload plus 64 bytes of header), and while the applications used on networks have changed quite a bit since the RFC was published, a great deal of traffic still consists of datagrams of this size or smaller.

Identification

Every IP packet receives an identification value to aid in reassembly of packets. Packets too large for the network must be segmented into smaller chunks for transmission. For example, the maximum transmission unit (MTU) for an Ethernet network is 1,500 bytes. Thus, while an IP packet can extend to 65,535 bytes, the packets must be broken up in order to fit into Ethernet frames. The ID field describes which fragments belong to the same packet. The value is chosen at random, but since it is a two-byte field, the values will be reused. However, in any particular conversation, the packets will typically have sequential IDs.

Flags

This small, three-bit field describes how the packet fragmentation is to be handled. Table 3-3 includes the possible values.

Table 3-3. Flag values

Bit	Values
Bit 0	Reserved (always 0)
Bit 1	If 0, the packet may be fragmented; if 1, do not fragment
Bit 2	If 0, this is the last fragment; if 1, there are more fragments to come

With small packets, the value of this field will be 000. If a packet is fragmented, the flags in the fragments will vary depending on their order. A node may specify that a packet is not to be fragmented. In this case, should the packet exceed the MTU for the network, there is a very good chance it will be dropped.

Fragment offset

This 13-bit field is used in conjunction with the identification field (or fragment ID). Once a packet has been broken up, each part is given the same ID. However, when the packets are collected together, some method must be used to determine their proper order. The fragment offset provides the value (in bytes) of a particular fragment's position. An example of this fragmentation is shown in Figure 3-5. Pinging the address 10.1.1.253 with a payload slightly larger than 1,500 bytes results in the conversation shown in Figure 3-6.

```
⊞ Ethernet II, Src: Intel_c8:ad:30 (00:0c:f1:c8:ad:30), Dst: Cisco_b5:05:40 (00:07:50:b5:05:40)
⊟ Internet Protocol, Src: 10.1.1.1 (10.1.1.1), Dst: 10.1.1.253 (10.1.1.253)
     Version: 4
     Header length: 20 bytes
  ⊞ Differentiated Services Field: 0x00 (DSCP 0x00: Default; ECN: 0x00)
     Total Length: 1500
     Identification: 0x1d66 (7526)
  ⊞ Flags: 0x02 (More Fragments)
     Fragment offset: 0
     Time to live: 128
     Protocol: ICMP (0x01)
  ⊞ Header checksum: 0xe0bb [correct]
     Source: 10.1.1.1 (10.1.1.1)
     Destination: 10.1.1.253 (10.1.1.253)
     Reassembled IP in frame: 17
⊞ Data (1480 bytes)
⊞ Ethernet II, Src: Intel_c8:ad:30 (00:0c:f1:c8:ad:30), Dst: Cisco_b5:05:40 (00:07:50:b5:05:40)
⊟ Internet Protocol, Src: 10.1.1.1 (10.1.1.1), Dst: 10.1.1.253 (10.1.1.253)
     Version: 4
     Header length: 20 bytes
  ⊞ Differentiated Services Field: 0x00 (DSCP 0x00: Default; ECN: 0x00)
     Total Length: 548
     Identification: 0x1d66 (7526)
  ⊞ Flags: 0x00
     Fragment offset: 1480
     Time to live: 128
     Protocol: ICMP (0x01)
  ⊞ Header checksum: 0x03bb [correct]
     Source: 10.1.1.1 (10.1.1.1)
     Destination: 10.1.1.253 (10.1.1.253)
  ⊞ [IP Fragments (2008 bytes): #16(1480), #17(528)]
⊞ Internet Control Message Protocol
```

Figure 3-5. Sequential fragmented packets

```
16 18.673969          10.1.1.1          10.1.1.253        IP      Fragmented IP protocol
17 18.673990          10.1.1.1          10.1.1.253        ICMP    Echo (ping) request
18 18.677451          10.1.1.253        10.1.1.1          IP      Fragmented IP protocol
19 18.677766          10.1.1.253        10.1.1.1          ICMP    Echo (ping) reply
```

Figure 3-6. Fragmentation conversation

Figure 3-6 is an ICMP echo request exchange between the two endpoints. Notice that two packets are sent in one direction before the corresponding response is received. The first two packets are then decoded. By examining the IP header in Figure 3-5, you can see that the two packets have the same ID number (7526), but the fragment offsets are different. This is because they are two parts of the same message. The first packet has an offset of 0 because it is the start of the message. The second has an offset of 1480. (The Ethernet MTU is 1500; subtracting 20 bytes for the IP header in the second packet fixes the offset at 1480.) The offset of this first packet must be a multiple of eight.

Examining the flags field, you can see that the first packet (packet 16) has a value of 0x02, indicating more fragments to come, while the second (packet 17) has a value of 0x00, indicating that there are no further packets. The value 0x02 may be a bit confusing, but recall that this is a three-bit field. Since hexadecimal numbers are four bits long, Wireshark is simply borrowing the neighboring bit, which is 0.

Time to live

At Layer 3, to provide some protection from routing loops and to remove continuously circulating datagrams, we use the time to live (TTL) value. This is the number of hops that this packet is permitted to make on the network. Each router decrements this field by 1, and when the value reaches 0, the packet must not be forwarded. RFC 791 refers to this as an actual lifetime in seconds, with each router taking approximately 1 second to process the packet. However, since modern routers process packets very quickly and no router will decrement the field by less than 1 (or more than 1), this value really indicates the hop count.

Protocol

This eight-bit field provides an indication as to what is being carried by the IP packet. This is necessary for the next process to correctly parse the subsequent header information. RFC 790 contains most of the assigned numbers used in networks today, including the values used in the protocol field. However, the most common values seen will be hexadecimal 0x01 (1—ICMP), 0x11 (17—UDP), and 0x06 (6—TCP). The value shown in Figure 3-3 indicates that ICMP is encapsulated.

Header checksum

This is a 16-bit one's complement of the one's complement sum of the 16-bit words in the header. The packet capture in Figure 3-3 returns the value 0x949d. Refer to Chapter 6 for an example of one's complement addition.

Source and destination IP addresses

The last two fields normally used are the IP addresses of the nodes involved in the transmission. In this case, the four-byte source is 192.168.15.103 and the destination is 192.168.15.1. Looking at the hexadecimal, the values c0a80f67 and c0a80f01 can be seen as the last part of the header. "Addressing" on page 56 provides greater insight into the various IP addresses seen in these fields.

Options

In comparing Figure 3-2 and Figure 3-3, you'll see that the options field is absent from the live packet. This is normal for standard network transmissions. RFC 791 specifies that while the options field must be supported, it may or may not appear in packets. This is a variable-length field consisting of the option type, option parameters, and any additional data required. Options can be used in the case where a particular feature or test is desired. For example, if an administrator wishes to use a particular pathway between two hosts, the specific routers to be followed can be specified in the IP packet. Additionally, there may be some security requirements for traffic that can be described in the options field. Options may also be configured to be part of any fragments that are created. In Figure 3-7, *ping* was used to recover the route taken by packets for the first couple of hops. Notice that the number of hops desired can vary, so the field size also varies. Figure 3-7 shows the result of running the command ping -r 2 172.30.100.1, which asks that the first two hops encountered be recorded.

```
C:\WINDOWS\system32\cmd.exe                                          - □ ×
     Minimum = 0ms, Maximum = 1ms, Average = 0ms

C:\Documents and Settings\Administrator>ping -r 2 172.30.100.1

Pinging 172.30.100.1 with 32 bytes of data:

Reply from 172.30.100.1: bytes=32 time<1ms TTL=63
    Route: 172.30.100.2 ->
           172.30.100.1
Reply from 172.30.100.1: bytes=32 time<1ms TTL=63
    Route: 172.30.100.2 ->
           172.30.100.1
Reply from 172.30.100.1: bytes=32 time<1ms TTL=63
    Route: 172.30.100.2 ->
           172.30.100.1
Reply from 172.30.100.1: bytes=32 time<1ms TTL=63
    Route: 172.30.100.2 ->
           172.30.100.1

Ping statistics for 172.30.100.1:
    Packets: Sent = 4, Received = 4, Lost = 0 (0% loss),
Approximate round trip times in milli-seconds:
    Minimum = 0ms, Maximum = 0ms, Average = 0ms

C:\Documents and Settings\Administrator>
```

Figure 3-7. Record route output

The accompanying packet capture shown in Figure 3-8 has been expanded to show the options field. This packet comes from the destination, meaning that the source host requested that the information be included in the response. In addition, the header length, normally 20 bytes, is now 32. The extra 12 bytes include the option type field (the record route option has a value of 7), the length field (1 byte with a value of 11), a pointer indicating the next route data entry to be processed, and the two addresses returned (8 bytes). The final byte is the end flag.

```
⊞ Ethernet II, Src: Cisco_1b:5c:00 (00:1a:30:1b:5c:00), Dst: Intel_10:61:8c (00:07:e9:10:61:8c)
⊟ Internet Protocol, Src: 172.30.100.1 (172.30.100.1), Dst: 10.110.100.41 (10.110.100.41)
     Version: 4
     Header length: 32 bytes
  ⊞ Differentiated Services Field: 0x00 (DSCP 0x00: Default; ECN: 0x00)
     Total Length: 72
     Identification: 0x1f63 (8035)
  ⊞ Flags: 0x00
     Fragment offset: 0
     Time to live: 63
     Protocol: ICMP (0x01)
  ⊞ Header checksum: 0x8670 [correct]
     Source: 172.30.100.1 (172.30.100.1)
     Destination: 10.110.100.41 (10.110.100.41)
  ⊟ Options: (12 bytes)
     ⊟ Record route (11 bytes)
        Pointer: 12
        172.30.100.2
        172.30.100.1
        EOL
⊞ Internet Control Message Protocol
```

Figure 3-8. IP header with options

Addressing

IP addresses are written in what is called *dotted quad* four-byte addressing. This simply means that there are four numbers in every IPv4 address and that these four values are each one byte in length and separated by a decimal point. For example, in Figure 3-3 the source IP address is 192.168.15.103. Because each number is a single byte in length, the range for each is 0–255. The corresponding binary and hexadecimal ranges are 00000000–11111111 and 00–ff, respectively. While it is not obvious, each IP address has a network portion and a host portion that is determined by the mask, which we'll look at shortly.

IP addresses are also grouped into *classes*. These classes vary in the size of the network and the number of hosts in each. Table 3-4 provides the ranges for each class.

Table 3-4. IP classes

Class	Range of the first octet	Value of the first bits in binary	Number of possible networks	Number of possible hosts per network
A	0–127	0	128	16,777,216
B	128–191	10	16,364	65,636
C	192–223	110	2,097,152	256
D	224–239	1110	NA	NA
E	240–255	1111	NA	NA

For example, Rochester Institute of Technology (RIT) has a network address of 129.21.0.0. This means all of the network hosts within RIT will begin with the same network ID, 129.21. In addition, based on the information in Table 3-4, there are 65,536 possible hosts within the RIT network, and there are fewer than 17,000 networks of this size or larger. Examining the binary for the first octet (129) returns 10000001, which corresponds to the binary pattern for a class B network.

Each class of address has a *mask* associated with it. The purpose of the mask is to determine the network for a particular address. Table 3-5 provides these values.

Table 3-5. IP class masks

Class	Mask	Network addressing	Host addressing
A	255.0.0.0	7 bits	24 bits
B	255.255.0.0	14 bits	16 bits
C	255.255.255.0	21 bits	8 bits

The method used to determine the network is called *ANDing*. By taking the IP address and ANDing it with the mask associated with the network, you can calculate the network ID. The logical AND operation takes two inputs and compares them. Anytime a value is ANDed with a 0, the result is 0. Converting an RIT address to binary results in the following:

129.21.199.200	10000001 .00010101 .11000111 . 11001000
255.255.0.0	*11111111 .11111111 .00000000 . 00000000*
After ANDing	10000001 .00010101 .00000000 . 00000000

The reason the network ID must be calculated is that forwarding decisions, for hosts and routers, are made based on the network ID. Every network device performs these calculations. Taken another way, the binary 1s indicate the network portion and the 0s indicate the host portion. This process is covered in greater detail in Chapter 7. The network and host portions are also referred to as the *prefix* and *suffix*. It is important to remember that the prefix and suffix are determined by the mask.

In addition to the classes of address, there are many special IP addresses that are reserved. These are described in Table 3-6.

Table 3-6. Reserved IP addresses

Binary prefix	Binary suffix	Type and example	Purpose
All zeros 00000...	All zeros 00000...	Identifies the host 0.0.0.0	Used for DHCP to obtain a working IP address
IP address (network portion)	All zeros 00000...	Network ID 129.21.0.0	Specifies a particular network
IP address (network portion)	All ones 11111...	Directed broadcast 129.21.255.255	Broadcast packet to a particular network
All ones 11111...	All ones 11111...	Limited broadcast	Broadcast packet to the current network
127	Anything	Loopback 127.0.0.1	Used for testing or identifying the local host

There are a couple of other special addresses that must be included in this discussion. Anyone running a network in his own home or small office probably recognizes the address 192.168.1.1. This address is part of a collection of addresses (one for each class) specified for use with network address translation, or NAT. While NAT is a subject for another chapter, the basic idea is that private addressing or addresses not present on the public Internet are used whenever NAT is deployed. Table 3-7 provides the complete list.

Table 3-7. Private IP address ranges

Class	Address range
A	10.0.0.0–10.255.255.255
B	172.16.0.0–172.31.255.255
C	192.168.0.0–192.168.255.255

For more information about NAT, good places to start are RFC 1918 for the addressing and RFC 1631 for NAT structure and operation.

There is one other address range that is quite common, but is often confused with what might be default settings or allocated to Microsoft. The address range in question is 169.254.0.0–169.254.255.255. This set of addresses is set aside for the IETF Zero Configuration standard. This standard describes operation and requirements for a network running without infrastructure support. This means that in the absence of DHCP or DNS, the network will still be operational (to a certain extent), because the nodes will still have IP addresses automatically assigned. Figure 3-9 depicts an example of Zero-Conf addressing.

```
Ethernet adapter Local Area Connection 1:

        Connection-specific DNS Suffix   . :
        Autoconfiguration IP Address. . . : 169.254.200.104
        Subnet Mask . . . . . . . . . . . : 255.255.0.0
        Default Gateway . . . . . . . . . :
```

Figure 3-9. IP ZeroConf example

Sample Host Configuration

When operating on a network, four numbers are typically required: IP address, mask, default gateway (router), and DNS server. These values are mostly commonly acquired via a DHCP server. The output shown in Figure 3-10 is a sample configuration from a Windows host. To do this yourself, open a command prompt (type **cmd** in the Run box and press Enter) and issue the command **ipconfig /all**.

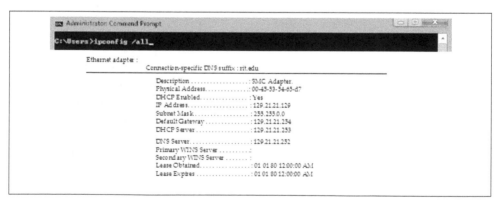

Figure 3-10. Sample host configuration

If any one of these numbers is missing, some portion of network communications will be hobbled. For example, without the DNS entry, names such as *www.rit.edu* or *www.google.com* couldn't be found. The IP addresses, if known, would have to be typed into the web browser. Without the default gateway entry, there would be no way to communicate with nodes outside of the current network, because the host would not know the address of the router used to send packets externally.

Operation

IP is one of the protocols that can really make you wonder at the success of the Internet, at least in terms of its operation. IP packets have no knowledge of the pathway to the endpoint, little in the way of error control, and nothing to ensure their delivery. To quote from RFC 791:

> The internet protocol treats each internet datagram as an independent entity unrelated to any other internet datagram. There are no connections or logical circuits (virtual or otherwise).

Yet, as packets are cast into the void of interconnected networks, somehow they reach their destinations. The key is that all routers and hosts follow the same set of rules. The amazing part is that these devices are run by humans who typically *do not* follow the rules.

Once a host initiates a communication via an application, some chunk of data, such as an email message, document, or Facebook post, is inserted into a TCP or UDP datagram. This datagram is in turn placed inside an IP packet. The result of this process can be seen in any of the TCP-based captures in this book, or in the encapsulation examples. The IP packet is created after examining the host routing table. This step is critical because the sending host must determine whether the packet is to be sent to a node on the local network or one that is outside, thus changing the content of the IP header.

If the packet belongs to the current network and the appropriate header is constructed, no more has to be done with the IP header except when it is received by the destination. Packets destined for the current network get to the destination via a local forwarding based on MAC addresses and ARP. Recall that ARP maps IP addresses to MAC addresses. When received, the header checksum will be calculated and the packet will be delivered to the proper application.

If the packet is to be sent off of the current network, the packet must be routed, so it is sent to the host's default gateway. The default gateway is a router interface that is reachable by the host. A simple example is a home gateway such as a Linksys router. Linksys provides (among other things) routing services for the internal hosts, meaning that computers on the home network send packets to the router for forwarding to either the next router in line (the next hop) or the final destination. Like hosts, routers participate in the ARP protocol, understand ICMP, and have a routing table. However, the router's routing table has a slightly different use than the host's routing table—it is filled with information about other networks rather than information about the current network.

In their basic form and operation, routers process the IP headers and simply forward the packets on—they do not modify the content of either the header or the IP packets. With advanced operations, certainly there are times when this is not the case.

Digging a Little Deeper—What Addressing Is Sufficient?

There are many types of addressing used in a modern communication network. These addresses may exist at different layers of our networking models, be encoded in hardware, or be easily manipulated in software. Addressing can even be dynamically generated as needed, as with TCP/UDP ports. But what addressing is actually required? Why does a typical communication use at least three different addresses?

To understand how we arrived at the current state of affairs, it might be appropriate to imagine scenarios in which networks try to get by with less. For example, eliminating either the MAC (hardware) or the IP (software) address would simplify things a bit. Headers and, therefore, packets would be smaller, improving network throughput. But is one address enough? Giving each host a single unique address might mean that all hosts would exist on the same network. This would also mean that broadcast and multicast messages would have the potential to propagate much farther. Node or service discovery could be much more time-consuming, as the hierarchy imposed by IP would now be missing. It turns out that in our current architecture, the additional addresses are required in order to provide some indication of location, or at least forwarding. MAC addresses do not contain any location information and IP addresses do not have a mechanism for locating individual hosts. IP also insulates the packet from the possible differences in Layer 2 technologies, providing the ability to move easily between Ethernet, Token Ring, or 802.11 networks.

But not everyone believes that this is the way it must be. The telephone system provides a single address for every telephone, and the location information is stored within the telephone number itself. The telephone network has built-in redundancy for many of its pathways and has successfully kept people connected for decades, albeit over very low-bandwidth lines. New ideas have begun to surface about Internet topologies following this sort of approach. IP addresses provide routing information, but a specific address may physically exist. By creating a system in which geographic regions have assigned addresses, the routing becomes very similar to the telephone system. Forwarding may be much faster and routing tables simpler to parse. If the test data works out, IPv6 may have a competitor or two. You can find some light reading on the subject at the National Science Foundation's NeTS FIND Initiative (*http://www.nets-find.net/*) and the European Future Internet Initiative (*http://initiative.future-internet.eu/*).

Security Warning

There are a number of security concerns with basic IP headers and operation. IP addresses are logical addresses configured within the software of the operating system. Between this and the ability to capture traffic, it is extraordinarily simple to pick a target IP address and change yours to match the target. This is called *spoofing* an address. The purpose of spoofing is to pass your system off as a valid node in order to bypass security or receive packets destined for someone else.

The IP header is almost always clear text. Even when operating in a system deploying virtual private networks (VPNs), such as those based on Internet Protocol Security (IPsec), the Secure Sockets Layer (SSL), or the elderly Point-to-Point Tunneling Protocol (PPTP), the IP header is clearly visible. This gives attackers the ability to read portions of any conversation in order to determine the probable locations of servers, hosts, and network devices. By understanding the network device types, attacks can be tailored for the appropriate target.

The basic operation of IP also lends itself to attack. Since IP does not have any inherent error or security checks, packets are forwarded according to the rules. This is the case for all traffic; thus, there is often no distinction between good traffic and bad traffic. A router will forward packets regardless of where they came from or where they are going to, unless it is specifically configured not to do so. But that is another subject entirely.

Organizations for Assigning Addresses and Names

The most notable and oldest group associated with the Internet as we know it is the Internet Assigned Numbers Authority, or IANA. The following information is taken from the IANA website (*http://www.iana.org*):

> IANA manages the DNS Root Zone (assignments of ccTLDs and gTLDs) along with other functions such as the .int and .arpa zones.

> IANA coordinates allocations from the global IP and AS number spaces, such as those made to Regional Internet Registries.

> IANA is the central repository for protocol name and number registries used in many Internet protocols.

IANA is, in turn, operated by the Internet Corporation for Assigned Names and Numbers (ICANN), which is a nonprofit partnership that organizes the public IP address space for the entire world. It is the central repository for all of the used and unused addresses. Formed in 1998, ICANN is also responsible for organizing all of the names and conventions used in the domain name servers. ICANN is the forum that grants stakeholders a voice in the administration process and policy building.

Interaction between ICANN and the other organizations can be a bit confusing, as there are several components. In addition to ICANN, there are five nonprofit Regional Internet Registries (RIRs) that manage the numeric resources and help develop policy:

- AfriNIC—Africa
- APNIC—Asia/Pacific
- ARIN—North America
- LACNIC—Latin America/Caribbean
- RIPE NCC—Europe, Middle East, Central Asia

The Number Resource Organization (NRO), created in 2005, brings these five groups together for joint projects and for coordinating the number allocation/protection and policy work.

The Domain Name System (DNS) provides the mapping between human-readable names, such as those used in web pages, and IP addresses, which are horrible to remember. IANA/ICANN manages significant parts of the DNS. The DNS is a very complex collection of servers, each providing answers related to the resolution of IP addresses. There are 13 main or *root* servers, each of which has a copy of the index for what amounts to the Internet phone book. Further down the chain are the servers running the top-level domains, such as those ending with *.com* or *.edu*. A *registry* is in charge of each top-level domain, and domain names such as *whatshouldicallmywebsite.com* are purchased from registrars. In practice, someone wishing to create her own domain might purchase the domain name from any number of companies (registrars), which will handle registering the new domain with the DNS. These companies are, in turn, charged by the registry.

You can find a wealth of information regarding DNS at the IANA (*http://www.iana.org/*) and InterNIC (*http://www.internic.net/*) websites. Run by ICANN, InterNIC provides facilities for searching for accredited registrars, operational information, and filing complaints.

Summary

While IPv6 (discussed further in Chapter 8) is beginning to see increased deployment, IPv4 continues to be the basis for contemporary networks. This chapter detailed the fields and addressing used within IP packets and provided several examples in which the fields were modified. However, it is not enough to simply understand the structure of the packets. IP is integrated into network operations and the forwarding of these packets throughout the global Internet. For this reason, this chapter also introduced some of the operational and security considerations that are part of any network. Finally, it provided an introduction to the many agencies that work together to manage the addressing and naming concerns associated with IP.

Additional Reading

- RFC 790: "Assigned Numbers"
- RFC 791: "Internet Protocol DARPA Internet Program Protocol Specification"
- RFC 796: "Address Mapping"
- RFC 1122: "Requirements for Internet Hosts—Communication Layers"

Review Questions

1. What is the length of a typical IP header?
2. IP ToS is commonly used to provide QoS to IP packets. True or false?
3. IP packets belonging to the same "conversation" are generally routed together. True or false?
4. The protocol field in the IP header uses the same values as the Ethernet control field. True or false?
5. Each class C network can contain 256 possible addresses. True or false?
6. An IP address consisting of a network ID followed by all 1s is used for what type of message?
7. What is the address space specified for use with the Zero Configuration Protocol?
8. What are the four dotted-quad numbers required for hosts operating on a network?
9. IP headers are almost always transmitted in the clear, regardless of the security employed. True or false?
10. What organization is responsible for managing critical DNS components such as the root servers?

Review Answers

1. 20 bytes
2. False
3. False
4. False
5. True

6. This is a directed broadcast aimed at a particular network.

7. 169.254.0.0–169.254.255.255

8. IP address, DNS server, mask, and default gateway

9. True

10. IANA

Lab Activities

Activity 1—Determining IP Address Components

Materials: A computer with an active Internet connection

1. Open up a command shell and run `ipconfig /all`.

2. Identify the IP address, mask, default gateway, and DNS server.

3. Where did these numbers come from?

4. Calculate the network ID for your computer.

Activity 2—IP Packet Capture

Materials: Wireshark and an active connection

1. Start Wireshark.

2. In the command shell, ping your default gateway.

3. Within Wireshark, examine the packets that result from this command.

4. Identify the individual fields in the IP packets.

5. What are the values for each field? Does the protocol ID match the payload?

6. Were other packets captured while you were doing this activity? If so, how are they different from the ICMP traffic?

Activity 3—Header Checksum

Materials: Wireshark and an active connection

1. If you haven't already, open Wireshark and capture an IP packet.

2. Find the value of the header checksum.

3. Take a look at the hexadecimal values in the bottom frame within Wireshark.

4. Using these values and the one's complement, calculate your own header checksum.

5. Did your value match that seen in Wireshark?

Activity 4—Fragmentation

Materials: Wireshark and an active connection

1. Within the command shell, run the `ping` command without an argument. This will provide you with the options available with `ping`.

2. Using the `-l` option, change the length of your next ping to the gateway to 2,000 bytes.

3. While capturing, issue the `ping` command.

4. Examine the packets generated and match the packets with the same identification value. Calculate the fragment offsets.

5. Do the fragment offsets match your calculations?

6. Would `ping -l 1000` accomplish the same goal of following the fragmentation? Why or why not?

Activity 5—Special Address Capture

Materials: Wireshark and an active connection

1. Start a packet capture on your local segment or your home network.

2. Table 3-6 identifies several special (reserved) addresses used on IP-based networks. Can you capture packets that use each one of these special addresses? Hint: what does a Windows host send out when trying to bring up a network connection?

3. Once you have captured the packets, can you determine the conversation or activity that generated the packets?

4. Convert these addresses to binary. Do they match the values shown in Table 3-6?

CHAPTER 4

Address Resolution Protocol

*"The world is a jungle in general, and the
networking game contributes many animals."*

—RFC 826

The operation of an IPv4 network requires not only the use of several kinds of addresses at different layers of the networking model, but also the resolution of these addresses. This chapter describes the address resolution process, gives real-world examples of the messaging used, and provides insight into potential security risks associated with its use.

The Problem

A vast majority of IP packet–based data transmission begins and ends on a LAN. This is true regardless of whether the IP packet is going to a neighbor on the same LAN or to the other side of the world. Chapter 3 describes how IP packets are encapsulated in LAN frames that use Layer 2 MAC addressing for both the source and the destination nodes. The source MAC address is easy to determine. The problem is the determination of the destination MAC address.

With Ethernet as a LAN infrastructure, a frame is constructed using the sender's own MAC address as the source at Layer 2 and its IP address as the source at Layer 3. The destination IP address (or at least the name) is usually known, leaving only the determination of the destination MAC address. Figure 4-1 is a packet-capture review of these addresses shown in an encapsulated ICMP message.

```
⊕ Frame 4 (74 bytes on wire, 74 bytes captured)
⊕ Ethernet II, Src: D-Link_c1:d2:01 (00:50:ba:c1:d2:01), Dst: Cisco_23:85:68 (00:19:06:23:85:68)
⊕ Internet Protocol, Src: 192.168.10.11 (192.168.10.11), Dst: 129.21.21.1 (129.21.21.1)
⊕ Internet Control Message Protocol
```

Figure 4-1. Addressing layers

This is an example of a transmitted frame where the source and destination MAC addresses have been previously determined.

Techniques

Methods for the determination of the destination MAC address include closed-form computation, table lookup, and message exchange. Some of these options are listed in RFC 894, which describes Ethernet encapsulation.

Closed-form computation calculates the unknown MAC address from the known IP address. The sending node fills in the destination MAC address in the Ethernet frame from the calculated value. This method is very quick and does not require outside resources or communication. It also allows reasonably tight control over the address space. However, it does require configurable MAC addresses and some level of management, as the addresses must all be assigned to the various hosts.

Table lookup provides each host with a list of MAC addresses and the corresponding IP addresses. This is also very fast, as the sender needs to consult the table only before building the Ethernet frame. Replacing even a single network card mandates that all tables be updated, though.

These methods have an advantage in terms of speed but impose heavy management oversight. Individual host addresses must be configured, and the hosts have to be notified of any changes. For this reason, networks today (with the exception of some WAN connections) rely on the distributed approach or message exchange using the Address Resolution Protocol, or ARP. Message exchange does add extra traffic to the network and is slower than the other methods. However, it is totally automated and therefore very attractive.

Protocol Description

ARP is built into the IP configuration of every node. This means that developers at Microsoft, Sun, Google, and in the open source community develop their operating systems for operation on an IPv4 network, and code for ARP is included.

The nice thing about ARP is that for basic operation, there are only two messages defined: an ARP request and an ARP reply. When a host must find the MAC address of the destination, it will send out an ARP request. This is after the node consults its ARP table and determines that the address is in fact unknown.

Upon receipt of the ARP request message, the destination will send back an ARP reply. Basically, the ARP request asks, "Can I have your MAC address?" and the reply says, "Sure, here it is." Hosts never say no if they can help it. Figure 4-2 shows this message exchange.

No. .	Time	Source	Destination	Protocol	Info
299	426.491695	Ibm_43:49:97	Broadcast	ARP	who has 192.168.1.254? Tell 192.168.1.1
300	426.492283	Cisco_35:1a:d0	Ibm_43:49:97	ARP	192.168.1.254 is at 00:19:55:35:1a:d0

Figure 4-2. ARP exchange

Wireshark interprets this conversation as a question followed by an answer. In the first line, one node (192.168.1.1) is asking about 192.168.1.254 and in the response, 192.168.1.254 gives its location as 00:19:55:35:1a:d0, which is a MAC address.

Structure

The construction of the ARP request message is shown in Figure 4-3. We'll look at the reply message shortly, in Figure 4-5. Consider the details of the two message types, paying special attention to the addressing used in both the frame and the ARP fields.

```
⊞ Frame 299 (42 bytes on wire, 42 bytes captured)
⊞ Ethernet II, Src: Ibm_43:49:97 (00:11:25:43:49:97), Dst: Broadcast (ff:ff:ff:ff:ff:ff)
⊟ Address Resolution Protocol (request)
    Hardware type: Ethernet (0x0001)
    Protocol type: IP (0x0800)
    Hardware size: 6
    Protocol size: 4
    Opcode: request (0x0001)
    [Is gratuitous: False]
    Sender MAC address: Ibm_43:49:97 (00:11:25:43:49:97)
    Sender IP address: 192.168.1.1 (192.168.1.1)
    Target MAC address: 00:00:00_00:00:00 (00:00:00:00:00:00)
    Target IP address: 192.168.1.254 (192.168.1.254)
```

Figure 4-3. ARP request

The ARP message format is straightforward and consists of the following fields:

Hardware type
    The type of MAC address being sought

Protocol type
    The Layer 3 protocol in use

Hardware size
    The length of the MAC address

Protocol size
The length of the protocol address

OpCode
The type of ARP message

Sender MAC address
The MAC address of the machine sending the request

Sender IP address
The protocol address of the machine sending the request

Target MAC address
The MAC address being sought

Target IP address
The protocol address of the destination

The terms *hardware address* and *protocol address* are used as general descriptions, but operationally these will almost always be Ethernet six-byte hardware addresses and IP four-byte addresses. The OpCode will be either a request or a reply.

Addressing in the ARP Request

Three of the four addresses in an ARP request packet are known: the source and destination IP and the source MAC. This leaves only the destination MAC unknown. The request packet is completed by padding the unknown address field with 0s. The reply will fill in the correct value.

Line 2 of Figure 4-3 shows that the Ethernet frame source MAC is the machine sending the request, but the frame destination MAC is a broadcast address. This ensures all nodes pay attention, thereby guaranteeing that if the destination is connected and powered up, it will respond.

While there are IP or protocol addresses used in this message, it does not actually have an IP header. The IP addresses seen are simply part of the ARP header. This means that ARP messages are not routable and that routers will not pass ARP traffic on to another network. Consequently, the MAC address of a node not on the source node's LAN cannot be determined.

It also means that the Ethertype in an Ethernet frame carrying an ARP message is different than in standard data traffic. This difference is shown in Figure 4-4.

```
⊞ Frame 17 (60 bytes on wire, 60 bytes captured)
⊟ Ethernet II, Src: Cisco_0d:18:57 (00:19:aa:0d:18:57), Dst: Broadcast (ff:ff:ff:ff:ff:ff)
  ⊞ Destination: Broadcast (ff:ff:ff:ff:ff:ff)
  ⊞ Source: Cisco_0d:18:57 (00:19:aa:0d:18:57)
    Type: ARP (0x0806)
    Trailer: 000000000000000000000000000000000000
⊞ Address Resolution Protocol (request)

⊞ Frame 12 (74 bytes on wire, 74 bytes captured)
⊟ Ethernet II, Src: D-Link_c1:d2:01 (00:50:ba:c1:d2:01), Dst: Cisco_23:85:68 (00:19:06:23:85:68)
  ⊞ Destination: Cisco_23:85:68 (00:19:06:23:85:68)
  ⊞ Source: D-Link_c1:d2:01 (00:50:ba:c1:d2:01)
    Type: IP (0x0800)
⊞ Internet Protocol, Src: 192.168.10.11 (192.168.10.11), Dst: 129.21.21.1 (129.21.21.1)
⊞ Internet Control Message Protocol
```

Figure 4-4. Ethertypes

Frame 17 in Figure 4-4 has a hexadecimal type value of 0x0806 and lacks an IP header. Frame 12 has a hexadecimal type value of 0x0800 and does have an IP header. This difference can affect packet filtering or the firewall rules in place, depending on the information sought.

Addressing in the ARP Reply

The ARP reply depicted in Figure 4-5 is the response to the request sent in Figure 4-3, with the missing MAC address filled in. The reply is heading in the opposite direction. Thus, the sender and target addresses are now reversed. The code field has also changed to a reply.

```
⊞ Frame 300 (60 bytes on wire, 60 bytes captured)
⊞ Ethernet II, Src: Cisco_35:1a:d0 (00:19:55:35:1a:d0), Dst: Ibm_43:49:97 (00:11:25:43:49:97)
⊟ Address Resolution Protocol (reply)
    Hardware type: Ethernet (0x0001)
    Protocol type: IP (0x0800)
    Hardware size: 6
    Protocol size: 4
    Opcode: reply (0x0002)
    [Is gratuitous: False]
    Sender MAC address: Cisco_35:1a:d0 (00:19:55:35:1a:d0)
    Sender IP address: 192.168.1.254 (192.168.1.254)
    Target MAC address: Ibm_43:49:97 (00:11:25:43:49:97)
    Target IP address: 192.168.1.1 (192.168.1.1)
```

Figure 4-5. ARP reply

In the Ethernet frame itself, instead of a broadcast destination, *both* MAC addresses are now unicast. The reply goes directly to the original sender from the target, and other nodes will ignore the frame.

Upon receiving this message, the original source host will do two things:

1. Build the data frame using the newly determined MAC address information in the destination field.
2. Populate the local ARP table.

Step 1 satisfies the original goal of sending a message to the destination. The second step populates an ARP table to save time during the next transmission to the same destination. The ARP table is a collection of recently learned MAC addresses and corresponding IP addresses. The next time the host must transmit a frame, it will search for the address in local memory and use the address found there instead of issuing another ARP request, if possible. An example of an ARP table is shown in Figure 4-6.

```
C:\>arp -a

Interface: 129.21.152.158 --- 0x10005
  Internet Address      Physical Address      Type
  11.11.11.11           23-34-45-56-67-78     static
  129.21.152.172        00-11-d8-d6-06-91     dynamic
  129.21.152.254        00-00-0c-07-ac-01     dynamic
```

Figure 4-6. ARP table

This output was obtained on a Windows machine with the command `arp -a` issued from the command shell. Notice the two types of entries—static and dynamic. The normal entry will be a dynamic entry. Static entries are uncommon.

The dynamic nature of these entries indicates that they are not permanent. Regardless of the underlying operating system, all nodes will age out ARP table entries in a matter of minutes. Windows, for example, removes these entries after approximately two minutes. If a node is to be addressed but has been aged out of the ARP table, the ARP process must be repeated for that node.

The time that an ARP table entry should be allowed to live has been debated, as there are differing opinions as to the perfect time. If the value is too short, the hosts will be reARPing at an increased rate and generating more network traffic. If the time is too long, bad or erroneous information may stick around longer and prevent hosts from reaching the proper destination.

Operation

With an understanding of what takes place under the hood, two examples will help illustrate ARP packet formation for near and far destinations when ARP table information is nonexistent.

Example 1—Sender and Target on the Same LAN

A common troubleshooting technique is to ping a target IP address as "proof of life." Ping generates an ICMP echo request packet that is encapsulated in an IP packet, which, in turn, is encapsulated in an Ethernet frame, as shown in Figure 4-7.

Figure 4-7. Basic frame encapsulation

Packet capture activity of the frame depicted in Figure 4-7 is shown in Figure 4-8.

```
    1 0.000000     Micro-St_eb:78:84  Broadcast          ARP    who has 192.168.15.1?  Tell 192.168.15.100
    2 0.000324     Cisco-Li_7f:fb:9d  Micro-St_eb:78:t   ARP    192.168.15.1 is at 00:14:bf:7f:fb:9d
    3 0.000347     192.168.15.100     192.168.15.1       ICMP   Echo (ping) request
    4 0.000862     192.168.15.1       192.168.15.100     ICMP   Echo (ping) reply

□ Frame 3 (74 bytes on wire, 74 bytes captured)
□ Ethernet II, Src: Micro-St_eb:78:84 (00:0c:76:eb:78:84), Dst: Cisco-Li_7f:fb:9d (00:14:bf:7f:fb:9d)
  ⊞ Destination: Cisco-Li_7f:fb:9d (00:14:bf:7f:fb:9d)
  ⊞ Source: Micro-St_eb:78:84 (00:0c:76:eb:78:84)
    Type: IP (0x0800)
  ⊞ Internet Protocol, Src: 192.168.15.100 (192.168.15.100), Dst: 192.168.15.1 (192.168.15.1)
  ⊞ Internet Control Message Protocol
```

Figure 4-8. ARP and ICMP on the same network

The MAC address requested in frame 1 is returned in frame 2. It is then used in frame 3 to build the Ethernet frame carrying the ping (ICMP echo), with Node A attempting to contact the router on its LAN (Figure 4-9). While this example uses ping with the associated ICMP echo request/reply messages, the same ARP request and reply would have been required had the sender issued a Telnet, FTP, or HTTP request to the target.

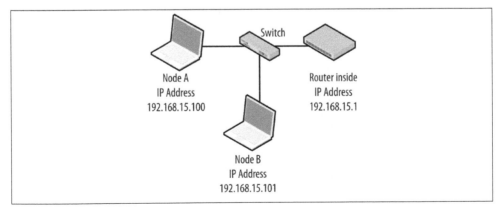

Figure 4-9. Single LAN topology

Example 2—Sender and Target on Separate LANs

As with our first example, when the sender and target are on separate LANs, the Ethernet frame's destination MAC address must be determined. In this case, the destination node is on a remote LAN. Since Layer 2 MAC addressing is restricted to the local network, assistance is required from the designated default gateway that will route the frame to the destination network. Router ARP behavior is similar to that of hosts. They respond to ARP messages and have to locate locally connected nodes.

To accomplish this, the sending node determines the gateway's MAC address and places it in the destination field, as shown in Figure 4-10. As before, frame 3 is expanded to show that in the ICMP echo request, the router MAC address is used.

```
  1 0.000000     Micro-St_eb:78:84  Broadcast           ARP    who has 192.168.15.1?  Tell 192.168.15.100
  2 0.000479     Cisco-Li_7f:fb:9d  Micro-St_eb:78:8  ARP    192.168.15.1 is at 00:14:bf:7f:fb:9d
  3 0.000503     192.168.15.100     129.21.3.17         ICMP   Echo (ping) request
  4 0.036549     129.21.3.17        192.168.15.100    ICMP   Echo (ping) reply

⊞ Frame 3 (74 bytes on wire, 74 bytes captured)
⊟ Ethernet II, Src: Micro-St_eb:78:84 (00:0c:76:eb:78:84), Dst: Cisco-Li_7f:fb:9d (00:14:bf:7f:fb:9d)
  ⊞ Destination: Cisco-Li_7f:fb:9d (00:14:bf:7f:fb:9d)
  ⊞ Source: Micro-St_eb:78:84 (00:0c:76:eb:78:84)
    Type: IP (0x0800)
⊞ Internet Protocol, Src: 192.168.15.100 (192.168.15.100), Dst: 129.21.3.17 (129.21.3.17)
⊞ Internet Control Message Protocol
```

Figure 4-10. ARP and ICMP exchange for different networks

To summarize, the sender is attempting to determine the target MAC address, but the ICMP echo request is heading for a destination on another network. So the ICMP echo request uses the default gateway MAC address (00:14:bf:7f:fb:9d), but the IP address is for the distant node. Shown in Figure 4-11, Node A is now trying to contact Node C.

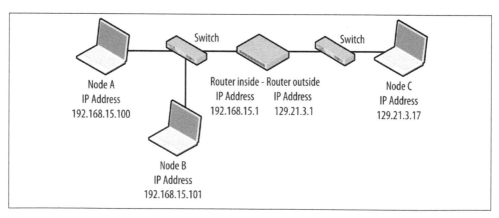

Figure 4-11. Two-network topology

The question to ask at this point is, "How did the original source node know that it had to replace the MAC address of the destination host with the MAC address of the router?" Hosts first process their own routing tables to determine if the host is on the same LAN. Then the ARP process takes over. The algorithm the hosts use is discussed in Chapter 7.

Additional Operations

The standard operation of ARP is pretty simple: broadcast a message requesting the MAC address for a particular IP address and receive an answer. However, there are a couple of key "helper" tasks accomplished by ARP that either add a little security or improve the performance of the network.

The Return ARP

The conversation shown in Figure 4-12 illustrates another important facet of ARP— only the host originating the conversation (generating the ARP request) will place an entry for the destination host in its local ARP table. That is, other stations hearing the exchange, even if they are receiving the ARP request, will not add these stations to their own ARP tables. However, many hosts (especially routers) are aggressive when it comes to populating their tables and, upon hearing ARP traffic or being involved in ARP messages, will subsequently generate their own ARP requests to populate their tables.

```
 1  0.000000    Micro-St_eb:78:84    Broadcast            ARP    Who has 192.168.15.1?  Tell 192.168.15.100
 2  0.000479    Cisco-Li_7f:fb:9d    Micro-St_eb:78:8     ARP    192.168.15.1 is at 00:14:bf:7f:fb:9d
 3  0.000503    192.168.15.100       129.21.3.17          ICMP   Echo (ping) request
 4  0.036549    129.21.3.17          192.168.15.100       ICMP   Echo (ping) reply
 5  0.993031    192.168.15.100       129.21.3.17          ICMP   Echo (ping) request
 6  1.045927    129.21.3.17          192.168.15.100       ICMP   Echo (ping) reply
 7  1.993023    192.168.15.100       129.21.3.17          ICMP   Echo (ping) request
 8  2.030664    129.21.3.17          192.168.15.100       ICMP   Echo (ping) reply
 9  2.992966    192.168.15.100       129.21.3.17          ICMP   Echo (ping) request
10  3.029049    129.21.3.17          192.168.15.100       ICMP   Echo (ping) reply
11  5.034065    Cisco-Li_7f:fb:9d    Micro-St_eb:78:8     ARP    Who has 192.168.15.100?  Tell 192.168.15.1
12  5.034091    Micro-St_eb:78:84    Cisco-Li_7f:fb:9     ARP    192.168.15.100 is at 00:0c:76:eb:78:84
```

Figure 4-12. Return ARP exchange

The packet capture sequence shown in Figure 4-12 shows the original host using ARP to determine its default gateway when attempting to send to an offsite host. After the conversation has been routed, the router (default gateway) issues its own ARP request for the original (sending) host. In this way, it populates its table with what it believes is a valid host address. This improves routing efficiency for future traffic forwarding.

Gratuitous ARP

When a host boots up, it either receives an IP address via DHCP or has one statically configured. But the host must make sure no other network node is using the same address. For this reason, network hosts will often ARP for themselves. If a device answers, the sender is alerted that another node is using the same IP address. Figure 4-13 shows a gratuitous ARP, where the target and sender IP addresses are the same.

```
⊞ Ethernet II, Src: Avaya_70:cf:66 (00:04:0d:70:cf:66), Dst: Broadcast (ff:ff:ff:ff:ff:ff)
⊟ Address Resolution Protocol (request/gratuitous ARP)
    Hardware type: Ethernet (0x0001)
    Protocol type: IP (0x0800)
    Hardware size: 6
    Protocol size: 4
    Opcode: request (0x0001)
    [Is gratuitous: True]
    Sender MAC address: Avaya_70:cf:66 (00:04:0d:70:cf:66)
    Sender IP address: 192.168.16.2 (192.168.16.2)
    Target MAC address: 00:00:00_00:00:00 (00:00:00:00:00:00)
    Target IP address: 192.168.16.2 (192.168.16.2)
```

Figure 4-13. Gratuitous ARP

Security Warning

The distributed approach to address resolution can be subject to attackers. Although hosts should populate their tables only with information they have requested, not all operating systems are programmed this way. Some older systems will allow unsolicited ARP traffic to fill a host's cache, accepting an ARP response even if it was not requested. This allows attackers to populate the ARP table with bogus data, resulting in hosts forwarding traffic based on erroneous information.

An attacker can also take advantage of a device's desire to populate its ARP table by providing an answer for every address on the network. In this way, it claims to have a valid MAC address for all hosts on the network, so hosts and routers on the network will believe that the attacker's address is to be used for all destinations. The effect is that the valid network hosts send their traffic to the attacker, who then makes copies of the data and sends the traffic on to the correct destination.

This is called a *man-in-the-middle* attack because the attacker has placed himself between the source and the proper destination and is effectively invisible. The technique of inserting bad data into unsuspecting host ARP tables is called *ARP poisoning*.

You can diagnose this type of attack by examining the ARP tables on the host machines and the routers, looking for multiple entries with identical MAC addresses. Security heuristics will also look for excessive ARP messages on the network. While these tables are easy to access, overworked network administrators do have to look, so this information is often missed.

IPv6

ARP is absent in IPv6. Rather, network hosts use a series of messages called redirects, solicitations, and advertisements in a process called *neighbor discovery*. Instead of using an approach that requires hosts to discover MAC addresses when they are needed, IPv6 adopts a slightly different process. Neighbor solicitation and advertisement messages help discover information about the network before it is needed. These messages are multicast out to all IPv6 nodes. Examples of these packets are given in Chapter 6.

Digging a Little Deeper—The Cost of a Distributed Approach

ARP, a distributed approach to address resolution and discovery, is not without problems. Consider the traffic generated in a 100-node network, where each host must discover every address on the network. If nodes do not cache information as a result of a transmission from a neighbor, every node has the potential to send 99 messages. Adding another 99 messages for the corresponding replies brings the total to 198 for that single requesting node. For n nodes, each node will generate $2(n-1)$ messages, or a total of $2n(n-1)$.

Half of the $2n(n-1)$ messages, $n(n-1)$, are broadcast frames traveling throughout the entire Layer 2 network (wired and wireless), and all of them are necessary, but they are considered overhead because they do not carry user data. It is unlikely that most of these frames will be generated at the same time, but there are times (for example, at the beginning and end of the workday) when a large number of network hosts will be transmitting concurrently. Complicating matters is the fact that ARP tables age out for nodes that are not routinely participating in message exchanges. Refreshing those tables further adds to network traffic.

Routers are burdened with the additional problem of resolving the addresses' next hop routers. Thus, when a router receives a message to be sent to a distant host, it must first determine the MAC address of the neighboring router. At the other end, the router receiving an IP packet may have to ARP for the destination host, further adding delays to the message traffic. As a result, it is not uncommon for the first packet of a transmission to be delayed or lost while addresses are being resolved. For this reason, routers will aggressively populate their ARP tables with known hosts.

IPv6 alleviates some of this, but it creates other traffic issues, as the discovery process uses several types of message (some of which are multicast). Switch behavior with multicast is similar in that multicast frames are sent everywhere throughout the Layer 2 domain. While routers, switches, and hosts have some ability to filter multicast traffic, we have increased the number of message types (redirects, router advertisements, router solicitations, neighbor advertisements, and neighbor solicitations), arguably increasing the overhead on the network.

Summary

In this chapter, we examined the problem of Layer 2 address resolution. After examining the packets themselves and the addressing used, you should now have a solid understanding of ARP. We have also examined several of the operations used and the security threat represented by this distributed approach.

Additional Reading

This chapter has taken you through the operation and structure of ARP. This information is about all you will need to handle ARP on almost any network. However, there are some operations or standards that you should familiarize yourself with, even though you are not likely to run into them very often. Useful resources include:

RFC 826: "Ethernet Address Resolution Protocol"
   This is the base address resolution standard. While not very descriptive, current operation is based on this RFC.

RFC 903: "A Reverse Address Resolution Protocol"
   This RFC approaches the issue of address resolution from the opposite direction. Instead of trying to learn a MAC address, RFC 903 describes how a host can discover a protocol (IP) address if it knows only the MAC address of the destination.

RFC 1293: "Inverse Address Resolution Protocol"
   This RFC allows a host to request a particular protocol address for a given hardware address.

RFC 1868: "ARP Extension—UNARP (Proxy ARP)"
   This RFC suggests some solutions for potential limits of the original ARP RFC.

Review Questions

1. How many addresses are defined in ARP?
2. Is an ARP message routable?
3. Describe the Ethernet addressing used in the standard ARP request. Are the source and destination addresses unicast, broadcast, or multicast?
4. Describe the Ethernet addressing used in the standard ARP reply. Are the source and destination addresses unicast, broadcast, or multicast?
5. What is a gratuitous ARP?
6. What information is stored in an ARP table?
7. Can we send standard ARP messages directly to computers that are not on our own network?

8. Is ARP included in IPv6?

9. Is ARP a secure protocol?

10. What is the Ethertype hexadecimal value for an ARP message?

Review Answers

1. 2

2. No, the messages do not contain an IP header.

3. The ARP request uses a unicast address for the source and a broadcast address for the destination.

4. The ARP reply uses a unicast address for the source and a unicast address for the destination.

5. This term refers to a node sending out an ARP request for its own IP address in order to determine if another node is using the same address.

6. The ARP table contains a mapping between host MAC and IP addresses. It also shows whether each entry is static or dynamic.

7. No, ARP is not routable.

8. No.

9. No. False ARP messages can be created to fool ARP tables. Hosts then make incorrect forwarding decisions. ARP transmissions are also sent in the clear.

10. 0806

Lab Activities

Activity 1—Determining Your IP Address and Your Default Gateway

Materials: A Windows computer with a network connection

1. In Windows, click the Start button.

2. In the run box, type **cmd** and press Enter. A command window opens.

3. Type **ipconfig /all**. This will display the IP address of your computer. The output will be similar to the following. This shows your IP address and the address of the default gateway:

```
Windows IP Configuration

Mini-PCI Express Adapter
    Physical Address. . . . . . . . . : 00-22-68-90-D5-DB
```

```
DHCP Enabled. . . . . . . . . . : Yes
Autoconfiguration Enabled . . . . : Yes
IPv4 Address. . . . . . . . . . : 192.168.15.100(Preferred)
Subnet Mask . . . . . . . . . . : 255.255.255.0
Default Gateway . . . . . . . . : 192.168.15.1
DHCP Server . . . . . . . . . . : 192.168.15.1
DNS Servers . . . . . . . . . . : 24.56.123.4
                                  106.12.34.56
NetBIOS over Tcpip. . . . . . . : Enabled
```

Activity 2—Examining the ARP Table

Materials: A Windows computer with a network connection

1. In the command window, type **arp -a**. This will provide the same output shown in Figure 4-6. This gives an idea about nodes on the network with which the computer has recently communicated.

2. Record the IP addresses you see in this table, as you'll need them later.

Activity 3—Packet Capture

Materials: A Windows computer with a network connection and packet capture software

1. To capture the ARP traffic, first clear the ARP table or cache. To do this, type **arp -d *** in the command window; then type **arp -a** to verify there are no entries.

2. In Wireshark, select your adapter and start a capture.

3. Back in the command window, ping one of the nodes previously listed in the ARP table. In the capture window, you should see the ARP request and ARP reply. These will be followed by the ICMP traffic. In pinging the default gateway, you may see the return ARP. That is, after pinging the gateway and seeing the associated traffic, the gateway generates its own ARP request directed back to you.

Activity 4—Gratuitous ARP

Materials: A Windows computer with a network connection, packet capture software, and a DHCP server like a Linksys router

To see a node ARPing for itself, typically the best time is right after an exchange with the DHCP server. This can be done on startup or by forcing the node to go through the IP address release and renewal process.

1. Start another capture.

2. In the command window, type **ipconfig /release**. This forces the node to give up its IP address.

3. In the command window, type **ipconfig /renew**. This causes the node to ask for an IP address again.

4. After the DHCP exchange has completed, you should see your node ARP for the very IP address it was assigned during the exchange. This is the gratuitous ARP.

Activity 5—How Long Does an ARP Table Entry Live?

Materials: A Windows computer with a network connection

1. In the command window, type **arp -a** to show the other nodes on the network.

2. Ping one of these nodes to refresh the ARP table entry.

3. Repeat the command **arp -a** at 30-second intervals until the entry disappears from the ARP table. How long did it take?

CHAPTER 5

Network Equipment

Every network needs a certain amount of equipment facilitating the transmission of data. Equipment selection is based on the task at hand. To select the best possible device, we have to understand operations and ask questions regarding the interconnection of networks and computers. In addition to handling a specific set of tasks, infrastructure devices are designed to operate at a particular layer of the TCP/IP model. This means that hubs (also called repeaters), switches (or bridges), routers, access points (APs), and gateways can be inserted into the model just like protocols. While contemporary networks continue to use devices that are clearly defined, newer equipment can cross layer boundaries.

This chapter examines the components of a typical network in terms of their operation and behavior. We will also take a look at some of the security concerns associated with each. This includes changes for contemporary equipment, small office/home office (SOHO) networks, and the ubiquitous home gateway.

Figure 5-1 provides the basis for most of this chapter. Both the OSI and TCP/IP models are represented, along with the major protocols at each layer. The hubs, switches, and router interconnect the two sides. The solid line at the bottom represents the physical connection between the devices, or what we might call the transmission path. However, devices may make decisions at upper layers, so they are logically connected via the dotted line. For example, switches process Layer 2 frames, which include MAC addresses.

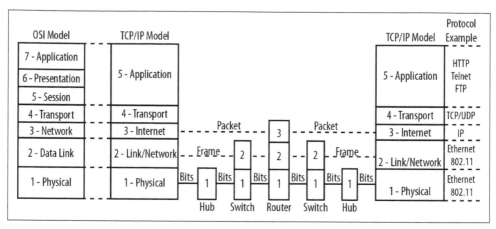

Figure 5-1. Models and equipment

Tables and Hosts

While this chapter is about network equipment, it wouldn't be complete without some mention of the hosts or nodes sitting on the network. Nodes have IP and MAC addresses, which are used to communicate over the network infrastructure. Almost without exception, devices use these addresses to forward packets or frames. It is also helpful to realize that within the network, almost everything follows a step-by-step process based on the same set of rules. The process can be traced through a series of tables and packets. All of the devices on the network, including the hosts, have these tables and are capable of generating and/or forwarding packets. In the following sections, we will discuss the major types of equipment and the tables they use to process frames. Table 5-1 lists these tables, along with each one's purpose and where it can be found on the network.

Table 5-1. Networking tables and purposes

Table	Location	Purpose
ARP table	Router and host	Maps IP addresses to MAC addresses
Source address table	Switch/bridge	Maps MAC addresses to switch ports
Routing table	Router and host	Determines correct interface and next hop
AP forwarding database	Access point	Collection of nodes managed by the AP

Many of these operations are covered in greater depth in other chapters in this book, but let's examine a general example. Figure 5-2 shows a basic network, illustrating the components covered in this chapter.

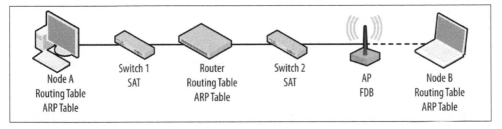

Figure 5-2. Basic network

If we assume that Node A is sending data to Node B, the following basic step-by-step process is followed:

1. Node A consults its host routing table to determine if the packet is for the local network or offsite.

2. Node A builds a frame for the Layer 2 destination by pulling the proper MAC address from its ARP table or by sending an ARP request and receiving the appropriate answer.

3. The frame is sent from Node A to the router via Switch 1.

4. Upon receiving the frame, Switch 1 consults its source address table (SAT) to determine the proper port for the destination.

5. The router receives the frame from Switch 1 and examines the IP header to determine the destination network.

6. The router processes its routing table to determine the correct interface to use for the destination.

7. The router builds a frame for the Layer 2 destination by pulling the proper MAC address from its ARP table or by sending an ARP request and receiving the appropriate answer.

8. The frame is sent from the router to Node B via Switch 2 and the AP.

9. Upon receiving the frame, Switch 2 consults its SAT to determine the proper port for the destination.

10. The AP receives the frame and, upon determining that Node B is in its forwarding database, sends the frame out to Node B.

It may seem like an awful lot of processing just to get a packet across two networks, but every single network transmission can follow a similar process.

Hubs or Repeaters

Starting from the bottom of the TCP/IP protocol stack and working our way up, the first device we come across is a hub. Hubs, or at least the need for hubs, are defined right along with the Layer 2 protocol standards. To clarify, let's start with the term *repeater*. IEEE 802.3 describes repeating as "the means used to connect segments of network medium together, thus allowing larger topologies and a larger multi-station access unit (MAU) base than are allowed by the rules governing individual segments."

The idea of a repeater has been around for a long time. The basic problem for a signal is that it tends to degrade over distance. A repeater is a point in the network where a weak but still readable signal can be cleaned up and retransmitted, thus extending the length of the network. According to the standards, repeaters "improve signal amplitude, waveform, and timing applied to the normal data and collision signals." However, it is important to remember that this is not without boundaries, as protocols such as Ethernet have rules regarding network size, particularly in the case of the collision domain. Repeaters may also permit the interconnection of dissimilar physical layers, such as UTP and fiber, and are used only in half-duplex environments. Hubs handle the same sort of operations and are defined in 802.3 as "device[s] used to provide connectivity between DTEs. Hubs perform the basic functions of restoring signal amplitude and timing, collision detection, and notification and signal broadcast to lower-level hubs and DTEs."

So what is a DTE? The term *data terminal equipment* typically refers to devices generating/terminating transmissions and, in this case, nodes. One other distinction is that hubs can generate some of the control signals used on the network. But with statements like "repeater sets are used as the hub in a star topology," it can get a little confusing. A little reality can help us here. First, you don't buy repeaters anymore; you buy hubs. Lots of networking folks think of hubs as multiport repeaters. Second, we don't like to buy hubs. Most organizations have moved away from hubs, so this discussion is included here only to be complete.

So what have we got against hubs? Generally, they do not possess a great deal of intelligence. Early managed versions like those from 3Com actually had a nice collection of tools for controlling network traffic, but this was unusual. Most hubs are not much smarter than your toaster. Hubs act like repeaters—they forward traffic out all ports except the source interface. Thus, any transmission is sent to anyone connected to the same collision domain. This makes the hub a significant security concern. This behavior can vary between manufacturers. For example, some vendors isolate slower connections, but the hub broadcast behavior makes jacks installed in conference rooms, seating areas, or spare offices a real threat to network security.

One positive aspect of hubs is that they are very fast. In a small network with a few nodes, it is tough to beat the performance of a hub. In some scenarios, they will actually outperform a switch. But as the number of nodes increases, we start to get collisions, which destroy the performance. As the network size increases, hub performance decreases, so hubs do not *scale* well. For these performance and security reasons, hubs have largely been replaced with switches.

Switches and Bridges

Moving up to the next TCP/IP layer, we have switches. Switches are the workhorses of modern networks. Where previously we might have used hubs to extend the network and add more nodes, we now use bridges and switches. The term *bridge* is used to describe a device that interconnects collision domains. Collisions that appear on one side of a switch are not allowed to propagate to the other. In Figure 5-3, a collision on Hub 4 will propagate to all of the nodes in the same collision domain. This includes PC 4, PC 5, PC 6, and the switch port itself. However, the switch/bridge will prevent further transmission. PC 1 and PC 2 will be blissfully unaware of the collision. Switches and bridges also filter out traffic that should not be forwarded. For example, if PC 1 and PC 2 are having a conversation, there is no reason to force the other nodes to listen, so PC 3, PC 4, PC 5, and PC 6 will not hear the frames.

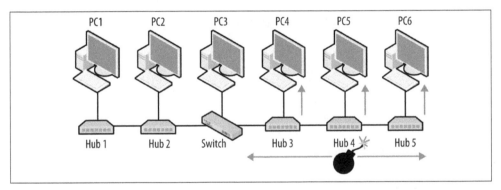

Figure 5-3. Collision boundary

Generally, switches are considered to be newer, high-powered versions of bridges, performing the same functions and bringing some extras to the table. In fact, we don't buy bridges anymore, except in the case of wireless bridges—but these are not typical and aren't used if it can be avoided. Early versions of bridges and bridging standards did not include many of the advanced features we have come to rely on. For these reasons, our discussion will center on switches.

As a replacement for hubs, switches have done very well. The purchase price (cost per port) of a switch has come down considerably and switches have many features that hubs (or early bridges) never possessed, including changes to the forwarding behavior, support for virtual LANs (VLANs), basic port security, and 802.1X.

The key difference between switches and hubs is that switches forward based on MAC addresses. To accomplish this, the switch consults a SAT before transmitting a frame to the destination. This means that for a significant portion of network traffic, only the proper destination receives the transmission. The operation of switches and bridges is defined in IEEE 802.1D, titled "IEEE Standard for Local and Metropolitan Area Networks: Media Access Control (MAC) Bridges." 802.1D provides the guidelines for support of the MAC layer, including interconnecting network segments, support for several Layer 2 protocols, handling of errors, and, of course, forwarding of frames. In addition, the standard describes the behavior of other Layer 2 protocols, such as Spanning Tree.

So, how does a switch work? Aside from a couple of rules for specialized frames, Ethernet switches operate in a very straightforward way: receive a frame, read the addresses, error check, and forward to the correct port. We will work through a couple of examples to explore the details. Figure 5-4 depicts a typical topology with a switch at the center.

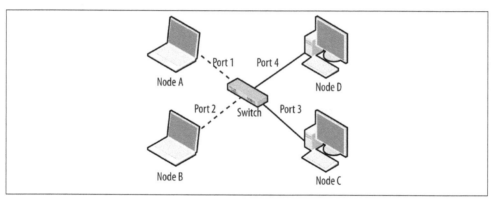

Figure 5-4. Basic switch topology

Switches keep track of the locations of network nodes via the SAT or MAC address table. Remember that all network nodes have a unique MAC address and each Ethernet frame identifies the source and destination by these MAC addresses. The table is a mapping between the MAC addresses and the switch ports. This table also keeps track of the VLANs configured on the switch. The SAT for the network shown in Figure 5-4 might look like Table 5-2. Typically, nodes all start out in VLAN 1.

Table 5-2. Basic switch SAT

MAC address	VLAN	Port
Node A MAC	1	1
Node B MAC	1	2
Node C MAC	1	3
Node D MAC	1	4

A switch has some basic procedures to follow:

1. When a frame is received, buffer the frame and perform the frame error check. If there are problems, discard the frame.

2. Copy the source address and port number into the SAT.

3. Look in the SAT for the destination MAC address.

4. If the address is known, forward to the correct port. If the address is not known, send the frame everywhere except the source port. This is called *flooding*.

5. If the destination is a broadcast address (ff:ff:ff:ff:ff:ff), send the frame everywhere except the source port. In many cases, this is also the behavior for multicast frames. Recall that multicast frames commonly begin with 01. VLANs can reduce the effect of flooding because they can be used to segment the switch into smaller logical network segments, but this is a story for another day.

 Switches will continue to forward broadcast frames from one another until the frame hits a Layer 3 boundary, like a router. The distance that a broadcast frame will travel is called the *broadcast domain*.

Let's take the example of a ping between Node A and Node B in Figure 5-4 and add a little more detail. For this example, we will assume the SAT entries in Table 5-2 are not present. SAT entries usually time out in five minutes or so. For this example, we will use the frame shown in Figure 5-5.

```
Ethernet II, Src: Ibm_43:49:97 (00:11:25:43:49:97), Dst: Cisco_35:1a:d0 (00:19:55:35:1a:d0)
⊞ Destination: Cisco_35:1a:d0 (00:19:55:35:1a:d0)
⊞ Source: Ibm_43:49:97 (00:11:25:43:49:97)
  Type: IP (0x0800)
Internet Protocol, Src: 192.168.1.1 (192.168.1.1), Dst: 192.168.1.254 (192.168.1.254)
Internet Control Message Protocol
```

Figure 5-5. Ethernet frame with ICMP echo request

When the ICMP echo request is received at the switch, the switch buffers the entire frame and calculates the CRC. If there are no problems with the error check, the switch places the MAC address of Node A (Src) into the SAT and notes the port number and VLAN ID:

```
MAC Address          VLAN     Port
00:11:25:43:49:97    1        1
```

Next, the destination MAC address is examined. Node B is currently missing from the SAT, so the switch forwards the frame out of all ports except the original source port. Here, the ICMP echo request is sent out ports 2, 3, and 4. Node B receives the frame and answers back. When the switch receives the ICMP echo reply (shown in Figure 5-6), the switch buffers the entire frame and calculates the CRC.

```
Ethernet II, Src: Cisco_35:1a:d0 (00:19:55:35:1a:d0), Dst: Ibm_43:49:97 (00:11:25:43:49:97)
⊞ Destination: Ibm_43:49:97 (00:11:25:43:49:97)
⊞ Source: Cisco_35:1a:d0 (00:19:55:35:1a:d0)
  Type: IP (0x0800)
Internet Protocol, Src: 192.168.1.254 (192.168.1.254), Dst: 192.168.1.1 (192.168.1.1)
Internet Control Message Protocol
```

Figure 5-6. Ethernet frame with ICMP echo reply

Take a look at the source and destination MAC addresses in Figure 5-6. They have flipped, indicating that this is a reply. The IP addresses have also flipped. If there are no problems with the error check, the switch places the MAC address of Node B into the SAT and notes the port number and VLAN ID:

```
MAC Address          VLAN    Port
00:11:25:43:49:97    1       1
00:19:55:35:1a:d0    1       2
```

As the destination is examined, we find that Node A has an entry in the SAT, so the frame can be directed to Port 1 only. This learning process is what makes a switch *transparent*. This is also what allows the switch to filter network traffic, prevent errors, and stop the propagation of collisions. Figure 5-7 shows the SAT from an operating Cisco switch. The term *dynamic* means that the switch learned the address.

```
Non-static Address Table:
Destination Address   Address Type   VLAN   Destination Port
-------------------   ------------   ----   ----------------
0004.9b4b.5701        Dynamic        1      FastEthernet0/1
0004.9b4b.5701        Dynamic        2      FastEthernet0/1
0004.9b4b.5701        Dynamic        3      FastEthernet0/1
000e.0c76.5ad4        Dynamic        2      FastEthernet0/7
000e.0c77.20e4        Dynamic        2      FastEthernet0/1
000e.0c77.2322        Dynamic        3      FastEthernet0/1
0011.212c.15e0        Dynamic        3      FastEthernet0/23
0011.212c.15e1        Dynamic        2      FastEthernet0/13
```

Figure 5-7. Cisco switch SAT

In this particular case, there are three VLANs, and we can see that Port 1 (FastEthernet0/1) has several associated MAC addresses. This is because another switch was connected at that point. This is reflected in the topology shown in Figure 5-8. Two switches are interconnected via Port 3 on Switch 1 and Port 3 on Switch 2. As normal traffic flows, the switches will learn where all of the MAC destinations are by recording the source MACs from Ethernet transmissions.

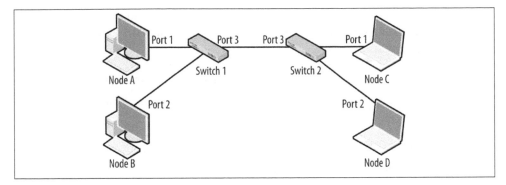

Figure 5-8. Two-switch topology

In topologies such as this, it is impossible for a switch to connect directly to each destination. The only piece of information a switch will possess is the source, from its perspective. So, from the perspective of Switch 2, all frames appear to have come from the single port connected to Switch 1. The reverse is also true. Building on what we know of SATs and the learning process, the SATs for the two switches would look like Table 5-3.

Table 5-3. SATs for a two-switch topology

Switch 1 SAT			Switch 2 SAT		
Node A MAC address	VLAN 1	Port 1	Node A MAC address	VLAN 1	Port 3
Node B MAC address	VLAN 1	Port 2	Node B MAC address	VLAN 1	Port 3
Node C MAC address	VLAN 1	Port 3	Node C MAC address	VLAN 1	Port 2
Node D MAC address	VLAN 1	Port 3	Node D MAC address	VLAN 1	Port 1

Node A sends traffic to Node D, and Switch 1 forwards the traffic out Port 3. Switch 2 receives the frame and forwards the frame to Port 1. If these nodes cease to generate traffic, their addresses will be removed from the SAT.

Ethernet nodes obey the CSMA/CD access method. By default, switches also engage in CSMA/CD because, until link negotiation is complete, the switch has no indication as to what might be downstream of a particular port. Finally, switches read and process the Ethernet frames, but they are not supposed to change them in any way. This means a frame that is forwarded by a switch looks exactly the same as it did when it was received by the switch. We will see that this is not always true when dealing with network devices.

Access Points

Before we leave Layer 2, let's talk about APs. APs are sometimes called *wireless hubs* because the medium is shared. While calling them hubs isn't exactly accurate, we can understand the confusion. Just like a hub, APs broadcast traffic to anyone capable of hearing it. But, again, this is more due to the type of media than the operation of the AP. Let's take a closer look at what an AP is supposed to do. The 802.11 standard describes several major responsibilities:

- Notifying network users of its presence and negotiating connections
- Forwarding traffic between the wired and wireless sections of the network
- Handling traffic for all of the wireless nodes currently connected
- Encrypting of data traffic if configured
- Handling nodes in power save mode

There have been several modifications to this standard, including 802.11b, 802.11a, 802.11g, and 802.11n. However, with the exception of 802.11n, there have not been very many changes to the Layer 2 behavior. Most of the changes have been to signaling and modulation, so the responsibilities outlined in the preceding list haven't changed.

Nodes use a three-step process when joining a wireless network. First, the network must be found either by passive or active scan. Second, the node must authenticate with the network. Third, the node is associated with the network. Actually, a node associates with an AP possessing the service set identifier (SSID) for the desired network. Once this has been completed, the node is entered into the AP's forwarding database. The association is a key relationship, because the nodes understand which AP is theirs, and the AP takes responsibility for the associated nodes. This means the AP will not forward traffic for nonassociated nodes, and when wireless laptops have traffic to send, one of the MAC addresses included in the frame is that of the AP. A wireless data frame is shown in Figure 5-9.

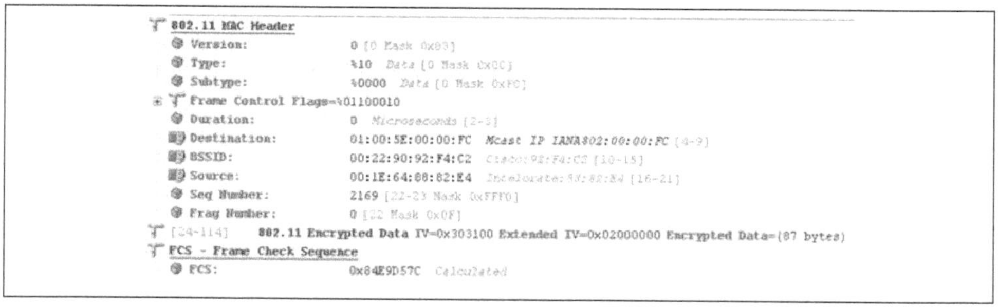

Figure 5-9. Wireless data frame

This frame was captured using OmniPeek. While the details of 802.11 operation and frame content are a little beyond the scope of this text, we can see that three addresses are used in an 802.11 data frame: destination, BSSID, and source. The destination and source MAC addresses are exactly the same as in an Ethernet frame and serve the same purpose. The BSSID (basic service set identification) is the MAC address of the AP. This allows the AP to determine which frames to process.

This brings us to the behavior of the AP. Based on these decisions, the AP is forwarding traffic after examining the MAC addresses used in the frame, so it operates similarly to a switch. We already know that traffic sent out by the AP is broadcast to anyone listening. This includes frames such as beacons and other wireless management traffic. In the case of Figure 5-10, the AP handles transmissions from Node C and Node D, because they are associated with the AP. When two wireless nodes communicate, as long as they are connected to the same AP, the transmission is limited to the wireless segment and does not cross to the wired side. The same can be said of two wired nodes (Node A and Node B) because the frames stay on their side of the network. When traffic from the wired-side switch arrives at the AP, it is buffered and sent out to the wireless network. If we know how a switch operates, we can understand how traffic finds its way to the AP.

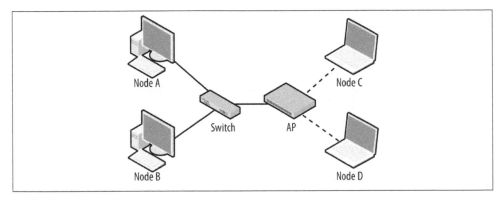

Figure 5-10. Small wireless topology

When Node A and Node B generate broadcast or multicast traffic, it will be forwarded by the switch. It turns out that the AP does the same thing. In addition, any traffic is destined for Node C and Node D will be forwarded to the AP from the switch because of the switch SAT. Again, close examination of this behavior reveals that most forwarding decisions are based on MAC addresses or handling of broadcast/multicast frames.

There are differences between the Layer 2 behavior seen on a switch and that seen on an AP. 802.11 frames have a greater number of control fields compared to Ethernet. In addition, 802.11 frames are larger. So, an AP is one network device that must modify the Layer 2 frame. However, like a switch, the AP does not care about Layer 3 addresses or headers.

Routers

As we move up the layers in our networking model, the biggest differences in device operation revolve around addressing and what the device "cares" about. Routers live at Layer 3, as they deal primarily with IP addresses. Building on Figure 5-1, we can see the area of concern for each type of device and the type of addressing processed. Unlike any other device, routers will forward traffic between IP-based networks after examining the Layer 3 header (Figure 5-11).

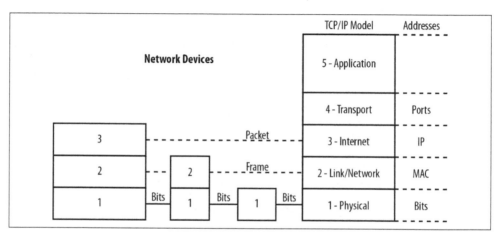

Figure 5-11. Device addressing

Though routers act on IP addresses, that doesn't mean they are not actively engaged in the network. A router can act much like a host in some situations. They require IP addresses in order to operate (switches and APs do not), they use and respond to ARP messages, and they listen to (but will not forward) all broadcast frames. This means that not only will a router forward traffic for hosts, but it can be contacted directly. Routers are also known by another name—*default gateway*. To be fully functional, a host must be able to communicate off of its LAN. So, when a host is configured, either statically or via DHCP, it has a default gateway, as shown in Figure 5-12. This default gateway is actually the router that will receive transmissions from the network nodes when sending traffic offsite.

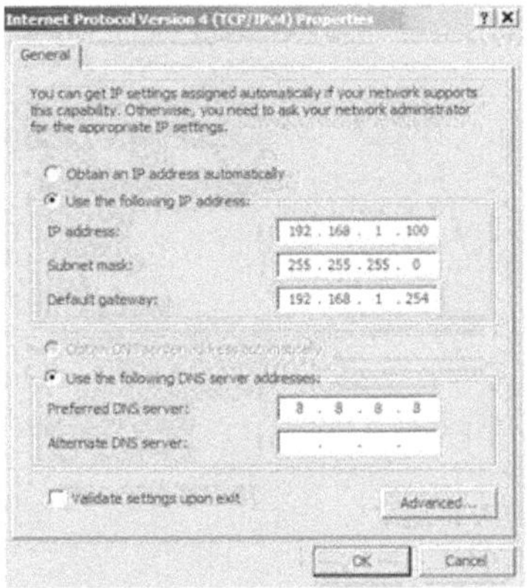

Figure 5-12. Host IP settings

There are three major operations/objects to think about on a router:

- Routing process
- Routing protocols
- Routing table

The routing process is the actual movement of IP packets from one port to another, the routing table holds the information used by the routing process, and routing protocols such as the Routing Information Protocol (RIP) or Open Shortest Path First (OSPF) might be used to communicate with other routers. Hosts, switches, and APs do not participate in these processes, although the SAT and forwarding database (FDB) do behave in similar fashion. A simple routing table appears in Figure 5-13.

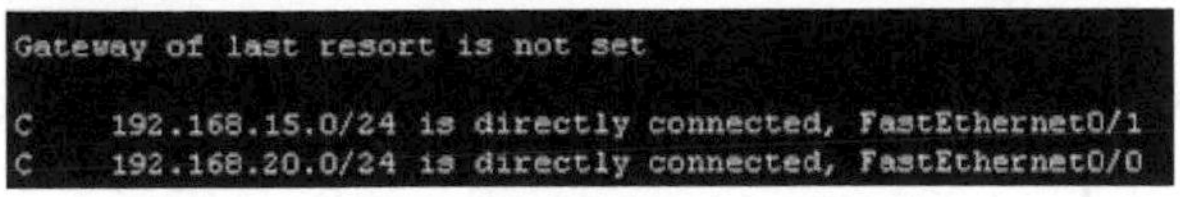

```
Gateway of last resort is not set

C    192.168.15.0/24 is directly connected, FastEthernet0/1
C    192.168.20.0/24 is directly connected, FastEthernet0/0
```

Figure 5-13. Router routing table

Another major difference between router behavior and the operation of lower-layer devices is that routers change the Layer 2 frames. When a transmission is destined for an offsite location, the frame on the incoming side is completely removed and replaced with an appropriate frame on the outgoing side. Consider the small network shown in Figure 5-14.

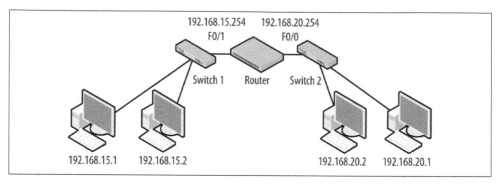

Figure 5-14. Routed topology

The two networks shown in Figure 5-14 have been interconnected via the router. Addresses for the nodes and router interfaces have been filled in. Node A and Node B use the leftmost router interface (192.168.15.254) as their default gateway. Node C and Node D use 192.168.20.254. We already know that if Node A and Node B communicate, the entire process is handled by these two nodes and Switch 1. Switch 1 will examine the MAC addresses. An important detail that we often gloss over is that the Ethernet frames will be addressed from the MAC address of Node A to the MAC address of Node B.

This changes as we go to the network on the other side of the router. Nodes on a particular network will never know the MAC addresses for nodes residing on distant networks. Instead, Layer 2 frames are addressed to router interfaces, and this is actually how we ask a router to forward something for us. So, when Node A wishes to communicate with Node D, it sends an IP packet encapsulated in an Ethernet frame to the router. The IP packet is addressed from Node A to Node D, but the Ethernet frame is addressed from the MAC address of Node A to the MAC address of the left router interface, or F0/1. As the router forwards the IP packet to the other network (192.168.20.0), the frame is rebuilt for the new network. The IP packet is still addressed from Node A to Node D, but the Ethernet frame is addressed from the router interface F0/0 to the MAC address of Node D. The MAC addresses are learned via ARP. If we now go back to the process described at the beginning of the chapter, the whole thing begins to come together.

Another Gateway

At the beginning of this chapter, there was mention of a device called a gateway. This is not to be confused with the default gateway or the home gateway. In this case, *gateway* refers to a device that understands and converts between two networking models. For example, a gateway is necessary when connecting IPX/SPX and TCP/IP and AppleTalk networks together. Since TCP/IP is the dominant model, the usage of this type of gateway is much diminished. However, VoIP breathes new life into this old term because now TCP/IP networks must talk directly with Signaling System 7 on the telephone network.

Multilayer Switches and Home Gateways

The network devices described so far behave in a very stratified manner. They rarely leave their networking model layers and do not share responsibilities. But, just as hubs and bridges are fading away, so too are the straightforward single-use switch and router. Multilayer switches are an attempt to achieve performance gains while collapsing the chassis a bit. If we consider the routed topology shown in Figure 5-14, we can see that there are three network devices and that the router takes up a port on each switch. However, if the switches understood a little more about routing, we could reduce the number of devices and power outlets, recover some network ports, use less A/C cooling, and save some space. Most vendors have a collection of products that accomplish exactly that. In fact, it is getting more and more difficult to find a device that is "just a router" or "just a switch." Another nice feature is that now a single device can route between VLANs. However, there is a bit more to the story than these improvements alone. Multilayer switches are also trying to improve the forwarding efficiency of the network.

The idea is that if the device understands something about the topology of the network (i.e., MAC addresses in addition to IP networks), this knowledge might be leveraged to improve forwarding times. For example, in Figure 5-14, a transmission from Node A to Node D would normally be processed by two SATs and a router routing table. With multilayer switching, one SAT and one routing table would be in use. Finally, if we take advantage of the topology information, it is possible that the routing table would not be necessary. With these modifications, the topology shown in Figure 5-14 might be rebuilt with a multilayer switch as shown in Figure 5-15.

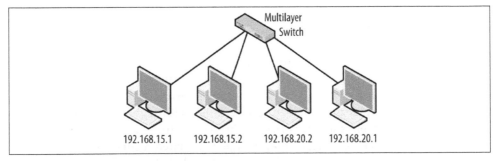

Figure 5-15. Multilayer switch topology

Home gateways are another interesting type of device, because they combine so many features from so many layers of the TCP/IP networking model. A typical unit includes four to eight switch ports and a wireless interface. All of the nodes connected to these interfaces are on the same network and receive IP addresses from the gateway. A common network address is 192.168.1.0. Since the gateway is providing addresses, it is a DHCP server. The gateway also routes traffic to the outside world, but before it forwards the traffic, the source IP addresses are translated by the gateway. The 192.168 address space is considered a private network and cannot be used on the public Internet. This translation is called network address translation (NAT) and is primarily concerned with the conservation of IP addresses. Different SOHO networks can use the same network addresses because of this translation. Finally, outside requests will not be forwarded to the internal network, because the gateway is preconfigured to block unsolicited packets. Thus, the gateway is performing the functions of a basic firewall. Figure 5-16 depicts a functional diagram of the gateway, including the switch, DHCP server, router, NAT operation, and firewall.

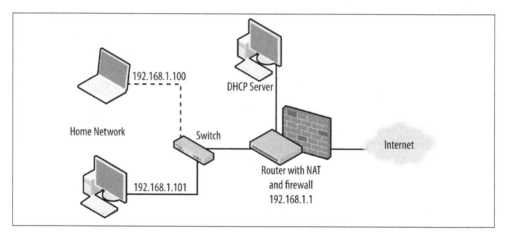

Figure 5-16. Home gateway

Security Warning

If we look at these devices and their topologies from a security standpoint, we can begin to understand potential attack vectors that might take advantage of their basic operation. Every single device and protocol that is part of the network can be attacked or used as an attack vector. If we imagine that an attacker might either plug into our network or be listening on the wireless side, we place the threat at the front door. Starting with Layer 1 hubs, the weakness is very clear—they operate in a shared media and make no effort to filter traffic. In Layer 2, switches filter traffic based on MAC address, but they are willing to forward broadcast frames everywhere. This means that over time, an attacker can learn quite a bit via passive eavesdropping. Common improvements are the addition of VLANs to reduce exposure and port-based security to prevent unauthorized MAC addresses from gaining access to the network.

Wireless networks present a completely different problem in that the traffic is broadcast out to the world. However, if the wireless APs are connected back to a switch configured with VLANs, we can minimize the amount of traffic that is broadcast. Wireless networks should also be protected with encryption. Historically, we had Wired Equivalent Privacy (WEP), followed by WiFi Protected Access with a Pre-Shared Key (WPA-PSK) for small networks. Since both of these have been cracked, the recommended minimum encryption for these network types is WPA2-PSK with a 20-character passphrase using number and letter combinations. This goes a long way to prevent dictionary or brute-force attacks.

Routers provide the greatest amount of inherent filtering because they will not forward anything unless the packets are destined for another network. So, broadcast frames are not allowed to pass. The problem is that, by default, routers are also very accommodating. If you send a router a packet for forwarding, it will do its best to see that it gets there, whether you are a bad guy or not. In addition, routers have an IP address. That is not to say that switches and APs never do—switches and APs will often be given IP addresses for the purpose of remote access and management protocols such as Telnet, Secure Shell (SSH), and the Simple Network Management Protocol (SNMP). But routers always have IP addresses and are often directly connected to the outside world. Like hosts, routers can be attacked, because they can be reached via the IP address. This also means routers, like hosts, must be secured in the areas of accounts, patch levels, shutting down access to services, and firewalls or filter rules. Finally, any protocol (such as a routing protocol) that involves the router should also be secured.

Summary

When building a network, you are going to use the same building blocks as most other networks: switches, APs, and routers. Newer implementations will see increased use of multilayer switches, though it is tough to justify throwing out perfectly good routers and switches. In this chapter, you have hopefully developed an understanding of not only the purpose of each device, but how it operates. Each device has a particular set of functions as it processes packets and frames.

When packets traverse a network, it is possible to track each and every decision along the way in order to determine the best device to use. The tables used to make these decisions can also be used to diagnose problems, optimize performance, and understand potential security threats.

Review Questions

1. Match the following devices to the proper networking model layer:

   a. Hub   A. Application
   b. Switch   B. Transport
   c. Access point   C. Internet
   d. Router   D. Link/Network
                   E. Physical

2. Match the following devices to the type of addressing processed:

   a. Hub   A. Port
   b. Switch   B. IP address
   c. Access point   C. MAC address
   d. Router   D. 1s and 0s

3. Match the following devices to the tables used to process packets or frames. For some devices, you may select more than one table:

   a. Host   A. Routing table
   b. Switch   B. Source address table
   c. Access point   C. Forwarding database
   d. Router   D. ARP table

4. Switches stop collisions from propagating. True or false?

5. APs stop broadcast frames from propagating. True or false?

6. A SAT is a mapping between MAC addresses and IP addresses. True or false?

7. While routers process packets, they do not change or manipulate the frames or packets themselves. True or false?

8. A default gateway is a router interface. True or false?

9. A multilayer switch is simply a switch that understands how to forward packets between VLANs. True or false?

10. One of the reasons switches are very fast even when connected to a wireless network is that Ethernet frames and 802.11 frames are almost identical. True or false?

Review Answers

1. a) E, b) D, c) D, d) C

2. a) D, b) C, c) C, d) B

3. a) A, D; b) B; c) C; d) A, D

4. True

5. False

6. False

7. False

8. True

9. False

10. False

Lab Activities

Activity 1—Traffic Comparison

Materials: Wireshark, switch, three computers

1. Configure the IP addresses for the computers.

2. Connect all three computers to the switch.

3. On all three machines, start Wireshark.

4. Ping between two of the computers.

5. Compare the traffic that is seen on the computers. What is the difference in the traffic? Why is there a difference?

Activity 2—Layer 2 Trace

Materials: Two computers, Wireshark, switch

1. Configure the IP addresses for the computers.

2. Connect both computers to the switch.

3. Start a capture on each machine.

4. Access the SAT on the switch.

5. Access the ARP (`arp -a`) and routing (`route print`) tables on the hosts.

6. Ping from one computer to another.

7. Using the tables and packet capture, explain exactly how the packet gets from one node to another. Include every device in your explanation.

Activity 3—Tables

Materials: AP, router, switch, wired host, wireless host (use devices that are available; not all are required)

1. Add a router and AP to the topology you created in Activity 2. This will give you two IP-based networks.

2. Connect a node to the AP.

3. Configure the IP addresses and ensure that all nodes can ping each other.

4. Establish a management connection to each of the devices used.

5. Pull up the tables discussed in this chapter for each of the devices.

6. Explain the content of these tables and how it got there.

Activity 4—Layer 3 Trace

Materials: Two computers, Wireshark, two switches, router (one switch may be used; however, configuring VLANs may add confusion)

1. Configure a topology similar to the one shown in Figure 5-14.

2. Start a capture on each machine.

3. Access the SAT on the switch.

4. Access the ARP (`arp -a`) and routing (`route print`) tables on the hosts.

5. Access the routing table for the router.

6. Ping from one computer to another.

7. Using the tables and packet capture, explain exactly how the packet gets from one node to another. Include every device in your explanation.

Activity 5—Traffic Comparison

Materials: Two computers, Wireshark, two switches, router (one switch may be used; however, configuring VLANs may cause confusion)

1. Using the topology from Activity 4, start a capture on both computers.

2. Ping from one node to another.

3. In the packet captures, compare the packets and frames seen on one side of the router to those seen on the other.

4. What are the differences? Why are they different?

CHAPTER 6

Internet Control Message Protocol

"ICMP error messages signal network error conditions that were encountered while processing an internet datagram. Depending on the particular scenario, the error conditions being reported might or might not get solved in the near term."

—RFC 4443

The Internet Control Message Protocol (ICMP) provides error messages and feedback during network operations. These messages provide insight into the current state of the network, making it simpler to troubleshoot network connectivity problems. An ICMP error message is often sent in response to a failed transmission attempt. In addition, ICMP messages allow us to ask the network for information. This chapter will explain ICMP by taking an in-depth look at several of the most common message types and the conditions that cause them. The basic tools used herein include captures from Wireshark, the output from the Windows command (DOS) shell, and output seen from a Cisco router.

RFC 792 defines several ICMP message types and forms the basis of our discussion. Contemporary networks typically use a handful of these message types to deal with standard issues. Several other RFCs have contributed to ICMP, most of which are designed to handle very particular situations. A list of these RFCs is included at the end of the chapter.

ICMP exists within the Internet Layer (Layer 3) of the TCP/IP model and is encapsulated in an IP datagram (shown in Figure 6-1). All IP-based nodes, regardless of operating system or device type, use ICMP for error and notification messages. However, the behavior can vary between systems.

```
Ethernet II, src: Cisco_28:1b:e1 (00:05:5e:28:1b:e1), Dst: HonHaiPr_12:1c:a9 (00:1f:e2:12:1c:a9)
Internet Protocol, src: 192.168.2.254 (192.168.2.254), Dst: 192.168.2.1 (192.168.2.1)
Internet Control Message Protocol
```

Figure 6-1. ICMP encapsulation

According to the RFC, to keep the error messages to a minimum, no ICMP error messages are sent about ICMP error messages and, in the case of fragmented IP packets, error messages are sent only regarding the first fragment (fragment 0) of the IP packet. So, if an ICMP error message is generated because of a problem, this message cannot inspire the creation of other error messages. However, in the case where the ICMP message is informational, other ICMP messages can result. For example, if you were to ping a node on another network via an ICMP echo request, and the intervening routers could not forward the traffic to the destination, the router might respond with an ICMP destination unreachable message. These ICMP message types are explained more fully later in this chapter.

Security is not often associated with ICMP, as many of the message types defined provide clear-text information about the network or its operation. In addition, many network devices and hosts are configured to answer ICMP questions without hesitation. In the case of *traceroute*, packets are normally permitted to traverse the network regardless of their source or purpose. Finally, the ICMP echo request is often used in packet injection attacks designed for breaking encryption schemes, because the alphabet is contained in the payload. This provides an easily recognizable pattern for the before-encryption and after-encryption snapshots.

Structure

Generally, ICMP messages have a similar structure. The next series of figures are Wireshark views of the same ICMP packet, each pointing out a different aspect. The ICMP echo request is the payload for the IP packet and is contained within the data field. ICMP does not possess a TCP or UDP header. Expanding the IP header shows us that the IP packet payload type is 01 for ICMP. This is highlighted in Figure 6-2.

```
Ethernet II, Src: Cisco_28:1b:e1 (00:05:5e:28:1b:e1), Dst: HonHaiPr_12:1c:a9 (00:1f:e2:12:1c:a9)
Internet Protocol, Src: 192.168.2.254 (192.168.2.254), Dst: 192.168.2.1 (192.168.2.1)
  Version: 4
  Header length: 20 bytes
⊞ Differentiated Services Field: 0x00 (DSCP 0x00: Default; ECN: 0x00)
  Total Length: 60
  Identification: 0x026d (621)
⊞ Flags: 0x00
  Fragment offset: 0
  Time to live: 255
  Protocol: ICMP (0x01)
⊞ Header checksum: 0x3304 [correct]
  Source: 192.168.2.254 (192.168.2.254)
  Destination: 192.168.2.1 (192.168.2.1)
Internet Control Message Protocol
```

Figure 6-2. IP payload type ICMP

In Figure 6-3, the expanded ICMP header depicts the general format for ICMP messages. This message happens to be an echo reply.

```
Ethernet II, Src: Cisco_28:1b:e1 (00:05:5e:28:1b:e1), Dst: HonHaiPr_12:1c:a9 (00:1f:e2:12:1c:a9)
Internet Protocol, Src: 192.168.2.254 (192.168.2.254), Dst: 192.168.2.1 (192.168.2.1)
Internet Control Message Protocol
  Type: 0 (Echo (ping) reply)
  Code: 0 ()
  Checksum: 0x5554 [correct]
  Identifier: 0x0001
  Sequence number: 7 (0x0007)
⊞ Data (32 bytes)
```

Figure 6-3. ICMP general format

The fields in the ICMP message are as follows:

Type
> The type of message. Common types include:

>> 0—Echo reply
>> 3—Destination unreachable
>> 4—Source quench
>> 5—Redirect
>> 8—Echo request
>> 9—Router advertisement
>> 10—Router solicitation message
>> 11—Time exceeded
>> 12—Parameter problem
>> 13—Timestamp
>> 14—Timestamp reply
>> 15—Information request
>> 16—Information reply

Code

Each type of message defines one or more codes that are used to indicate the operation of or variation in the message type. If there is only one code, its value will typically be 0.

Checksum

The 16-bit one's complement of the one's complement sum of the ICMP message, starting with the ICMP type. When computing the checksum, the checksum field should be 0.

Identifier

This field is not always present. In this case (Figure 6-3), it provides a reference point for matching the correct echo reply to the original echo request.

Sequence number

This value is also used in matching requests and replies.

Internet header + 64 bits of data datagram

In the case where an ICMP message is generated in response to a message from a network node, the ICMP message will include a copy of the original IP header plus 64 bits of the original message payload. This is to help the source host in identifying the reason for the ICMP message. As shown in Figure 6-3, not all ICMP messages contain this field.

Payload

In the case of an echo request, this is the data generated by the ICMP process. It is present only in some of the ICMP message types.

Operations and Types

This section covers the common ICMP behavior, the purposes of the various messages, and the scenarios in which they are produced.

Echo Request (Type 0) and Echo Reply (Type 8)

A common tool for testing connectivity is the *ping* program, which generates ICMP echo request packets. By sending an ICMP echo request, the sender is asking the receiving node to send an ICMP echo reply back. This is called the *responder function*. *ping* program behavior varies between operating systems, but the basic rules are the same. An example of the Windows exchange is shown in Figure 6-4. By default, Windows *ping* sends four ICMP echo requests, each having a payload size of 32 bytes.

```
C:\Users\bruce>ping 192.168.15.1

Pinging 192.168.15.1 with 32 bytes of data:
Reply from 192.168.15.1: bytes=32 time=1ms TTL=255
Reply from 192.168.15.1: bytes=32 time=1ms TTL=255
Reply from 192.168.15.1: bytes=32 time=2ms TTL=255
Reply from 192.168.15.1: bytes=32 time=1ms TTL=255

Ping statistics for 192.168.15.1:
    Packets: Sent = 4, Received = 4, Lost = 0 (0% loss),
Approximate round trip times in milli-seconds:
    Minimum = 1ms, Maximum = 2ms, Average = 1ms
```

Figure 6-4. ping command-line output

The packets resulting from this command are shown in Figure 6-5. In this case, the entire conversation includes the ARP request, the ARP reply, four ICMP echo requests (type 8), and the four corresponding ICMP replies (type 0). The ARP messages are generated because the ARP table on the sender does not include the address of the destination.

20 26.889800	HonHaiPr_90:d5:db	Broadcast	ARP	Who has 192.168.15.17 Tell 192.168.15.103
21 26.892093	Cisco-Li_7f:fb:9d	HonHaiPr_90:d5:db	ARP	192.168.15.1 is at 00:14:bf:7f:fb:9d
22 26.892134	192.168.15.103	192.168.15.1	ICMP	Echo (ping) request
23 26.893278	192.168.15.1	192.168.15.103	ICMP	Echo (ping) reply
24 27.892528	192.168.15.103	192.168.15.1	ICMP	Echo (ping) request
25 27.894209	192.168.15.1	192.168.15.103	ICMP	Echo (ping) reply
26 28.906559	192.168.15.103	192.168.15.1	ICMP	Echo (ping) request
27 28.908002	192.168.15.1	192.168.15.103	ICMP	Echo (ping) reply
28 29.920400	192.168.15.103	192.168.15.1	ICMP	Echo (ping) request
29 29.921921	192.168.15.1	192.168.15.103	ICMP	Echo (ping) reply

Figure 6-5. ICMP echo conversation

The ARP messages are not specific to the *ping* program and are generated anytime a network device communicates with another when corresponding ARP table entries are absent. Figure 6-6 is an expansion of the echo request and reply messages, and a direct comparison shows their differences and commonalities.

```
⊞ Ethernet II, Src: HonHaiPr_90:d5:db (00:22:68:90:d5:db), Dst: Cisco-Li_7f:fb:9d (00:14:bf:7f:fb:9d)
⊞ Internet Protocol, Src: 192.168.15.103 (192.168.15.103), Dst: 192.168.15.1 (192.168.15.1)
⊟ Internet Control Message Protocol
    Type: 8 (Echo (ping) request)
    Code: 0 ()
    Checksum: 0x4d42 [correct]
    Identifier: 0x0001
    Sequence number: 25 (0x0019)
  ⊟ Data (32 bytes)
      Data: 6162636465666768696A6B6C6D6E6F707172737475767761...
      [Length: 32]
⊞ Ethernet II, Src: Cisco-Li_7f:fb:9d (00:14:bf:7f:fb:9d), Dst: HonHaiPr_90:d5:db (00:22:68:90:d5:db)
⊞ Internet Protocol, Src: 192.168.15.1 (192.168.15.1), Dst: 192.168.15.103 (192.168.15.103)
⊟ Internet Control Message Protocol
    Type: 0 (Echo (ping) reply)
    Code: 0 ()
    Checksum: 0x5542 [correct]
    Identifier: 0x0001
    Sequence number: 25 (0x0019)
  ⊟ Data (32 bytes)
      Data: 6162636465666768696A6B6C6D6E6F707172737475767761...
      [Length: 32]
```

Figure 6-6. ICMP echo request and reply packets

First, the echo request is a type 8, while the echo reply is a type 0. Notice that the
identifiers and sequence numbers for these two packets are the same, since they are part
of the same conversation. Finally, the data, or payload, is a series of numbers from 61
to 76, repeating. These are the hexadecimal values for the ASCII table characters. As an
example, the hexadecimal value 61 corresponds to the base 10 value of 97, which in turn
corresponds to a lowercase *a* in the ASCII table. Windows sends the letters *a* through
w in the payload, and these values will repeat for larger payload sizes. Other devices
send different characters. However, with the responder function, whatever is sent is
supposed to be returned. The payload decode for this example is shown in Figure 6-7.

```
⊞ Ethernet II, Src: HonHaiPr_90:d5:db (00:22:68:90:d5:db), Dst: Cisco-Li_7f:fb:9d (00:14:bf:7f:fb:9d)
⊞ Internet Protocol, Src: 192.168.15.103 (192.168.15.103), Dst: 192.168.15.1 (192.168.15.1)
⊟ Internet Control Message Protocol
    Type: 8 (Echo (ping) request)
    Code: 0 ()
    Checksum: 0x4d42 [correct]
    Identifier: 0x0001
    Sequence number: 25 (0x0019)
  ⊟ Data (32 bytes)

0000  00 14 bf 7f fb 9d 00 22  68 90 d5 db 08 00 45 00   ......." h.....E.
0010  00 3c 06 6b 00 00 80 01  94 9d c0 a8 0f 67 c0 a8   .<.k.... .....g..
0020  0f 01 08 00 4d 42 00 01  00 19 61 62 63 64 65 66   ....MB.. ..abcdef
0030  67 68 69 6a 6b 6c 6d 6e  6f 70 71 72 73 74 75 76   ghijklmn opqrstuv
0040  77 61 62 63 64 65 66 67  68 69                     wabcdefg hi
```

Figure 6-7. ICMP echo payload

Echo fun

ping is a favored diagnostic tool and is used everywhere. However, using *ping* while
sitting behind a router performing network address translation (NAT) brings up an
interesting question. With basic NAT, the router modifies the IP header of outbound
packets by changing the source IP address to the outside interface of the router. In effect,

all of the traffic appears to have come from the router rather than the original source host. Figure 6-8 depicts a topology in which the middle router is running NAT. All of the traffic from the 192.168.1.0 and 192.168.2.0 networks is translated on the outside interface of this router. If the right side of the NAT router has an IP address of 192.168.3.253, all of the traffic from these two networks will appear to have come from this one IP address. When a message comes back in response, the router remaps the IP header back to the original IP address and forwards it on.

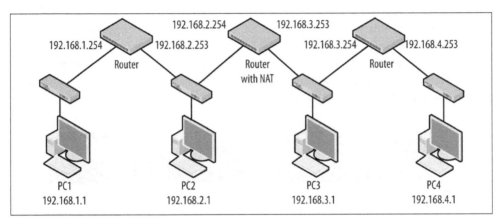

Figure 6-8. Three-router topology with NAT

The usual way to keep track of all these conversations is by the source and destination IP addresses, in addition to the Layer 4 port numbers (TCP and UDP). But *ping* can be used through a NAT device, and in fact, a node can run several instances of *ping* at the same time. However, ICMP does not have a Layer 4 header. In other words, the port numbers are missing. If this is true, how are the different ICMP conversations tracked through the NAT router? How do the packets return to the correct source?

The answer lies in the header of the ICMP packet. In this case, we are actually going to use the identifier value along with the IP addresses to keep track of the conversations. Figure 6-9 depicts an example of an ICMP echo request. The corresponding translation seen in a NAT table is shown in Figure 6-10. PC 1 has an IP address of 192.168.1.1 and attempts to ping PC 3, which has an IP address of 192.168.3.1. Since the middle router in Figure 6-8 is running NAT, it translates this packet so that it appears to have come from 192.168.3.253.

```
Ethernet II, Src: Cisco_28:1b:e0 (00:05:5e:28:1b:e0), Dst: Standard_08:e0:27 (00:e0:29:08:e0:27)
Internet Protocol, Src: 192.168.3.253 (192.168.3.253), Dst: 192.168.3.1 (192.168.3.1)
Internet Control Message Protocol
  Type: 8 (Echo (ping) request)
  Code: 0 ()
  Checksum: 0x195c [correct]
  Identifier: 0x0400
  Sequence number: 12288 (0x3000)
⊞ Data (32 bytes)
```

Figure 6-9. ICMP echo after translation

The identifier for this packet has a value 0f 0x0400, which is in hexadecimal, and converting this to base 10 numbers returns 1024. The translation table for the router is shown in Figure 6-10, where we can see the original source and destination, and the addresses used in the translation. In addition, the identifier value is clearly visible as the replacement for the TCP or UDP port number.

```
Router#
Router#sh ip nat translations
Pro Inside global      Inside local      Outside local      Outside global
icmp 192.168.3.253:1024 192.168.1.1:1024  192.168.3.1:1024   192.168.3.1:1024
Router#
```

Figure 6-10. Cisco translation table

Redirect (Type 5)

The goal of a redirect message is to inform a host that there is a better path to the destination than the one just tried. The diagram in Figure 6-11 depicts a topology in which a redirect often occurs, but according to RFC 792, a couple of conditions must first be satisfied:

- The new forwarding router and the host identified by the source IP address of the datagram must be on the same network.

- The datagram in question must not be using the IP source route options and the gateway address must not be in the destination address field.

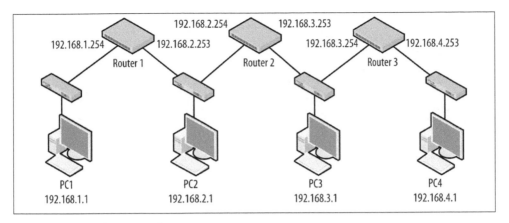

Figure 6-11. Redirect topology

The topology shown in Figure 6-11 can be used to demonstrate a redirect. Instead of NAT, the interesting characteristic is that PC 2 and PC 3 are connected between routers. This means that possible destinations can be found in both directions from these machines. In the case of PC 1 and PC 4, all destinations can be reached by traveling in one direction.

PC 3 on the 192.168.3.0 network is configured with Router 2 as its default gateway. Regardless of the destination, PC 3 will send traffic to this router. However, if PC 3 attempts to connect to PC 4 on the 192.168.4.0 network, the router must send this transmission right back out the same interface it came in.

When the packet arrives at Router 2, the router will consult its routing table and learn that the destination is connected back the other way, via Router 3. Since the source host (PC 3) and the left interface of Router 3 are both on the same network, the first condition for a redirect is satisfied.

The IP source route options are used when a host attempts to specify the path a packet will take. In that case, the IP header will expand to include as many as five additional hops or routers. However, using IP source route information is unusual (condition 2), so Router 2 will typically generate an ICMP redirect message back to PC 3. The redirect message instructs the host to use Router 3 the next time PC 4 or the 192.168.4.0 network is the destination. An example of a redirect message is shown in Figure 6-12.

```
Ethernet II, Src: Cisco_28:1b:e0 (00:05:5e:28:1b:e0), Dst: Standard_08:e0:27 (00:e0:29:08:e0:27)
Internet Protocol, Src: 192.168.3.253 (192.168.3.253), Dst: 192.168.3.1 (192.168.3.1)
Internet Control Message Protocol
   Type: 5 (Redirect)
   Code: 0 (Redirect for network)
   Checksum: 0xe0fc [correct]
   Gateway address: 192.168.3.254 (192.168.3.254)
⊟ Internet Protocol, Src: 192.168.3.1 (192.168.3.1), Dst: 192.168.4.254 (192.168.4.254)
     Version: 4
     Header length: 20 bytes
   ⊞ Differentiated Services Field: 0x00 (DSCP 0x00: Default; ECN: 0x00)
     Total Length: 60
     Identification: 0x02d0 (720)
   ⊞ Flags: 0x00
     Fragment offset: 0
     Time to live: 127
     Protocol: ICMP (0x01)
   ⊞ Header checksum: 0xafa1 [correct]
     Source: 192.168.3.1 (192.168.3.1)
     Destination: 192.168.4.254 (192.168.4.254)
⊞ Internet Control Message Protocol
```

Figure 6-12. ICMP redirect

There are a few more details to the process that are worth noting. First is that Router 2 will forward the original packet to the proper destination (192.168.4.254) to avoid losing any packets. The redirect is sent to the source host. Second, once the redirect has been sent to the original source host, the host installs a new local routing table entry so that the next time, it will use the proper router.

A majority of these local routing table updates will be host- or network-specific, and the redirect messages will typically have a code of 1 or 0, as shown in Figure 6-12. This is the default behavior of many routers. RFC 792 includes several codes to go along with the type 5 message:

> 0—Redirect datagrams for the network
> 1—Redirect datagrams for the host
> 2—Redirect datagrams for the type of service and network
> 3—Redirect datagrams for the type of service and host

A host like PC 3 could have many of these dynamically created routing table entries. A large number of redirects can mean that the network design or location of resources may have to be reviewed. An example of a host routing table with a host-specific entry is shown in Figure 6-13.

```
=============================================================================
Active Routes:
Network Destination        Netmask          Gateway        Interface  Metric
          0.0.0.0          0.0.0.0    192.168.3.253      192.168.3.1   1000
        127.0.0.0        255.0.0.0        127.0.0.1        127.0.0.1      1
      192.168.3.0    255.255.255.0      192.168.3.1      192.168.3.1     30
      192.168.3.1  255.255.255.255        127.0.0.1        127.0.0.1     30
    192.168.3.255  255.255.255.255      192.168.3.1      192.168.3.1     30
    192.168.4.254  255.255.255.255    192.168.3.254      192.168.3.1      1
        224.0.0.0        240.0.0.0      192.168.3.1      192.168.3.1     30
  255.255.255.255  255.255.255.255      192.168.3.1      192.168.3.1      1
Default Gateway:       192.168.3.253
=============================================================================
```

Figure 6-13. Host routing table with host-specific route

Most routing table entries are for networks, hosts, or special addresses. In this case, there has been an entry installed for one destination in particular—192.168.4.254. This is the host-specific entry.

Finally, an ICMP redirect has a different set of fields than the echo request/reply combination discussed earlier. In addition to the code change, the request also contains the new router address for the specified host (which also appears in the routing table entry), the original IP header, and 64 bits of the payload. The redirect not only informs the source of the new path, but also copies part of the original message. In Figure 6-12, the new gateway (192.168.3.254), the original IP header, and eight bytes of the ICMP initial echo request are all visible.

Time to Live Exceeded (Type 11)

Every single IP packet has a time to live (TTL) field. This is the number of hops or router interfaces the packet is permitted to traverse before it is removed from the network. When the TTL reaches zero, the packet is removed from the network and an ICMP "time to live exceeded" message is generated, indicating that the packet was dropped. This is sent back to the original source host as feedback. Figure 6-14 shows an ICMP time exceeded message. This is a type 11 code 0. Aside from adding a checksum, the rest is simply the original IP header and 64 bits of the dropped packet.

```
Ethernet II, Src: Cisco_28:1b:e0 (00:05:5e:28:1b:e0), Dst: Standard_08:e0:27 (00:e0:29:08:e0:27)
Internet Protocol, Src: 192.168.3.253 (192.168.3.253), Dst: 192.168.3.1 (192.168.3.1)
  Version: 4
  Header length: 20 bytes
⊞ Differentiated Services Field: 0xc0 (DSCP 0x30: Class Selector 6; ECN: 0x00)
  Total Length: 56
  Identification: 0x02db (731)
⊞ Flags: 0x00
  Fragment offset: 0
  Time to live: 255
  Protocol: ICMP (0x01)
⊞ Header checksum: 0x2fdb [correct]
  Source: 192.168.3.253 (192.168.3.253)
  Destination: 192.168.3.1 (192.168.3.1)
Internet Control Message Protocol
  Type: 11 (Time-to-live exceeded)
  Code: 0 (Time to live exceeded in transit)
  Checksum: 0x9fa3 [correct]
⊞ Internet Protocol, Src: 192.168.3.1 (192.168.3.1), Dst: 192.168.1.254 (192.168.1.254)
⊞ Internet Control Message Protocol
```

Figure 6-14. ICMP time exceeded

Time exceeded messages can occur anywhere there is a configuration problem on the
network that results in routers trying to forward traffic back and forth, or when topologies have loops. One common example occurs when neighboring routers are configured with each other as the forwarding router. A less obvious problem occurs when a
link or route goes down, resulting in a path being removed from a routing table.
Figure 6-15 shows this topology. Router 2 is using Router 3 as a default route. Both
Router 2 and Router 3 believe that the 192.168.1.0 network is available to the left via
Router 1.

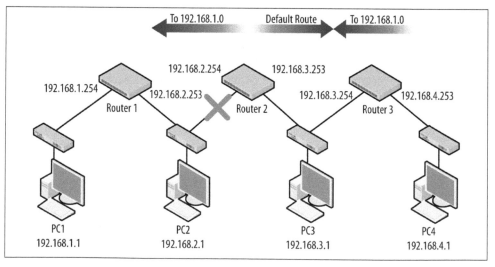

Figure 6-15. Time exceeded topology

During normal operation, the traffic for hosts on the 192.168.1.0 network will be handled by Router 1. However, if a network is shut down, the behavior of the routers will change dramatically. If the connection between Router 2 and Router 1 is lost, it is common to have Router 2 remove the 192.168.1.0 and 192.168.2.0 networks from its local routing table. If a network host (192.168.3.1) attempts to contact 192.168.1.1, Router 2 will send this traffic to its default route (Router 3), because this entry no longer exists in the routing table. The problem is that Router 3 is still configured to connect to the 192.168.1.0 network via Router 2 and thus sends the traffic back to Router 2. The process then begins again, eventually resulting in an ICMP time exceeded message.

Tracing a Route

You can use time exceeded messages for diagnostic purposes (for example, by using path discovery programs). *tracert* is a program built into Windows (*traceroute* is the equivalent for Linux and Cisco) that sends out ICMP messages with the TTL field in the IP header incremented by 1 in subsequent packets. So, the first ICMP echo request for the destination goes out with a TTL of 1. This echo request is repeated three or four times, depending on the operating system. The very first router decrements the TTL field to 0 and returns the ICMP time exceeded message. This informs the sender of the first outbound router interface.

As the transmission moves out from the source host, the IP TTL field goes up by one so that the next router returns the time exceeded message. In this way, we eventually work our way to the destination with the router interfaces that face the source host reporting their presence. An example of the Windows *tracert* output is shown in Figure 6-16.

```
C:\Documents and Settings\Administrator>tracert 192.168.1.1

Tracing route to 192.168.1.1 over a maximum of 30 hops

  1     *        1 ms    <1 ms   192.168.3.253
  2     1 ms     1 ms     1 ms   192.168.2.253
  3     1 ms    <1 ms    <1 ms   192.168.1.1

Trace complete.
```

Figure 6-16. Windows tracert output

Referring back to the topology in Figure 6-11, a host on the 192.168.4.0 network attempts to discover the path to the 192.168.1.0 network, and specifically the host 192.168.1.1. The resulting output displays the router interfaces receiving the ICMP echo request trace packets.

Destination Unreachable (Type 3)

Just as the name suggests, the type 3 message tells a source host that the pathway to the destination is unknown. When a router is missing information that will allow a packet to be forwarded, the feedback provided to the source host is the ICMP destination unreachable message. This is a very common occurrence when a router does not have a default route (gateway of last resort), because it will not be able to forward traffic to any network not configured via directly connected, static, or dynamic routes. As with a redirect, there are several codes for the destination unreachable message:

0—Net unreachable
1—Host unreachable
2—Protocol unreachable
3—Port unreachable
4—Fragmentation needed and DF (do not fragment) set
5—Source route failed

The most common of these messages are the host (code 1) and port (code 3) unreachable messages. These are shown in Figure 6-17. The messages share the following fields: type, code, checksum, the original IP header, and 64 bits of the data from the original packet. The difference between these two is that the host unreachable message is generated because the router does not know the path, while the port unreachable message is generated because the service is not available via the router. Incidentally, a router or firewall can generate a type 3 message with a code of 13, which means that the packet has been administratively filtered or actively blocked.

```
⊞ Ethernet II, Src: Cisco_23:85:68 (00:19:06:23:85:68), Dst: D-Link_c1:d2:01 (00:50:ba:c1:d2:01)
⊞ Internet Protocol, Src: 192.168.10.254 (192.168.10.254), Dst: 192.168.10.11 (192.168.10.11)
⊟ Internet Control Message Protocol
    Type: 3 (Destination unreachable)
    Code: 1 (Host unreachable)
    Checksum: 0xa7a2 [correct]
  ⊞ Internet Protocol, Src: 192.168.10.11 (192.168.10.11), Dst: 129.21.21.1 (129.21.21.1)
  ⊞ Internet Control Message Protocol


⊞ Ethernet II, Src: Cisco-Li_7f:fb:9d (00:14:bf:7f:fb:9d), Dst: HonHaiPr_90:d5:db (00:22:68:90:d5:db)
⊞ Internet Protocol, Src: 10.241.128.1 (10.241.128.1), Dst: 192.168.15.103 (192.168.15.103)
⊟ Internet Control Message Protocol
    Type: 3 (Destination unreachable)
    Code: 3 (Port unreachable)
    Checksum: 0x50f5 [correct]
  ⊞ Internet Protocol, Src: 192.168.15.103 (192.168.15.103), Dst: 10.241.128.1 (10.241.128.1)
  ⊞ User Datagram Protocol, Src Port: netbios-ns (137), Dst Port: netbios-ns (137)
```

Figure 6-17. ICMP destination unreachable types

Operating system versus ICMP

There is another situation in which the phrase "destination unreachable" is used. When a bad or missing default gateway is configured on a network host, the operating system returns this text to the user. This informs the user that the host (not the router) does not know a path to the destination. This output, and therefore its value to us in troubleshooting, is quite a bit different from the ICMP message.

Pinging a destination that is unknown to the router will result in an ICMP destination unreachable message, and the output in the command window will look like that shown in Figure 6-18. However, if the host does not have a default gateway and we attempt to transmit to a host on another network, the output changes to that shown in Figure 6-19. In the latter case, no packets are transmitted at all—the destination unreachable message comes from the operating system. The value in these different messages is that they both provide vital information about the source of the problem, and the sources couldn't be more different.

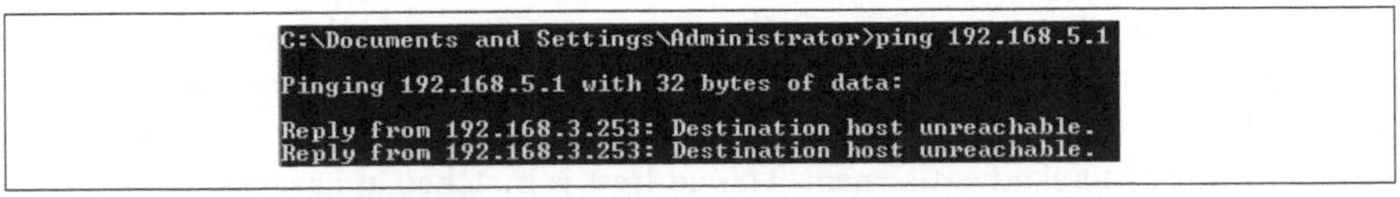

```
C:\Documents and Settings\Administrator>ping 192.168.5.1

Pinging 192.168.5.1 with 32 bytes of data:

Reply from 192.168.3.253: Destination host unreachable.
Reply from 192.168.3.253: Destination host unreachable.
```

Figure 6-18. ICMP destination unreachable command output

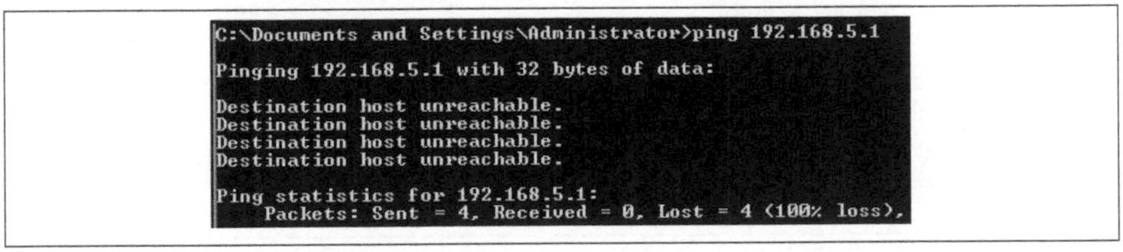

```
C:\Documents and Settings\Administrator>ping 192.168.5.1

Pinging 192.168.5.1 with 32 bytes of data:

Destination host unreachable.
Destination host unreachable.
Destination host unreachable.
Destination host unreachable.

Ping statistics for 192.168.5.1:
    Packets: Sent = 4, Received = 0, Lost = 4 (100% loss),
```

Figure 6-19. Command shell output from a missing gateway

Another interesting point is that while Windows is reporting that four packets were sent, no network traffic is generated as a result of this request, because the destination is off the network and the host is missing a default gateway.

Router Solicitation (Type 10) and Router Advertisements (Type 9)

Type 10 and type 9 messages are not as common as they once were, because they have been largely supplanted by the Dynamic Host Configuration Protocol (DHCP). Their purpose is to provide or request information regarding the routers on the LAN. If a host has an IP address but does not have a default gateway, it can ask the network for an answer by sending out an ICMP router solicitation (type 10) message, as shown in Figure 6-20. Notice that the Layer 3 destination address is the all-routers multicast of 224.0.0.2, and Layer 2 addressing is also multicast.

```
Ethernet II, Src: Standard_08:e0:27 (00:e0:29:08:e0:27), Dst: IPv4mcast_00:00:02 (01:00:5e:00:00:02)
Internet Protocol, Src: 192.168.3.1 (192.168.3.1), Dst: 224.0.0.2 (224.0.0.2)
Internet Control Message Protocol
  Type: 10 (Router solicitation)
  Code: 0 ()
  Checksum: 0xf5ff [correct]
```

Figure 6-20. ICMP router solicitation

This type of ICMP message is also very small and requires extra padding at the end to reach the minimum Ethernet frame size.

Routers periodically announce themselves or answer solicitations by sending out router advertisements like the one shown in Figure 6-21. In this case, the broadcast address is used. While a unicast address works well when answering a particular host, a broadcast is best for the general advertisement. This address is matched at Layer 2.

```
Ethernet II, Src: Cisco_28:1b:e1 (00:05:5e:28:1b:e1), Dst: Broadcast (ff:ff:ff:ff:ff:ff)
Internet Protocol, Src: 192.168.2.254 (192.168.2.254), Dst: 255.255.255.255 (255.255.255.255)
Internet Control Message Protocol
  Type: 9 (Mobile IP Advertisement)
  Code: 0 ()
  Checksum: 0x2b4f [correct]
  Number of addresses: 1
  Address entry size: 2
  Lifetime: 30 minutes
  Router address: 192.168.2.254
  Preference level: 0
```

Figure 6-21. ICMP router advertisement

With the widespread use of DHCP, there is no reason to ask about or receive router information if the default gateway was given along with the IP address. However, router solicitations and advertisements still have use in some wireless applications. In the case of a wireless node roaming from one network to another, the Mobile IP architecture still uses these messages.

A wireless node traveling from its home network to another while utilizing Mobile IP does not get a new IP address via DHCP when it arrives. Instead, it contacts a device called a *foreign agent*. This foreign agent acts as a proxy for the visiting node in that it forwards all transmissions to and from the visiting host. The visiting host and the foreign agent find each other via ICMP router advertisement and solicitation. The messages are modified or extended to include the additional Mobile IP–specific information. However, since most organizations do not permit roaming into and out of their networks, ICMP type 9 and 10 messages are not likely to make a big comeback. IPv6 also makes use of these message types, albeit in the ICMPv6 format.

Digging a Little Deeper—The One's Complement

The checksum in both the IP header and the ICMP message are calculated using the one's complement of the one's complement sum of the 16-bit words in either the header or the message itself. This means that the calculation called the one's complement is completed, and then the complement, or inverse, is used as the checksum value.

For example, suppose the following 16-bit binary streams are added together. The leading zeros are placeholders:

```
0000  1001  1010  1110  1010
0000  1011  0100  0011  0001
0001  0100  1111  0001  1011
```

As you can see, a 1 is carried over to the 17th bit. With the checksum one's complement, this carryover is added back in, as follows:

```
0000  1001  1010  1110  1010
0000  1011  0100  0011  0001
0000  0100  1111  0001  1011
                        0001
      0100  1111  0001  1100
```

Now that the sum (the one's complement) has been completed, the complement or inverse is taken:

```
1011  0000  1110  0011
```

This is the value that is actually used for the checksum, as seen in the ICMP packets—the 16-bit one's complement of the one's complement sum of the ICMP datagram.

IPv6

ICMP will continue to be of use as networks migrate to IPv6. The structure and many of the message types are similar to those used in IPv4. However, ICMPv6 is governed by the rules established in RFC 4443. One change is that the IP header "next header" field changes from a value of 1 to 58. Messages will also continue to be categorized as either informational or error and, where appropriate, will contain some of the original message. The major types of ICMPv6 messages are as follows:

- Type 1—Destination unreachable
- Type 2—Packet too big
- Type 3—Time exceeded

- Type 4—Parameter problem
- Type 128—Echo request
- Type 129—Echo reply

As you can see, many of these messages are performing similar functions to the IPv4 ICMP messages. There have also been a couple of new additions. These newer message types have more to do with changes to the operation of IPv6 than changes to ICMP.

Neighbor discovery is an example of an operational change that has significant impact on ICMP. IPv6 nodes take a very active role in learning about their local topology. During this process, the nodes seek out the Link Layer addresses of neighbors and routers willing to forward traffic, and will age out old information. There are several ICMPv6 message types involved, including router advertisement and solicitation, neighbor advertisement, and solicitation and redirects. Recall that ARP is not a part of IPv6. Some ICMPv6 examples are shown in Figure 6-22, which includes an ICMPv6 router solicitation with the IPv6 header expanded. Notice the "next header" field.

```
Ethernet II, Src: HonHaiPr_12:1c:a9 (00:1f:e2:12:1c:a9), Dst: IPv6mcast_00:00:00:02 (33:33:00:00:00:02)
Internet Protocol version 6
⊞ 0110 .... = version: 6
   .... 0000 0000 .... .... .... .... = Traffic class: 0x00000000
   .... .... .... 0000 0000 0000 0000 0000 = Flowlabel: 0x00000000
   Payload length: 16
   Next header: ICMPv6 (0x3a)
   Hop limit: 255
   Source: fe80::f077:1f25:cf06:ec54 (fe80::f077:1f25:cf06:ec54)
   Destination: ff02::2 (ff02::2)
Internet Control Message Protocol v6
   Type: 133 (Router solicitation)
   Code: 0
   Checksum: 0xb25a [correct]
⊟ ICMPv6 Option (Source link-layer address)
   Type: Source link-layer address (1)
   Length: 8
   Link-layer address: 00:1f:e2:12:1c:a9
```

Figure 6-22. ICMPv6 router solicitation

The ICMPv6 echo request and neighbor solicitation messages are shown in Figure 6-23 and Figure 6-24. The echo request uses the standard addressing at Layer 2, but the neighbor solicitation uses an address reserved for IPv6 multicast.

```
⊞ Frame 7 (94 bytes on wire, 94 bytes captured)
⊞ Ethernet II, Src: Intel_c8:b9:a0 (00:0c:f1:c8:b9:a0), Dst: Intel_c8:b4:1e (00:0c:f1:c8:b4:1e)
⊞ Internet Protocol Version 6
⊟ Internet Control Message Protocol v6
    Type: 128 (Echo request)
    Code: 0
    Checksum: 0x8489 [correct]
    ID: 0x0000
    Sequence: 0x0005
  ⊟ Data (32 bytes)
      Data: 6162636465666768696A6B6C6D6E6F707172737475767761...
      [Length: 32]
```

Figure 6-23. *ICMPv6 echo request*

```
⊞ Frame 5 (86 bytes on wire, 86 bytes captured)
⊞ Ethernet II, Src: Intel_c8:b9:a0 (00:0c:f1:c8:b9:a0), Dst: IPv6mcast_ff:c8:b4:1e (33:33:ff:c8:b4:1e)
⊞ Internet Protocol Version 6
⊟ Internet Control Message Protocol v6
    Type: 135 (Neighbor solicitation)
    Code: 0
    Checksum: 0xc8d7 [correct]
    Target: fe80::20c:f1ff:fec8:b41e (fe80::20c:f1ff:fec8:b41e)
  ⊟ ICMPv6 Option (Source link-layer address)
      Type: Source link-layer address (1)
      Length: 8
      Link-layer address: 00:0c:f1:c8:b9:a0
```

Figure 6-24. *ICMPv6 neighbor solicitation*

Summary

There are many types of ICMP messages defined in the RFCs, but only a subset of these are used with any regularity. On most networks, the ICMP echo request, echo reply, time exceeded, destination unreachable, and redirect messages are common. ICMP is broken down into informational and error messages. In the case of messages generated for feedback, a portion of the original IP packet is included. Several diagnostic programs, such as *ping* and *tracert*, use ICMP for path discovery and troubleshooting. IPv6 extends the life of ICMP and makes use of the less-common router solicitation and advertisement in a process called neighbor discovery.

Additional Reading

- RFC 792: "Internet Control Message Protocol"
- RFC 1256: "ICMP Router Discovery Messages"
- RFC 2461: "IPv6 Neighbor Discovery"
- RFC 4443: "Internet Control Message Protocol (ICMPv6) for the Internet Protocol Version 6 (IPv6) Specification"

Review Questions

1. What is the payload of an ICMP echo request from Windows?

2. Provide two examples of ICMP messages that include 64 bits of the original message.

3. What is the "all routers multicast" address?

4. What is the IP "next header" or protocol value for ICMP?

5. Router solicitations and advertisements are not very common. What protocol is used instead?

6. What is the IPv6 process that replaces ARP and uses several types of ICPv6 messages?

7. What are the type and code values of the ICMP network destination unreachable message?

8. What event causes an ICMP time exceeded message to be generated?

9. Instead of a TCP or UDP port number, what value is used when forwarding ICMP packets through a NAT router?

10. On the receiving host, what is the effect of an ICMP redirect message?

Review Answers

1. The alphabet

2. Redirect, destination unreachable, time exceeded

3. 224.0.0.2

4. 01

5. DHCP

6. Neighbor discovery

7. 3 and 0

8. The IP TTL field is decremented to 0.

9. The ICMP identifier

10. A route is added to the local host routing table for use in subsequent transmissions.

Lab Activities

Activity 1—ping

Materials: A computer with a connection to another network device or node

1. On the computer, start a Wireshark capture.

2. Open a command window or shell.

3. Using the `ping` command, ping the other device. For example, `ping 192.168.1.1`.

4. Take a look at the ICMP packets generated as a result of this ping. What are the type, code, and payload of each message?

Activity 2—tracert

Materials: A computer with a connection to the Internet or routed topology

1. On the computer, start a Wireshark capture.

2. Open a command window or shell.

3. Using the `tracert` command, perform path discovery to another node or a website. For example, `tracert www.google.com`.

4. What messages are generated as a result of this command?

5. Examine the TTL field of the IP packets and determine exactly what is happening.

6. What ICMP message results from the exchange?

7. What other packets are generated as a result of using a name instead of an IP address?

Activity 3—Startup Packet Capture

Materials: Two computers, Wireshark, and a connection to a router

1. To start, have one computer up and running and the other shut down.

2. Connect the router and both computers together. If using a home gateway, use the ports on the switch module. If not, another device such as a hub or switch may be required.

3. Start a Wireshark capture on the running machine.

4. Start up the second machine and observe the packets generated.

5. This particular exercise is concerned with the ICMP messages that are generated; however, the other types of traffic are very interesting as well. See if you can

determine the reasons for all of the traffic present. Depending on the operating system, you will see a variety of packets, including IPv4 and IPv6 ICMP messages.

Activity 4—Destination Unreachable from the OS

Materials: A computer with an active connection

1. Configure this computer with an IP address, but leave the default gateway line blank.
2. On the computer, start a Wireshark capture.
3. Open a command window or shell.
4. Ping a device or address that is not on your network.
5. What was the response? Where did this message come from?
6. Were there any packets generated as a result of this ping?

Activity 5—Destination Unreachable from the Router

Materials: A computer with an active connection to a router or home gateway

1. Configure the computer with an IP address, but this time, give the node a gateway.
2. Remove the outside connection to the home gateway.
3. On the computer, start a Wireshark capture.
4. Open a command window or shell.
5. Ping a device or address that is not on your network.
6. What was the response? Where did this message come from?
7. Were there any packets generated as a result of this ping?

CHAPTER 7

Subnetting and Other Masking Acrobatics

"While these problems could be avoided by attempting to restrict the growth of the Internet, most people would prefer solutions that allow growth to continue. Fortunately, it appears that such solutions are possible, and that, in fact, our biggest problem is having too many possible solutions rather than too few."

—RFC 1380

A network can be defined in many ways. From a Layer 3 perspective, a network is a group of nodes that all share the same IP addressing scheme. The original vision for the IP-based Internet was a two-tier system in which a collection of networks were all connected to a single Internet or catenet. Confusion arises because it can be difficult to tell what the network boundaries are. The answer, and perhaps the source of the confusion, lies in the network mask. Many networking decisions are made based on the mask—host and router routing, classful and classless address space, security, QoS provisioning, and the overall design are all affected by the masks applied to the nodes.

A device operating on a network requires four numbers to ensure basic connectivity: IP address, network mask, gateway, and domain name server address. Their purpose is straightforward. IP addresses provide logical locations, masks determine the network, the gateway is a router providing a pathway off of the current network, and the domain name server converts between IP addresses and more human-friendly addresses/words such as those used in web pages. The focus of this chapter is the network mask and the corresponding network.

How Do We Use the Mask?

The early IP network address assignments were based on the three main classes—A, B, and C—that varied in size, and the sizes were based on the mask. Each class had a normal, or *natural* mask, a specific number of hosts, and a range, as shown in Table 7-1.

Table 7-1. IP classes and masks

Class	Address range	Mask	Number of possible networks	Number of possible hosts
A	0–127	255.0.0.0	128	16,777,216
B	128–191	255.255.0.0	16,364	65,536
C	192–223	255.255.255.0	2,097,152	256

Many of these addresses are not actually valid on the public network (e.g., 127 is used for loopback), but generally, a network can be identified by looking at its IP address and the corresponding mask. An IP address beginning with 36 in the first octet (e.g., 36.45.197.223) resides on a class A network, regardless of the rest of the address. Table 7-1 shows that class A networks are few in number, but each contains millions of hosts. Class A networks also have a default mask of 255.0.0.0.

When a node is assigned an IP address, the IP address, when combined with the mask, actually includes not only the address for the host, but information about the network as well. The method used to determine the network address from the host address using the mask is a logical AND operation. This is shown in Figure 7-1.

Logical AND

The truth table for the logical AND is show below.
Anything "ANDed" with a 0 results in a 0 (shown in red);
the only to way obtain a 1 is if a 1 is ANDed with a 1.

```
                Mask bit
                 0     1
Address 0        0     0
bit     1        0     1
```

Figure 7-1. Logical AND

An organization wishing to connect to others via TCP/IP will be assigned a particular network based on this class structure. Smaller organizations will be given a class C network, while much larger ones might be given a class B or even a class A network. All of the nodes within the organization will be given IP addresses within the same scheme and all of them will have the same mask. Assigning addresses based on these classes is called *classful addressing*.

For example, if a smaller organization is given a class C network address of 200.150.100.0, it will use a mask of 255.255.255.0. The 0 in the last octet of the IP address is significant. Since the possible values for any octet in an IP address are from 0 (binary 00000000) to 255 (binary 11111111), the range of possible addresses for this particular network is 200.150.100.0 to 200.150.100.255.

All of the hosts on this network will have this same network address, and this is determined by the mask. The following calculations show how this is determined (assume Host A has IP address 200.150.100.95 and mask 255.255.255.0):

1. Convert the host address to binary:

   11001000.10010110.01100100.01011111

2. Convert the class mask to binary:

   11111111.11111111.11111111.00000000

3. Perform a bitwise AND using the host address and the mask to get the network address:

   11001000.10010110.01100100.01011111

   11111111.11111111.11111111.00000000

   11001000.10010110.01100100.00000000

4. Convert back to base 10 numbers:

   200.150.100.0

The last octet is converted to all 0s as a result of the logical AND. Any host address in the range described above will result in the same network address. *Hosts are not assigned this particular address.* When the mask octet value is 255, the IP address value is simply brought down to the result, as was the case for the 200, 150, and 100. This process is required because IP packets do not include any information regarding the network itself. Figure 7-2 shows a standard IP packet—notice that the mask is not even included.

```
Ethernet II, Src: Pentacom_5a:94:00 (00:d0:04:5a:94:00), Dst: IPv4mcast_7f:ff:fa (01:00:5e:7f:ff:fa)
⊞ Destination: IPv4mcast_7f:ff:fa (01:00:5e:7f:ff:fa)
⊞ Source: Pentacom_5a:94:00 (00:d0:04:5a:94:00)
  Type: IP (0x0800)
Internet Protocol, Src: 129.21.185.28 (129.21.185.28), Dst: 239.255.255.250 (239.255.255.250)
  Version: 4
  Header length: 20 bytes
⊞ Differentiated Services Field: 0x00 (DSCP 0x00: Default; ECN: 0x00)
  Total Length: 299
  Identification: 0xf2f6 (62198)
⊞ Flags: 0x00
  Fragment offset: 0
  Time to live: 3
  Protocol: UDP (17)
⊞ Header checksum: 0x999f [correct]
  Source: 129.21.185.28 (129.21.185.28)
  Destination: 239.255.255.250 (239.255.255.250)
User Datagram Protocol, Src Port: ssdp (1900), Dst Port: ssdp (1900)
  Source port: ssdp (1900)
  Destination port: ssdp (1900)
  Length: 279
⊞ Checksum: 0x0b26 [validation disabled]
Hypertext Transfer Protocol
⊟ NOTIFY * HTTP/1.1\r\n
  ⊞ [Expert Info (Chat/Sequence): NOTIFY * HTTP/1.1\r\n]
    Request Method: NOTIFY
    Request URI: *
    Request Version: HTTP/1.1
  LOCATION: http://129.21.185.28:8089/\r\n
  HOST: 239.255.255.250:1900\r\n
  SERVER: POSIX, UPnP/1.0, Intel MicroStack/1.0.1347\r\n
  NTS: ssdp:alive\r\n
  USN: uuid:1c852d10-b80b-1f08-98c5-02bad0d9b366::upnp:rootdevice\r\n
  CACHE-CONTROL: max-age=1800\r\n
  NT: upnp:rootdevice\r\n
  \r\n
```

Figure 7-2. Packet with all headers expanded

Within the network mask, there are two components. The binary ones (1) indicate the network portion, and the zeros (0) indicate the host portion. In this case, the network portion has been allocated three bytes. The host portion has been allocated a single byte of address space, as shown in Figure 7-3.

Binary	11111111.	11111111.	11111111.	0
Base 10	255.	255.	255.	0
	Network portion			Host portion

Figure 7-3. Network mask sections

Now that the binary digits have been exposed, another way of describing the mask is to count the number of 1s. Thus, class A networks have an 8-bit mask, class B networks have a 16-bit mask, and class C networks have a 24-bit mask.

Another special address for this particular network is 200.150.100.255, which is called the *directed broadcast address*. It is used to reach all hosts on the network, so it must not be assigned to any particular host. The network address contains all 0s in the host portion of the IP address. The directed broadcast address contains all 1s in the host portion of the IP address:

Network address: 11001000.10100000.01100100.**00000000** (200.150.100.0)
Directed broadcast address: 11001000.10100000.01100100.**11111111** (200.150.100.255)

Summarizing for this class C network:

Network address or ID: 200.150.100.0
Network mask: 255.255.255.0
Directed broadcast address: 200.150.100.255
Possible address space: 256 (200.150.100.0–200.150.100.255)
Usable address space: 254 (200.150.100.1–200.150.100.254)

Hosts in this network, such as computers, routers, and printers, will use addresses between 200.150.100.1 and 200.150.100.254. In our exercise, the organization is using all of the IP addresses within the class C network space and has not manipulated the mask, thus using *classful* addressing.

The nodes on a network typically use the same router to forward packets externally, and that router must also use an IP address on the network. Routers commonly use an address that is on either the low end or the high end of the range, such as 200.150.100.1 or 200.150.100.254, which cannot be given to computers or other network devices. Figure 7-4 shows what this network might look like. Each host uses the router as the default gateway for packets exiting the network, and the router itself has an additional address associated with the outside connection.

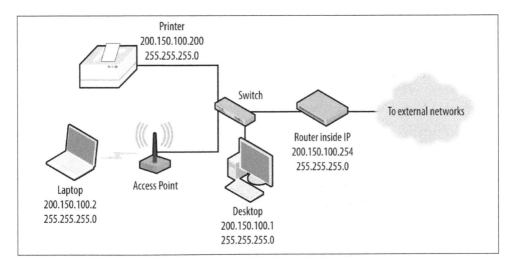

Figure 7-4. Network addressing

What Is a Subnet?

Subnets work exactly like classful networks in that they require a router to get to other networks and have a network address, a directed broadcast address, and a specific set of hosts. To quote from RFC 917:

> We discuss the utility of "subnets" of Internet networks, which are logically visible subsections of a single Internet network. For administrative or technical reasons, many organizations have chosen to divide one Internet network into several subnets, instead of acquiring a set of Internet network numbers.

Subnets are created by manipulating the mask of the classful address space and are often utilized to create separation between departments or interconnect different LAN technologies or device types. For example, if the organization shown in Figure 7-4 has a security policy requiring that the traffic from departmental nodes be isolated, a subnetting plan might be very useful. The previous address space consisting of 256 (0–255) possible addresses must be broken up into smaller networks or *subnetworks*.

When subnetting is implemented, there are changes to the mask, which will now be referred to as a *subnet mask* (netmask). The last nonzero octet in the mask will no longer be the friendly 255, which means that the results of the ANDing process are not as easy to predict. The mask now has a subnet field in addition to the network and host portions. Subnetting slightly modifies the ANDing process outlined earlier.

To create the new netmask, the number of desired subnets must be determined. Assume four subnets will be created for different departments. Each subnet will be smaller than the classful address space, so the number of bits allocated to hosts in each subnet will be fewer. For this reason, bits used to describe the subnets are said to be "stolen" from the host address space. *The number of bits stolen is determined by the number of subnets required.* These stolen bits also become the subnet field in the mask. This creates the new mask that all nodes within the subnetted classful address space will use. In order to create four subnets, we have to steal two bits from the host portion of the address space. We steal two because there are four possible values that can be represented with the two bits. What follows are the binary and base 10 values for the new subnet mask achieved as a result of stealing the two bits:

| Binary | 11111111. | 11111111. | 11111111. | **11**000000 |
| New mask | 255. | 255. | 255. | 192 |

Subnet bit stealing is accomplished by changing 0s to 1s as you move from left to right in the mask. This change impacts the ANDing process results. In our example, instead of returning a 0, the ANDing process will not accept whatever is in the IP address for these two bits. Stated another way, the ANDing process pays attention to these two values instead of overwriting them. The change in these bits also changes the IP addresses of the networks (subnets) and inserts the subnet field. The subnet field will use

---

the different binary patterns offered by the two bits: 00, 01, 10, and 11. These changes are shown in Table 7-2.

Table 7-2. Subnet mask patterns and allocations

Class A			Class B			Class C		
Mask	Subnets	Hosts	Mask	Subnets	Hosts	Mask	Subnets	Hosts
255.0.0.0	1	16777216	255.255.0.0	1	65536	255.255.255.0	1	256
255.128.0.0	2	8388608	255.255.128.0	2	32768	255.255.255.128	2	128
255.192.0.0	4	4194304	255.255.192.0	4	16384	255.255.255.192	4	64
255.224.0.0	8	2097152	255.255.224.0	8	8192	255.255.255.224	8	32
255.240.0.0	16	1048576	255.255.240.0	16	4096	255.255.255.240	16	16
255.248.0.0	32	524288	255.255.248.0	32	2048	255.255.255.248	32	8
255.252.0.0	64	262144	255.255.252.0	64	1024	255.255.255.252	64	4
255.254.0.0	128	131072	255.255.254.0	128	512	255.255.255.254	128	2
255.255.0.0	256	65536	255.255.255.0	256	256	255.255.255.255	256	0

The first entry in the table is for the classful address space and is not really a subnet.

Subnet Patterns

Regardless of which octet has been changed, subnet masks all use the same collection of values. Familiarity with these patterns makes subnetting and the manipulation of the address space much easier. Table 7-2 shows these patterns and the number of subnets and hosts that are created. The first row is for the classful address space.

Here are some items to take note of in Table 7-2:

- This is a table of possible values, not usable ones. For example, it doesn't make much sense to create 256 subnets in a class C address space.
- The masks use the same values, but in different octets, so the sizes of subnets vary between the classes.
- Multiplying the maximum number of hosts in each subnet by the number of subnets created will always result in the total number of hosts in the classful address space.
- The number of subnets and the number of hosts will always be a power of 2.
- The mask values result from stealing successive bits on the right side of the mask (for example, 10000000 = 128, 11000000 = 192, 11100000 = 224, 11110000 = 240).

Due to these changes, hosts that were originally on the same classful network will now reside on different subnetworks. Subnets behave just like classful networks and have the same requirements. To determine the new addressing, the subnet field is applied to the IP addresses, but using the combinations offered by the binary patterns.

Subnet IP Addressing

As stated earlier, subnetting steals bits from the host portion of the address space, and the bits stolen are described by changes in the subnet mask. Once the size and location (which octet) of the subnet field are known, all that remains is the starting point. The first subnet always has the same address as the classful address space, but it will be smaller. Using two stolen bits as an example, Figure 7-5 depicts the subnets, the subnet field, and the new ranges.

Network Address		Directed Broadcast		Subnet Range
	Binary Pattern		Binary Pattern	
200.150.100.	00 000000	200.150.100.	00 111111	200.150.100.0-63
200.150.100.	01 000000	200.150.100.	01 111111	200.150.100.64-127
200.150.100.	10 000000	200.150.100.	10 111111	200.150.100.128-191
200.150.100.	11 000000	200.150.100.	11 111111	200.150.100.192-255

⌐———— Subnet Field ————⌐

Figure 7-5. Subnet field with binary patterns

For simplicity's sake, the first three octets will not be converted to binary, but the last octet will be expanded to show the effect of the subnet field. Changes to the mask indicate the location of the subnet field, as shown in Figure 7-6. Once this is defined, we simply insert the different binary possibilities, as shown in Figure 7-5. Like classful networks, the subnet address places all 0s in the host portion. The directed broadcast address places all 1s in the host portion. These two values provide the subnet range.

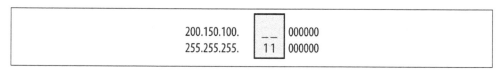

Figure 7-6. Masking in the subnet field

A check of the network ID using the previous process would work in the same way, but the results may be quite a bit different. The network for the same node is now 200.150.100.64, calculated as follows, assuming Host A has IP address 200.150.100.95 and mask 255.255.255.192:

1. Convert the host address to binary:

   11001000.10010110.01100100.01011111

2. Convert the subnet mask to binary:

   11111111.11111111.11111111.11000000

---

3. Perform a bitwise AND using the host address and the mask to get the network address:

11001000.10010110.01100100.01011111

11111111.11111111.11111111.11000000

11001000.10010110.01100100.01000000

4. Convert back to base 10 numbers:

200.150.100.64

Checking this value against the range for the subnet in Figure 7-5 proves this to be the correct answer. Figure 7-7 shows what a network topology might look like given this set of subnets. The central node is a router that now has additional interfaces.

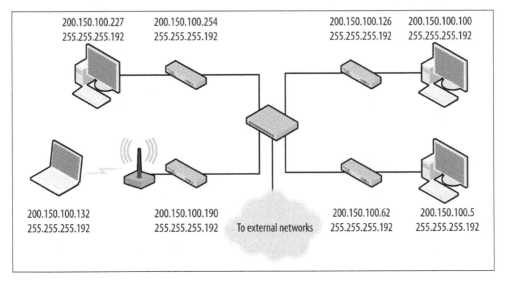

Figure 7-7. Subnetted topology

A Shorthand Technique

For a subnetting problem as straightforward as this one, there is another technique you can use to determine the addresses and ranges for each subnet. For this problem, the only given information is the classful address space (200.150.100.0 255.255.255.0) and the fact that four subnets were required. This means the 256 addresses will be divided into four equal parts of 64 (256/4 = 64).

This simple calculation and some basic understanding of the structure provide the basis for all of the subnets. Since the first subnet is always the same as the classful address space, the next step is simply to start counting at 0 to get the first set of 64, and then add 1 to get the start of the next range until the end of the address space is reached:

1. Counting to 64 starting from 0 gives the first set of 64.

   200.150.100.0–63

2. Adding 1 (63 + 1 = 64) gives the start of the next subnet. At this point, the range expands to a total of 64 addresses. Intuitively, counting now starts at 64, so adding 63 provides the endpoint for the next range (64 + 63 = 127).

   200.150.100.64–127

3. Repeat this process to get the third subnet (127 + 1 = 128, 127 + 63 = 191).

   200.150.100.128–191

4. Finally, 191 + 1 = 192, and 191 + 63 = 255.

   200.150.100.192–255

 Be careful when using this shorthand technique. It works well with simpler problems, but for more-complex subnetting (or supernetting) schemes, it is easy to lose your way. When in doubt, go back to the binary method.

The Effect on Address Space

In the classful example, the number of addresses that are unusable by hosts is two: one for the network itself and one for the directed broadcast address. To be complete, it could be said that the router also requires an address, leaving 253 of 256 addresses for networked computers, printers, etc. in that class C network. With subnetting, the number of addresses lost this way is greater, because each subnet has the same requirements. Figure 7-5 shows that creating four subnets loses eight addresses—four to the network and four to the directed broadcast. If you include the router interfaces, this means that of the original 256, only 244 host addresses are available. Pushing this a little further, creating 32 subnets in this address space results in a loss of more than 25 percent of the address space, without even counting the routers.

Theory Versus Reality

Table 7-3 indicates what can happen if we follow the traditional letter of the law when creating subnets. Again, we'll assume that we need four subnets. Examining the classful address space of 200.150.100.0 (mask of 255.255.255.0) and the subnetted address space of 200.150.100.0 (mask of 255.255.255.192), you can see that the first subnet has the same address as the classful address space. Based on the binary values, this is sometimes called the *all 0s* subnet. In addition, the directed broadcast for the last subnet has the same address (200.150.100.255) as the classful address space, and is often called the *all 1s* subnet. Since masks are not present in packets traveling on the network, these two addresses can lead to confusion with routing tables and design of the network, because the subnet addressing is not distinct from the classful addressing. As a result, some documentation recommends that network administrators refrain from using the subnets that include these addresses—namely, the lowest and highest subnets. In fact, RFC 950, which attempts to standardize subnetting procedures, states:

> This means the values of all zeros and all ones in the subnet field should not be assigned to actual (physical) subnets.

In the four-subnet example, eliminating these two subnets will result in a 50 percent loss of address space because the addresses 200.150.100.0–63 and 200.150.100.192–255 will no longer be available. Due to the loss of the subnet and directed broadcast addresses from the remaining subnets, less than 50 percent of the IP addresses are actually available for network hosts. Things can get even worse in terms of efficiency. The traditional model requires that more subnets be created in order to obtain the correct number of usable subnets. This is shown in Table 7-3.

Table 7-3. Subnet address efficiency

Subnet range	Result	Addresses lost due to subnets
200.150.11.0–200.150.100.31	Not allowed	32
200.150.100.32–200.150.100.63	Used	2
200.150.100.64–200.150.100.95	Used	2
200.150.100.96–200.150.100.127	Used	2
200.150.100.128–200.150.100.159	Used	2
200.150.100.160–200.150.100.191	Unused	32
200.150.100.192–200.150.100.223	Unused	32
200.150.100.224–200.150.100.255	Not allowed	32

If, as in this example, four subnets are desired, but the guidelines prohibit the use of the all 0s and all 1s subnets, stealing two bits no longer provides four subnets, but two. To obtain four usable subnets, three bits have to be stolen, which will result in eight possible and six usable subnets. If only four are used, and with the effect of subnets on address space, less than 47 percent of the address space is used. This approach is suboptimal at best.

From a practical perspective, this loss of address space makes this practice unpalatable for many veterans in the field and has forced changes to vendor networking equipment and design. The all 0s and all 1s subnets are no longer off-limits.

Supernetting

Supernetting is defined in RFC 1338 and works in an opposite manner to subnetting. This process combines chunks of address space together. A large number of nodes may be grouped together because they are not simultaneously active, because network load is small, or out of a desire for route aggregation. In terms of the masks used, the process is very similar, but instead of stealing bits from the host portion, bits are stolen from the network portion of the address. However, when stealing from the network portion, the opposite process takes place. Instead of converting the bits in the mask from 0 to 1, the bits are converted from 1 to 0. The effect is that the ANDing process no longer accepts the address information from the IP address, because more of the information will be converted to 0. The key is that in order to supernet networks together, the remaining binary patterns in the network portion of the address must be the same.

Using the same class C address space as the previous section (200.150.100.0, mask 255.255.255.0), this example will now supernet eight networks together. Eight networks will require changing three bits in the mask. Figure 7-8 will help you determine the appropriate mask, the new network address, and the range of hosts in the network. For simplicity, the table will only convert the octets affected by the mask change and the last octet of all 0s will be removed. Columns three and four are both part of the third octet. Like the subnet field, a supernet field will be created in the mask.

		Supernet Field	
Mask: 11111111 .11111111 .11111 ___ .00000000			

Network Address	First and Second Octets	Unchanged by Mask	Bits Stolen 1 2 3
200.150.96.0	200.150	011000	0 0 0
200.150.97.0	200.151	011000	0 0 1
200.150.98.0	200.152	011000	0 1 0
200.150.99.0	200.153	011000	0 1 1
200.150.100.0	200.154	011000	1 0 0
200.150.101.0	200.155	011000	1 0 1
200.150.102.0	200.156	011000	1 1 0
200.150.103.0	200.157	011000	1 1 1
200.150.104.0	200.158	011001	0 0 0
200.150.105.0	200.159	011001	0 0 1

Figure 7-8. Supernetted networks

After the conversion to binary, you can see that the patterns in the third octet start off the same, but begin to vary after moving to the right. For example, networks 200.150.96.0 and 200.150.100.97.0 are the same until the eighth bit of the third octet. If one bit (indicated by the first column from the right) was stolen from the network portion of the address, the mask would change from 255.255.255.0 to 255.255.254.0 because the bit stolen back would be changed to a 0:

11111111.11111111.1111111**1**.00000000 → 1111111.11111111.1111111 **0** .00000000

255.   255.   255.   0   255.   255.   254.   0

When this is done, the last bit of the network address is ignored—otherwise, the ANDing process would always result in a 0. Thus, the 96 and 97 networks would have the same pattern to the left of the stolen bit and effectively be in the same network. The same is true of the 98 and 99 networks, the 100 and 101 networks, and the 102 and 103 networks.

Stealing two bits changes the mask to 255.255.252.0 and causes the last two bits of the network addresses to be ignored. At this point, four networks would be supernetted together if their binary patterns to the left of the stolen bits were the same. From Figure 7-8, you can see that networks 96–99 would be supernetted together, as would networks 100–103. Stealing three bits would cause 200.150.100.96–200.150.100.103 to be supernetted together.

When stealing bits from the network portion, the values are similar to those used in subnetting, but they decrease as more bits are stolen or converted to 0s (Table 7-4).

Table 7-4. Supernet mask patterns

Bits stolen	Mask	This example	Class B example
0	255	255.255.255.0	255.255.0.0
1	254	255.255.254.0	255.254.0.0
2	252	255.255.252.0	255.252.0.0
3	248	255.255.248.0	255.248.0.0
4	240	255.255.240.0	255.240.0.0
5	224	255.255.224.0	255.224.0.0
6	192	255.255.192.0	255.192.0.0
7	128	255.255.128.0	255.128.0.0
8	0	255.255.0.0	255.0.0.0

The Supernetted Network

In order to determine the network address for the networks supernetted together, the lowest-numbered network matching the pattern is used. Remember that supernetting actually increases the size of the network in terms of the number of hosts and will extend to the end of highest network matching the binary pattern. In this case, stealing three bits results in a mask of 255.255.248.0. The lowest-numbered network matching this pattern is 200.150.96.0 and the highest is 200.150.103.0. This means that the network range is 200.150.96.0–200.150.103.255.

200.150.96.0 is the network address and 200.150.103.255 is the directed broadcast address for the network. To verify this, the same ANDing process is used. Given the original host address of 200.150.100.95 and the new mask of 255.255.248.0, the ANDing process resolves as shown in Figure 7-9.

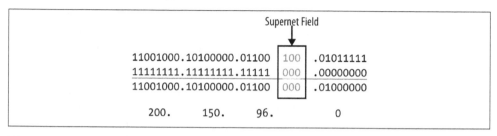

Figure 7-9. Supernet binary

Any address in this range will have the same result after ANDing.

Classless Inter-Domain Routing

As the number of networks attached to the Internet passed 10,000, it became apparent that if every organization wanted its own network, it wouldn't take long to run out of possible network addresses. Clearly, classful addressing did not have much of a future. The information in Table 7-1 shows that there are slightly more than 2 million possible networks in total, and most of these are small class Cs. A longer-term problem was the eventual exhaustion of the entire IPv4 address space because it is based on 32 bits.

Compounding the issue is the fact that the classful architecture was horribly inefficient. An organization might receive a class C network even if it only had a dozen network nodes. Making matters worse, an organization possessing 300 nodes, or believing that it might possess 300 nodes, would receive a class B network. The ability to manipulate the mask helps, so with supernetting, this organization might receive two class Cs instead. This was an improvement, but still resulted in low address space utilization efficiency and there was no guarantee that the address space would be continuous. A contemporary example exists in high-speed Internet connections to the home. The traditional viewpoint might be that everyone connecting a small home network to the Internet should be granted their own network. Clearly, this is not possible.

In addition to inefficient management of a very large address space, we would have had an explosion in routing table size. Routers are tasked with forwarding packets based on the destination network address. If every single organization were given a separate network, there would also be corresponding routing table entries. Routing tables across the Internet would grow until performance for routers on the interconnected networks was severely hampered. It takes time to construct and maintain a routing table, and additional time to find the correct routing table entry for a particular packet by searching the entries and completing the mask-based operations. This is also referred to as *traversing the routing table*. The speed of these calculations is dependent on a number of factors, including the processing power of the router, the installed memory, and the size of the routing table. Now imagine that the router is doing this for millions of packets per second, and the scope of the problem becomes clear.

The previous section describes how supernetting works, but supernetting was actually introduced as a scheme to contend with the issues of address space conservation and controlling the size of routing tables. Specific attention was paid to the routers that do not use default routes and the class B address space. The class B address space is of a size that appears to fit no one, as midsize organizations require more addresses than a class C network can offer, but cannot make use of an entire class B network of 65,536 (65,634) addresses. By manipulating the mask lengths, routing can depart from the stratified class structure, in effect becoming classless. Classless Inter-Domain Routing, or CIDR, was originally described in RFC 1519 and obsoletes RFC 1338 (supernetting), but the language is nearly identical.

Aggregation is a technique in which a reduced number of routing table entries can be used to forward traffic to downstream routers, because each entry encompasses several smaller networks due to variable-length subnet masks. The number of routes that must be advertised via a routing protocol is reduced correspondingly. Figure 7-10 shows a topology in which aggregation might be deployed.

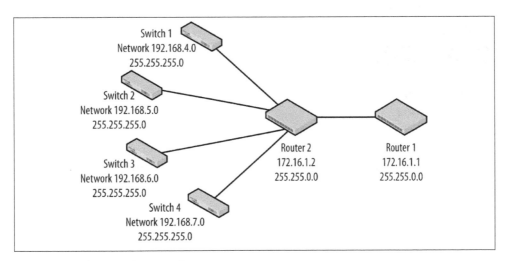

Figure 7-10. Aggregation topology

To get to all of the networks shown, the routing tables might be constructed as shown in Table 7-5.

Table 7-5. Router routing tables

Router 2			Router 1		
Address	Mask	Connection	Address	Mask	Connection
192.168.4.0	255.255.255.0	Directly connected	192.168.4.0	255.255.255.0	via 172.16.1.2
192.168.5.0	255.255.255.0	Directly connected	192.168.5.0	255.255.255.0	via 172.16.1.2
192.168.6.0	255.255.255.0	Directly connected	192.168.6.0	255.255.255.0	via 172.16.1.2
192.168.7.0	255.255.255.0	Directly connected	192.168.7.0	255.255.255.0	via 172.16.1.2
172.16.0.0	255.255.0.0	Directly connected	172.16.0.0	255.255.0.0	Directly connected
Default route via 172.16.1.1					

Router 1 must have all of the networks beginning with 192 included in its routing table, and all of these networks are using a 24-bit mask. The network connecting the two routers (172.16.0.0) is a class B and uses a 16-bit mask. As demonstrated in the earlier discussion on supernetting, networks sharing a common binary pattern can be collected together to form a larger network. The same is true of routing table entries. CIDR allows the use of variable-length masks to help slow the growth of routing tables. One other important point is that the four networks beginning with 192 are all accessible via the same pathway—172.16.1.2. This means that traffic destined for the four networks must travel through the same router interface.

Examining the binary of the third octet for the networks in question demonstrates that the first six bits have the same pattern (Table 7-6).

Table 7-6. Routing table binary patterns

Network	Byte 3 in binary
192.168.4.0	00000100
192.168.5.0	00000101
192.168.6.0	00000110
192.168.7.0	00000111

Based on this information, the routing table entry can be modified as shown in Table 7-7.

Table 7-7. Updated router routing table

Router 2			Router 1		
Address	Mask	Connection	Address	Mask	Connection
192.168.4.0	255.255.255.0	Directly connected	192.168.4.0	255.255.**252**.0	via 172.16.1.2
192.168.5.0	255.255.255.0	Directly connected	172.16.0.0	255.255.0.0	Directly connected
192.168.6.0	255.255.255.0	Directly connected			
192.168.7.0	255.255.255.0	Directly connected			
172.16.0.0	255.255.0.0	Directly connected			
Default route via 172.16.1.1					

Changing the mask means that this entry now refers to a larger chunk of address space: 192.168.4.0–192.168.7.255. Again, it is important to note that the pathway for all of the traffic is the same as the forwarding router interface—172.16.1.2. Counting the number of binary 1s in the entry mask (255.255.252.0), it can be said that this entry has a 22-bit mask.

CIDR and Aggregation Implementation

Given the problems outlined so far, there are some limits to a plan like this one. In Figure 7-4, the networks are very neatly arranged to allow the aggregation of the routing table information. Unfortunately, networks are not typically this organized. RFC 1519 mentions this particular problem, but specifies that network addresses will not be re-assigned. However, newly added addresses/networks can certainly be from aggregated address space. As an example, large ISPs, such as Time Warner, may control a block of addresses within the class A 24 network. Customers of Time Warner receive a portion of the 24 network rather than their own separate networks. In this way, the routing tables and the advertisements can be aggregated through the Time Warner paths. Both RFC 1338 and 1519 contain the following statement:

> For these reasons, and in the interest of providing a consistent procedure for obtaining Internet addresses, it is recommended that most, if not all, network numbers be distributed through service providers.

A second problem is that many networks may be multihomed. A basic part of good network design is to have redundant or backup connections to the outside world. Thus, the availability of the network will be maintained by a second entry in another router and the number of advertisements required may not be as low as hoped. So, while aggregation and the variable-length masks available via CIDR certainly help, there are limits on the ability to slow routing table growth. At the time of its writing, the authors were concerned with routing tables growing to 10,000 routes and, in their wildest imaginations, perhaps reaching 100,000 entries. Today routing tables on some core Internet routers have actually gotten much larger. According to the CIDR Report (*http://*

www.cidr-report.org) the number of entries in some routers has passed 200,000 after aggregation via CIDR and the number of network prefixes exceeds 300,000.

Along with the manipulation of the mask length is the use of *CIDR notation*. This usually refers to another way of indicating the mask length by counting the number of ones in the mask. For example, the class C network of 200.150.100.0 with a mask of 255.255.255.0 can be referred to as 200.150.100.0/24. Converting the base 10 values of the mask (255 = 11111111) returns 24 1s. CIDR notation is often used to abbreviate descriptions, providing a clear indication of different mask lengths. The number following the slash (/) indicates the network or prefix length, and is commonly used in routing tables. The following is from a router running OSPF:

```
O IA 192.168.4.0/24 [110/20] via 192.168.2.252, 00:02:48, FastEthernet0/0
O IA 192.168.5.0/24 [110/30] via 192.168.2.252, 00:02:44, FastEthernet0/0
O 192.168.1.0/24 [110/11] via 192.168.3.254, 00:09:46, FastEthernet0/1
C 192.168.2.0/24 is directly connected, FastEthernet0/0
C 192.168.3.0/24 is directly connected, FastEthernet0/1
```

RFC 4632

RFC 1519 (CIDR) and its predecessor, 1338 (supernetting), are very similar in that they both address aggregation and routing table growth. RFC 1519 adds sections to handle class D addressing, intradomain routing, and extending CIDR to class A networks. Recall that one of the primary problems was a reduced number of available class B networks. Much of the work done was to alleviate this stressor by manipulation of the masks specific to class B and C networks. Class A networks (and DNS) were discussed, but not to be affected upon adoption of the new addressing plan.

RFC 4632 obsoletes 1519 and includes updated discussions, clarifications, and a report on the effectiveness of the CIDR addressing scheme. It also provides the definition of the CIDR notation. The decade spanning 1994 to 2004 indicated that the CIDR effort was successful. With the possible exception of the "dot com bubble," the growth in routing table entries and advertised routes was linear rather than exponential. Since that time, more rapid growth has been observed and, as noted earlier, the number of entries in some core routers exceeds 300,000. A nice resource that depicts the current growth of core routing tables can be found at *http://bgp.potaroo.net*. The rapid growth may be a factor of increasing adoption of technology or service providers not adhering to the recommendations published for CIDR deployments.

Summary

The major topics of this chapter (subnetting, supernetting, and CIDR) are all related in their manipulation of network masks. They differ in scope and application. Generally, an organization owning a small amount of address space may opt to break it up into smaller chunks via subnetting. Internet service providers (ISPs) controlling much larger sections of IPv4 address space collect customer networks together via aggregation through supernetting or CIDR. Support of these techniques requires that the routing protocols and the equipment support classless advertisements. Aggregation is a technique employed on the Internet as a whole in order to slow routing table growth and deal with the limited number of available class B networks. These techniques have been successful in both endeavors. However, in recent years, this growth has again accelerated and new solutions must be found.

There are other forces at work that may have helped slow the growth of Internet routing tables and allowed the IPv4 address space to survive this long. NAT has created an environment in which multiple private addresses can share a single public address. Adoption of IPv6 (discussed in the next chapter), while relatively light, may have had some impact as well.

Additional Reading

- RFC 917: "Internet Subnets"
- RFC 950: "Internet Standard Subnetting Procedure"
- RFC 1338: "Supernetting: an Address Assignment and Aggregation Strategy"
- RFC 1519: "CIDR: an Address Assignment and Aggregation Strategy"
- RFC 1817: "CIDR and Classful Routing"
- RFC 4632: "CIDR: an Address Assignment and Aggregation Strategy"
- The CIDR Report (*http://www.cidr-report.org/as2.0/*)

Review Questions

Given an IP address of 150.125.100.1 and a mask of 255.255.248.0, answer the following questions.

1. To what class does this IP address belong, and what is the class mask?
2. What is the network address of this node, given the mask?
3. Is this a subnetting or a supernetting problem?
4. How many subnets/networks have been created?
5. How many possible and usable hosts exist in this subnet/supernet?
6. What is the range of host addresses for this network?
7. What are the directed broadcast addresses for the classful and network address, respectively?

8. What are possible high and low router addresses for this network?

9. What are the two problems addressed by RFCs 1338 and 1519?

10. Define aggregation in the context of routing tables and CIDR.

Review Answers

1. Class B, 255.255.0.0

2. 150.125.96.0

3. Subnetting

4. 32

5. 2,048 possible and 2,046 usable

6. 150.125.96.0–150.125.103.255

7. 150.125.255.255 and 150.125.103.255

8. 150.125.103.254 and 150.125.96.1

9. Routing table growth and a lack of class B network addresses

10. Using variable-length network masks in order to collapse smaller address chunks into larger address spaces for the purpose of reducing routing table and routing advertisement size

Lab Activities

Activity 1—What Is Your Network?

Materials: A computer with an active network connection

1. Within Windows, click on the Start button.

2. In the run box, type **cmd** and press Enter. This will open a command window.

3. Type **ipconfig /all**. This will display the IP address of your computer.

4. Perform the ANDing operation of your IP address and mask. What is your network?

Activity 2—Change Your Network

Materials: A computer with an active network connection

1. Within Windows, go to the properties of your network adapter.
2. Open up the Internet Protocol (TCP/IP) properties.
3. Give your adapter an IP address of 192.168.1.100 and a mask of 255.255.255.192.
4. Click OK to save your changes.
5. Repeat Activity 1. Is there a difference? Why/why not?

Activity 3—What Is the Address Given to You by Your ISP?

Materials: A home network

1. Most of us have home gateways such as a Linksys router. The outside address of this box is provided by your ISP. See if you can determine what the IP address is and then determine the size of your network segment.
2. What would the CIDR notation be for your network?

Activity 4—Subnet Calculator

Materials: A computer with a spreadsheet program

Using Excel or your favorite programming language, create a subnet calculator. Your calculator should allow the user to do the following:

- Input the IP address and mask.
- Select either the new mask or the number of subnets/supernets desired.
- Calculate the range of possible and usable host addresses per subnet/supernet.
- Provide the networked and directed broadcast address for each subnet.
- Provide possible router addresses.
- As a bonus, display the binary for the fields affected by the mask changes.

CHAPTER 8

Internet Protocol Version 6

"This proliferation of class C network numbers may aid in preserving the scarcity of class A and B numbers, but it is sure to accelerate the explosion of routing information carried by Internet routers...These recommendations for management of the current IP network number space only profess to delay depletion of the IP address space, not to postpone it indefinitely."

—RFC 1366

As we have already discussed, the language of the World Wide Web is the Internet Protocol (IP), or more specifically, IP version 4. But for a long time, folks have been talking about the demise of IPv4, primarily due to IP address space exhaustion. This meant that eventually there would not be any more addresses that could be assigned, begged, borrowed, or stolen for the public address space. So, an idea was born that would solve that problem and add features to the system. The year 1995 saw the publication of RFC 1752, which summarized the concerns and research of the previous five years —namely, that the IPv4 address space would not last forever. It had been predicted that the world would reach IP address exhaustion sometime between 2005 and 2011. While this prediction was not embraced by everyone, in February 2011 the Number Resource Organization (NRO) announced the following:

> As of 3 February 2011, the central pool of available IPv4 addresses managed by the Internet Assigned Numbers Authority (IANA) has been depleted.

The NRO stated that for the foreseeable future, we wouldn't notice changes to the operation of the Internet. But change is certainly coming, in the form of the next-generation Internet Protocol (IPng/IPv6) and really long addresses.

Protocol Description

There is a bewildering collection of RFCs associated with IPv6. To keep us sane, this chapter focuses on a couple of key documents, beginning with RFC 2460, entitled "Internet Protocol, Version 6 (IPv6) Specification"—though even this document has been updated by several others. As with IPv4, there are a couple of major aspects to IPv6 that must be covered in order to ensure a good understanding of the protocol, including packet structure, addressing, and operation. Many articles about IPv6 focus on addressing because this is such a visible topic. However, IPv6 has several other goals, such as these:

- Simplified header format
- Improved support for options and/or extensions
- Flow labeling capability
- Authentication and privacy

The operation of IPv6 relies on ICMPv6 (Internet Control Message Protocol version 6), so this chapter also spends some time on this protocol.

Part of the difficulty in understanding IPv6 is that even though IPv6 and IPv4 share some ideas and operations, there are also a significant number of differences that can make the transition confusing at best. So, in an effort to ease the pain, let us take a look at a small network (Figure 8-1) that we will use as the basis of our discussion, starting with a reminder about IPv4 basic network operation.

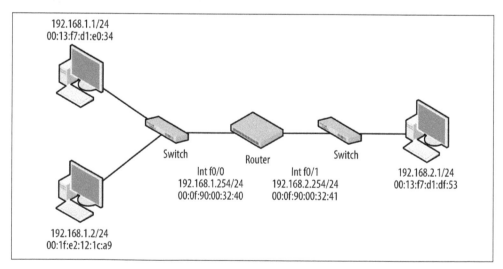

Figure 8-1. Small IPv4 network

This is a typical IPv4 network comprising computers, switches, and a router. The media access control (MAC) addresses have been included. If you have already gone through the earlier chapters, you should have a good understanding of the protocols involved and how they operate. In addition, you should understand where the addresses come from and how they are used. For example, MAC addresses are known only on the local area network (LAN), and nodes typically receive their IP addresses and knowledge of their default gateways either statically or via a Dynamic Host Configuration Protocol (DHCP) server. Since this is a small example, we have left off additional servers, printers, and the connection to the Internet. Traffic generated on a network like this should provide very little in the way of surprises.

But what happens if we simply strip off the IPv4 addresses and enable IPv6 on the hosts, as shown in Figure 8-2?

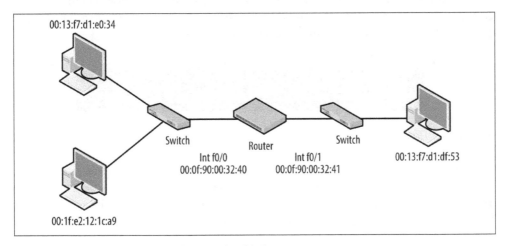

Figure 8-2. Small topology with IPv4 disabled

To begin, no static or dynamic configuration has been done regarding the IPv6 addressing. If we were to capture traffic on the hosts depicted in this topology, we would see a lot of activity as soon as IPv6 was enabled. For Windows 7 and many other operating systems, IPv6 is "ON" by default, so what I've actually done for this topology is *disable* IPv4. Initially, the router interfaces were shut down. The traffic captured by a host on the left side is shown in Figure 8-3. As can be seen, there are a number of IPv6 packets even though no configuration has been done and a DHCP server for DHCPv6 is not present.

```
No.   Source                    Destination       Protocol  Info
  1 fe80::f077:1f25:cf06:ec54  ff02::1:2         DHCPv6    Solicit XID: 0x2af8ba CID: 0001000112c1bd4b001fe2121ca9
  4 ::                         ff02::1:ff06:ec54 ICMPv6    Neighbor Solicitation for fe80::f077:1f25:cf06:ec54
  5 fe80::f077:1f25:cf06:ec54  ff02::2           ICMPv6    Router Solicitation from 00:1f:e2:12:1c:a9
  6 fe80::f077:1f25:cf06:ec54  ff02::16          ICMPv6    Multicast Listener Report Message v2
  7 fe80::f077:1f25:cf06:ec54  ff02::16          ICMPv6    Multicast Listener Report Message v2
 10 fe80::f077:1f25:cf06:ec54  ff02::1:2         DHCPv6    Solicit XID: 0x2af8ba CID: 0001000112c1bd4b001fe2121ca9
 11 fe80::f077:1f25:cf06:ec54  ff02::16          ICMPv6    Multicast Listener Report Message v2
 12 fe80::f077:1f25:cf06:ec54  ff02::1:3         LLMNR     Standard query ANY Shadowhawk
 13 fe80::f077:1f25:cf06:ec54  ff02::16          ICMPv6    Multicast Listener Report Message v2
 14 fe80::f077:1f25:cf06:ec54  ff02::c           UDP       Source port: 50614  Destination port: ws-discovery
 15 fe80::f077:1f25:cf06:ec54  ff02::1:3         LLMNR     Standard query ANY Shadowhawk
 16 fe80::f077:1f25:cf06:ec54  ff02::c           UDP       Source port: 50614  Destination port: ws-discovery
```

Figure 8-3. Left-side IPv6 traffic

Examining this traffic, we can see both source and destination addresses in use by the host. It turns out that the source address is called a *link-local address* (it begins with FE80), and the destinations are all multicast addresses (see Figure 8-4). Our task in this chapter is to understand the structure of these addresses, the operation of IPv6, and how these packets came to be on this network. The last thing we'll look at before moving to the next step is the addressing used by one of the nodes, via `ipconfig`. The %10 at the end of the line is an indicator of the interface in use.

```
Ethernet adapter Local Area Connection:

    Connection-specific DNS Suffix  . :
    Link-local IPv6 Address . . . . . : fe80::f077:1f25:cf06:ec54%10
    Default Gateway . . . . . . . . . :
```

Figure 8-4. IPv6 host link-local address

We know that this address is called link-local, but we still have to figure out how it is used and where the rest of the numbers come from. We can also take a look at the host routing table to see the collection of addresses currently in use via the `route print` command (see Figure 8-5). At this point, the host is aware of three IPv6 address types.

```
C:\>route print -6
===========================================================================
Interface List
 11...00 22 68 90 d5 db ......11a/b/g/n Wireless LAN Mini-PCI Express Adapter
 10...00 1f e2 12 1c a9 ......Intel(R) 82566MM Gigabit Network Connection
  1...........................Software Loopback Interface 1
 20...00 00 00 00 00 00 00 e0 Microsoft ISATAP Adapter
 18...00 00 00 00 00 00 00 e0 Teredo Tunneling Pseudo-Interface
===========================================================================

IPv6 Route Table
===========================================================================
Active Routes:
 If Metric Network Destination      Gateway
  1    306 ::1/128                  On-link
 10    276 fe80::/64                On-link
 10    276 fe80::f077:1f25:cf06:ec54/128
                                    On-link
  1    306 ff00::/8                 On-link
 10    276 ff00::/8                 On-link
===========================================================================
Persistent Routes:
  None
```

Figure 8-5. IPv6 host routing table

The next step in our discovery process is to assign some IPv6 addresses to the router. It would be unusual for a router to get its address from a DHCP server. While routing is not part of this book, it helps to understand a little about what is going on at the router. We will be using values from the 2001 address space. The IP addressing for North America is handled by the American Registry for Internet Numbers (ARIN), and the 2001:0400::/23 address block was allocated here. If you do not understand the numbers, don't panic: we're getting there. On a network like this, we can still use ping (ping -6), and Ethernet is still the local area network protocol, so all of those rules and the basic network behavior stay the same. However, we will see that there are some noticeable differences in operation.

Our diagram is now modified as shown in Figure 8-6.

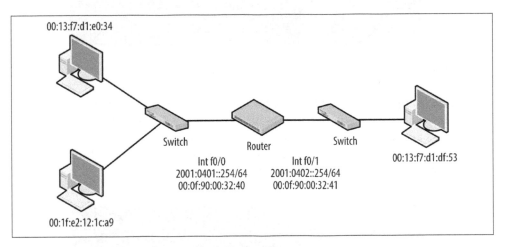

Figure 8-6. Updated topology with an IPv6 router

As a result of this change, the router is now an active member in an IPv6 topology and we see some additional traffic being generated, all from the router and all via ICMPv6.

In Figure 8-7, not only are there additional address types, such as the very strange double colon seen in the third packet, but there are also messages that directly impact the operation of the network. The router advertisement indicates a potential default gateway to the hosts. By the way, did you notice that the source address seen in the very first packet includes part of the MAC address? This is actually a link-local address that has been converted to the 64-bit Modified Extended Unique Identifier (EUI-64) format. This and other formatting will be explained later in this chapter.

```
Source                          Destination        Protocol  Info
fe80::20f:90ff:fe00:3240        ff02::16           ICMPv6    Multicast Listener Report Message v2
fe80::20f:90ff:fe00:3240        ff02::16           ICMPv6    Multicast Listener Report Message v2
::                              ff02::1:ff00:254   ICMPv6    Neighbor Solicitation for 2001:401::254
2001:401::254                   ff02::1            ICMPv6    Neighbor Advertisement 2001:401::254 (rtr, ovr)
fe80::20f:90ff:fe00:3240        ff02::16           ICMPv6    Multicast Listener Report Message v2
fe80::20f:90ff:fe00:3240        ff02::16           ICMPv6    Multicast Listener Report Message v2
fe80::20f:90ff:fe00:3240        ff02::16           ICMPv6    Multicast Listener Report Message v2
fe80::20f:90ff:fe00:3240        ff02::1            ICMPv6    Router Advertisement from 00:0f:90:00:32:40
```

Figure 8-7. Additional traffic after the addition of the router

Let's take another look at the output from the `ipconfig` command on our host, shown in Figure 8-8.

```
Ethernet adapter Local Area Connection:

   Connection-specific DNS Suffix  . :
   IPv6 Address. . . . . . . . . . . : 2001:401::f077:1f25:cf06:ec54
   Temporary IPv6 Address. . . . . . : 2001:401::c83f:b51:3d5d:2a95
   Link-local IPv6 Address . . . . . : fe80::f077:1f25:cf06:ec54%10
   Default Gateway . . . . . . . . . : fe80::20f:90ff:fe00:3240%10
```

Figure 8-8. ipconfig after router advertisement

Immediately apparent is that the host now has an IPv6 address (global unicast) that is not a link-local address. Another link-local address and a default gateway that matches the address are advertised by the router. We can see that similar information has been installed for the nodes on the opposite network. Note the change in the third and fourth octets from 401 to 402 (see Figure 8-9).

```
Ethernet adapter Student NIC:

   Connection-specific DNS Suffix  . :
   IPv6 Address. . . . . . . . . . . : 2001:402::f4e7:a9d1:f621:88ee
   Temporary IPv6 Address. . . . . . : 2001:402::e55b:b751:1aa3:ad5a
   Link-local IPv6 Address . . . . . : fe80::f4e7:a9d1:f621:88ee%24
   Default Gateway . . . . . . . . . : fe80::20f:90ff:fe00:3241%24
```

Figure 8-9. ipconfig for a node on the 2001:402 network

The temporary address seen in the output of the `ipconfig` command is exactly that—temporary. This can make things a little confusing, because nodes can have more than one IPv6 address, *and* these addresses can change. Figure 8-10 depicts the output from the `ipconfig` command run twice on the same machine. Before the second set of results was obtained, the computer was unplugged from the switch and then plugged back in. This forces the update on a Windows host.

```
Ethernet adapter Local Area Connection:

   Connection-specific DNS Suffix  . :
   IPv6 Address. . . . . . . . . . . : 2001:401::f077:1f25:cf06:ec54
   Temporary IPv6 Address. . . . . . : 2001:401::c83f:b51:3d5d:2a95
   Link-local IPv6 Address . . . . . : fe80::f077:1f25:cf06:ec54%10
   Default Gateway . . . . . . . . . : fe80::20f:90ff:fe00:3240%10

Ethernet adapter Local Area Connection:

   Connection-specific DNS Suffix  . :
   IPv6 Address. . . . . . . . . . . : 2001:401::f077:1f25:cf06:ec54
   Temporary IPv6 Address. . . . . . : 2001:401::1d3:c39e:75a0:f52b
   Link-local IPv6 Address . . . . . : fe80::f077:1f25:cf06:ec54%10
   Default Gateway . . . . . . . . . : fe80::20f:90ff:fe00:3240%10
```

Figure 8-10. Changes to the temporary IPv6 address

Some of the IPv6 addresses—the global unicast, link-local, and default gateway addresses—have not changed. However, the temporary address now has a different value. This change is an effort to protect the host from outside tracking. Reexamining the host routing table from the previous figure, we can see that there are some additional entries there as well (Figure 8-11).

```
C:\>route print -6
===========================================================================
Interface List
 11...00 22 68 90 d5 db ......11a/b/g/n Wireless LAN Mini-PCI Express Adapter
 10...00 1f e2 12 1c a9 ......Intel(R) 82566MM Gigabit Network Connection
  1...........................Software Loopback Interface 1
 20...00 00 00 00 00 00 00 e0 Microsoft ISATAP Adapter
 18...00 00 00 00 00 00 00 e0 Teredo Tunneling Pseudo-Interface
===========================================================================

IPv6 Route Table
===========================================================================
Active Routes:
 If Metric Network Destination      Gateway
 10    276 ::/0                     fe80::20f:90ff:fe00:3240
  1    306 ::1/128                  On-link
 10     28 2001:401::/64            On-link
 10    276 2001:401::c4ff:7d50:414a:116c/128
                                    On-link
 10    276 2001:401::f077:1f25:cf06:ec54/128
                                    On-link
 10    276 fe80::/64                On-link
 10    276 fe80::f077:1f25:cf06:ec54/128
                                    On-link
  1    306 ff00::/8                 On-link
 10    276 ff00::/8                 On-link
===========================================================================
Persistent Routes:
  None
```

Figure 8-11. Changes to the host routing table

At this point, we can also test connectivity on the network through the ping command, as shown in Figure 8-12. The ping command works with IPv6 without any arguments, but you can specify IPv6 by using the ping -6 option. Using the command shown and pinging a neighbor, the results are very similar to those seen on an IPv4 network. The first line shows a successful ping to the link-local address of the router. This matches the address seen in the output from ipconfig on the host.

```
C:\>ping -n 1 fe80::020f:90ff:fe00:3240

Pinging fe80::20f:90ff:fe00:3240 with 32 bytes of data:
Reply from fe80::20f:90ff:fe00:3240: time=1ms

Ping statistics for fe80::20f:90ff:fe00:3240:
    Packets: Sent = 1, Received = 1, Lost = 0 (0% loss),
Approximate round trip times in milli-seconds:
    Minimum = 1ms, Maximum = 1ms, Average = 1ms

C:\>ping -n 1 2001:0401::254

Pinging 2001:401::254 with 32 bytes of data:
Reply from 2001:401::254: time=2ms

Ping statistics for 2001:401::254:
    Packets: Sent = 1, Received = 1, Lost = 0 (0% loss),
Approximate round trip times in milli-seconds:
    Minimum = 2ms, Maximum = 2ms, Average = 2ms
```

Figure 8-12. Ping to router

Halfway down, we can seen another successful ping to the assigned global unicast address of the router. This second ping also shows the zero-suppressed (double colon) address for the router. This is not to be confused with the double colon address seen in the earlier packet capture. We'll talk about this in "Addressing" on page 163.

If you are a little confused or are panicking, take a deep breath and relax. In both the IPv4 and IPv6 network examples, the routers separate different networks, and the networks are distinguished by prefixes and the netmask. So far, the only obvious difference is the form that the addresses take and the longer masks. To be complete, the topology can be redrawn with the learned addresses installed (see Figure 8-13).

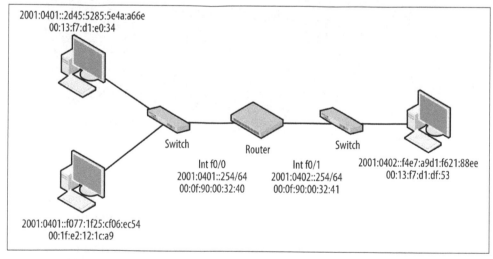

Figure 8-13. Topology with learned addresses installed

The addresses for the nodes are certainly starting to grow in size. Trying to keep track of and work with these longer addresses can be a bit of a pain. For example, connecting to a node on the other side of the router would require that the entire address be used, as shown in Figure 8-14.

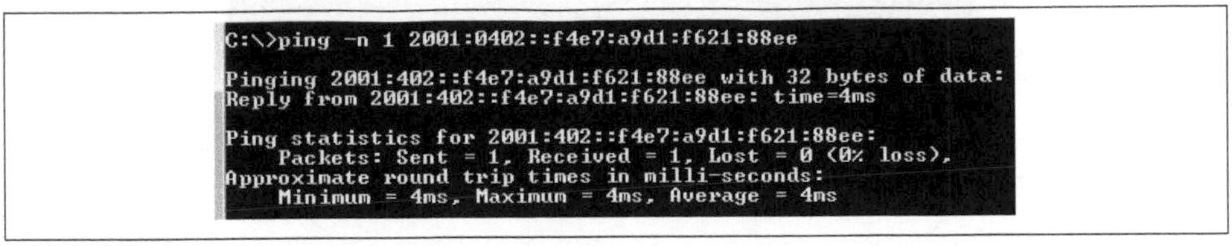

```
C:\>ping -n 1 2001:0402::f4e7:a9d1:f621:88ee

Pinging 2001:402::f4e7:a9d1:f621:88ee with 32 bytes of data:
Reply from 2001:402::f4e7:a9d1:f621:88ee: time=4ms

Ping statistics for 2001:402::f4e7:a9d1:f621:88ee:
    Packets: Sent = 1, Received = 1, Lost = 0 (0% loss),
Approximate round trip times in milli-seconds:
    Minimum = 4ms, Maximum = 4ms, Average = 4ms
```

Figure 8-14. Connecting to a node on another network

This can be quite cumbersome. So, it is not uncommon to depart from the automatic configuration somewhat in order to assign addresses that are a little easier to work with. This addressing is similar to that already used on the router. In the next IPv6 example, the addresses have been manually configured in much the same way that the addresses for an IPv4 network might be. You are already familiar with the Windows 7 interface for IPv4 addresses, and the IPv6 interface is shown in Figure 8-15.

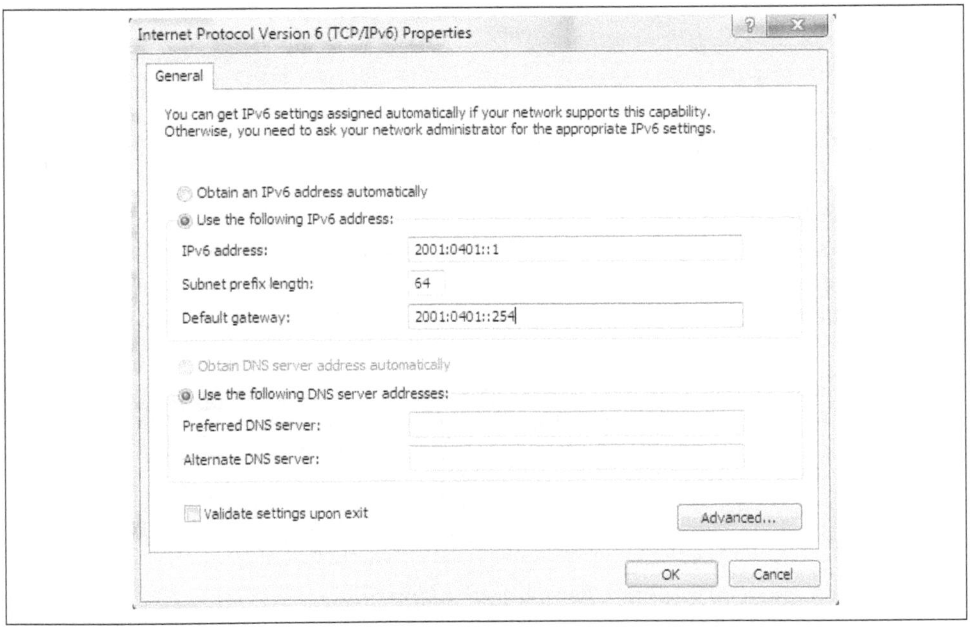

Figure 8-15. Windows 7 IPv6 configuration interface

Once this manual configuration has been completed, we can again test via ping but use the shorter addresses. In Figure 8-16, 2001:0401::2 is pinging 2001:0401::1.

```
C:\>ping -6 2001:0401::1

Pinging 2001:401::1 with 32 bytes of data:
Reply from 2001:401::1: time=1ms
Reply from 2001:401::1: time<1ms
Reply from 2001:401::1: time<1ms
Reply from 2001:401::1: time<1ms

Ping statistics for 2001:401::1:
    Packets: Sent = 4, Received = 4, Lost = 0 (0% loss),
Approximate round trip times in milli-seconds:
    Minimum = 0ms, Maximum = 1ms, Average = 0ms
```

Figure 8-16. Test via ping using manual addresses

The ICMP traffic that results from this command is very similar to that in an IPv4 network, except of course that it is accomplished via ICMPv6, as shown in Figure 8-17. In this example, two nodes on the same network (2001:401::1 and 2001:401::2) are pinging each other. You may have noticed that the address 2001:0401::2 does not appear in these packets as we would normally expect. This is the first indication of an operational difference between IPv6 and IPv4. The source node (in this case, 2001:0401::2) is using what is called its link-local address because the destination node is on the same network.

Source	Destination	Protocol	Info
2001:401::e19e:9cf6:6051:477d	2001:401::1	ICMPv6	Echo (ping) request id=0x0001, seq=362
2001:401::1	2001:401::e19e:9cf6:6051:477d	ICMPv6	Echo (ping) reply id=0x0001, seq=362
2001:401::e19e:9cf6:6051:477d	2001:401::1	ICMPv6	Echo (ping) request id=0x0001, seq=363
2001:401::1	2001:401::e19e:9cf6:6051:477d	ICMPv6	Echo (ping) reply id=0x0001, seq=363

Figure 8-17. ICMPv6 traffic resulting from ping

But what has happened to the addressing now that the static addresses have been added? The changes to `ipconfig` and the host routing table as a result of the manual configuration are shown in Figure 8-18 and Figure 8-19. From these two images, we can see that both the host and the router can now be identified by yet another IPv6 address.

```
Ethernet adapter Local Area Connection:

    Connection-specific DNS Suffix  . :
    IPv6 Address. . . . . . . . . . . : 2001:401::2
    IPv6 Address. . . . . . . . . . . : 2001:401::f077:1f25:cf06:ec54
    Temporary IPv6 Address. . . . . . : 2001:401::c4ff:7d50:414a:116c
    Link-local IPv6 Address . . . . . : fe80::f077:1f25:cf06:ec54%10
    Default Gateway . . . . . . . . . : fe80::20f:90ff:fe00:3240%10
                                        2001:401::254
```

Figure 8-18. Change to ipconfig after manual addressing

```
C:\>route print -6
========================================================================
Interface List
  11...00 22 68 90 d5 db ......11a/b/g/n Wireless LAN Mini-PCI Express Adapter
  10...00 1f e2 12 1c a9 ......Intel(R) 82566MM Gigabit Network Connection
   1...........................Software Loopback Interface 1
  20...00 00 00 00 00 00 00 e0 Microsoft ISATAP Adapter
  18...00 00 00 00 00 00 00 e0 Teredo Tunneling Pseudo-Interface
========================================================================

IPv6 Route Table
========================================================================
Active Routes:
 If Metric Network Destination      Gateway
 10   276 ::/0                      fe80::20f:90ff:fe00:3240
 10   276 ::/0                      2001:401::254
  1   306 ::1/128                   On-link
 10    28 2001:401::/64             On-link
 10   276 2001:401::2/128           On-link
 10   276 2001:401::c4ff:7d50:414a:116c/128
                                    On-link
 10   276 2001:401::f077:1f25:cf06:ec54/128
                                    On-link
 10   276 fe80::/64                 On-link
 10   276 fe80::f077:1f25:cf06:ec54/128
                                    On-link
  1   306 ff00::/8                  On-link
 10   276 ff00::/8                  On-link
========================================================================
Persistent Routes:
 If Metric Network Destination      Gateway
  0 4294967295 ::/0                          2001:401::254
========================================================================
```

Figure 8-19. Changes to the host routing table after manual configuration

Another common tool used to test connectivity is *tracert*. It is used to identify the hops or router interfaces (tracing a route) between the source and destination. The output in Figure 8-20 indicates that the command works in IPv6 as well. In this case, the computer was discovering the path to a node on the other network. This command can also be written as tracert -6.

```
C:\>tracert 2001:0402::1

Tracing route to 2001:402::1 over a maximum of 30 hops

  1    1 ms     1 ms     1 ms   2001:401::254
  2    2 ms     1 ms     1 ms   2001:402::1

Trace complete.
```

Figure 8-20. IPv6 tracert

Through the process of building this small network, we can see that while there are several unique aspects to IPv6 addressing, the operation is largely the same as on an IPv4 network. In the next couple of sections, we will further discuss the structure of and addressing used in this protocol.

Structure

Before we examine the structure of the IPv6 header, perhaps a little review of the IPv4 header is in order. Figure 8-21 displays a packet and includes fields for version, header length, type of service (differentiated services), total length, identification, flags, fragment offset, time to live, protocol, and a header checksum on top of the IP addresses. In all, there are 12 separate fields, though some of them—such as the identification, flags, and fragment offset—work together. Figure 8-21 also shows the encapsulation used on an IPv4 network with the payload (ICMP) enclosed within IP, which is wrapped by Ethernet.

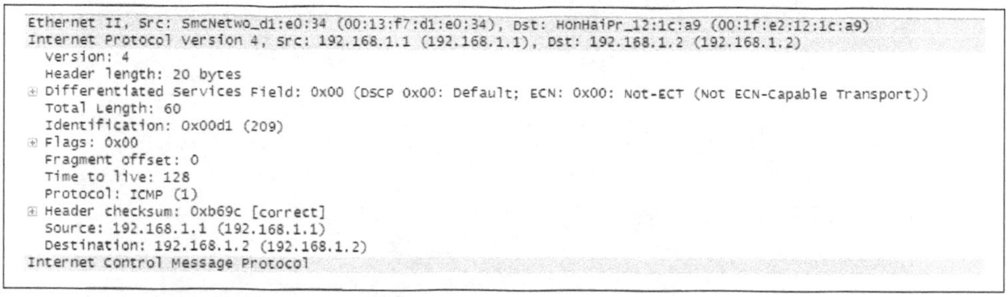

```
Ethernet II, Src: SmcNetwo_d1:e0:34 (00:13:f7:d1:e0:34), Dst: HonHaiPr_12:1c:a9 (00:1f:e2:12:1c:a9)
Internet Protocol Version 4, Src: 192.168.1.1 (192.168.1.1), Dst: 192.168.1.2 (192.168.1.2)
   Version: 4
   Header length: 20 bytes
 ⊞ Differentiated Services Field: 0x00 (DSCP 0x00: Default; ECN: 0x00: Not-ECT (Not ECN-Capable Transport))
   Total Length: 60
   Identification: 0x00d1 (209)
 ⊞ Flags: 0x00
   Fragment offset: 0
   Time to live: 128
   Protocol: ICMP (1)
 ⊞ Header checksum: 0xb69c [correct]
   Source: 192.168.1.1 (192.168.1.1)
   Destination: 192.168.1.2 (192.168.1.2)
Internet Control Message Protocol
```

Figure 8-21. IPv4 packet header

The encapsulation used with IPv6 is shown in Figure 8-22. The encapsulation works in the same way, except for the addition of the v6 for IP and ICMP.

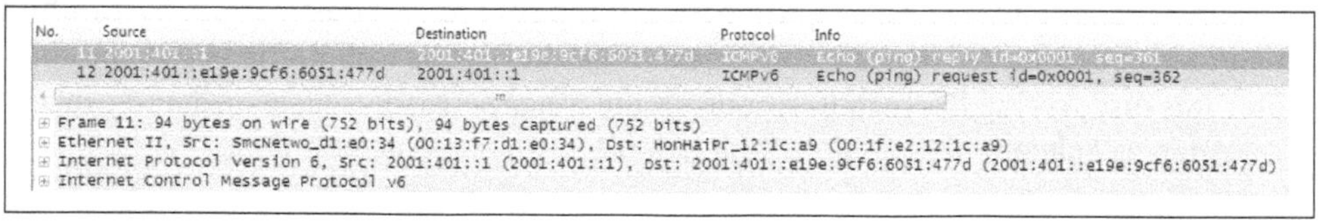

```
No.      Source                        Destination              Protocol    Info
    11 2001:401::1                     2001:401::e19e:9cf6:6051:477d   ICMPv6    Echo (ping) reply id=0x0001, seq=361
    12 2001:401::e19e:9cf6:6051:477d   2001:401::1              ICMPv6    Echo (ping) request id=0x0001, seq=362
◀                                       III
⊞ Frame 11: 94 bytes on wire (752 bits), 94 bytes captured (752 bits)
⊞ Ethernet II, Src: SmcNetwo_d1:e0:34 (00:13:f7:d1:e0:34), Dst: HonHaiPr_12:1c:a9 (00:1f:e2:12:1c:a9)
⊞ Internet Protocol Version 6, Src: 2001:401::1 (2001:401::1), Dst: 2001:401::e19e:9cf6:6051:477d (2001:401::e19e:9cf6:6051:477d)
⊞ Internet Control Message Protocol v6
```

Figure 8-22. IPv6 encapsulation

Compare the fields shown in Figure 8-21 to the RFC 2460 IPv6 header shown in Figure 8-23. The IPv6 header is simplified to include only fields for version, traffic class, flow label, payload length, next header (protocol), hop limit, and the addresses. However, as we will see in a later section, the complexity of this header can increase as advanced capabilities are implemented.

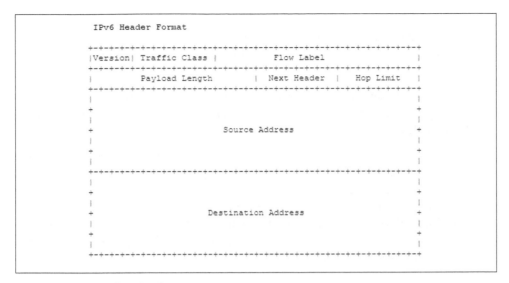

```
IPv6 Header Format

+-+-+-+-+-+-+-+-+-+-+-+-+-+-+-+-+-+-+-+-+-+-+-+-+-+-+-+-+-+-+-+-+
|Version| Traffic Class |                  Flow Label                   |
+-+-+-+-+-+-+-+-+-+-+-+-+-+-+-+-+-+-+-+-+-+-+-+-+-+-+-+-+-+-+-+-+
|          Payload Length        |   Next Header  |   Hop Limit   |
+-+-+-+-+-+-+-+-+-+-+-+-+-+-+-+-+-+-+-+-+-+-+-+-+-+-+-+-+-+-+-+-+
|                                                               |
+                                                               +
|                                                               |
+                     Source Address                            +
|                                                               |
+                                                               +
|                                                               |
+-+-+-+-+-+-+-+-+-+-+-+-+-+-+-+-+-+-+-+-+-+-+-+-+-+-+-+-+-+-+-+-+
|                                                               |
+                                                               +
|                                                               |
+                  Destination Address                          +
|                                                               |
+                                                               +
|                                                               |
+-+-+-+-+-+-+-+-+-+-+-+-+-+-+-+-+-+-+-+-+-+-+-+-+-+-+-+-+-+-+-+-+
```

Figure 8-23. IPv6 header from RFC 2460

Several of these fields are very similar to their IPv4 counterparts, and this becomes more apparent with an actual IPv6 header, as shown in Figure 8-24. In this case, the hexadecimal has been included so that we can see that some of the decoded fields have been shortened in the decoded view. It is immediately apparent that while the overall header length might be greater, the number of fields and therefore the complexity of the header is reduced.

```
⊞ Ethernet II, Src: HonHaiPr_12:1c:a9 (00:1f:e2:12:1c:a9), Dst: SmcNetwo_d1:e0:34 (00:13:f7:d1:e0:34)
⊟ Internet Protocol Version 6, Src: 2001:401::9f6:4c79:a2cf:7d5c (2001:401::9f6:4c79:a2cf:7d5c), Dst: 2001:401::1 (2001:401::1)
   ⊞ 0110 .... = Version: 6
   ⊞ .... 0000 0000 .... .... .... .... .... = Traffic class: 0x00000000
     .... .... .... 0000 0000 0000 0000 0000 = Flowlabel: 0x00000000
     Payload length: 40
     Next header: ICMPv6 (0x3a)
     Hop limit: 128
     Source: 2001:401::9f6:4c79:a2cf:7d5c (2001:401::9f6:4c79:a2cf:7d5c)
     Destination: 2001:401::1 (2001:401::1)
⊞ Internet Control Message Protocol v6

0000  00 13 f7 d1 e0 34 00 1f  e2 12 1c a9 86 dd 60 00   .....4........`.
0010  00 00 00 28 3a 80 20 01  04 01 00 00 00 00 09 f6   ...(:. .........
0020  4c 79 a2 cf 7d 5c 20 01  04 01 00 00 00 00 00 00   Ly..}\ .........
0030  00 00 00 00 00 01 80 00  14 d4 00 01 01 84 61 62   ..............ab
0040  63 64 65 66 67 68 69 6a  6b 6c 6d 6e 6f 70 71 72   cdefghij klmnopqr
0050  73 74 75 76 77 61 62 63  64 65 66 67 68 69         stuvwabc defghi
```

Figure 8-24. IPv6 packet header from Wireshark

IPv6 Fields

The header of an IPv6 packet is made up of the fields described in this section (Figure 8-24 is used as a reference).

Version

4 bits, indicating the protocol version number (value = 6, binary 0110).

Traffic class

8 bits, used in quality of service (QoS) deployment in order to differentiate between various classes or types of traffic. As in IPv4, the default value is 0.

Flow label

20 bits, used to tag packets for special handling. Typically, a flow is a group of packets sharing some commonality, such as source and destination addresses. As in IPv4, the default value is 0.

There are many methods used to provide priority handling of traffic, but most "label" the packets in some way. These labels appear in both the IPv4 ToS field and the IPv6 traffic class field described above. After traffic is labeled, network devices provide resources such as bandwidth in order to ensure that the packets are in fact prioritized. QoS deployments use Differentiated Services (provisioned) or Integrated Services (signaled) as the model, but techniques such as queuing can also take advantage of packet labels.

Payload length

16-bit unsigned integer, indicating the length of the payload after the address fields in octets. In our example, this is 40 bytes and in the lower hexadecimal this corresponds to the bytes containing 0028.

Unsigned integers are specified when we do not differentiate between positive and negative numbers. An unsigned integer in a binary will be based on the number of bits available for the numbers and must start counting at 0. For example, the range of possible values in four bits would be 0000–1111, or 0–15 in base 10 numbers. These values can be also represented using $2^4 - 1$.

Next header

8 bits, indicating the protocol that is encapsulated within the IP datagram. This field uses the same values as IPv4. These numbers were originally listed in RFC 790, which has been obsolete for quite some time. The values are now online (per RFC 3232) at *www.iana.org*. Common examples include:

6—TCP (06 in hexadecimal)
17—UDP (11 in hexadecimal)
1—ICMP (01 in hexadecimal)
58—ICMPv6 (3a in hexadecimal)

In this example, we can see that this packet encapsulates ICMPv6. This is verified by counting in six bytes and seeing that the "next header" hexadecimal value is 3a.

Hop limit

8-bit unsigned integer, reduced by 1 in every router forwarding the packet. When the field gets to 0, the packet is dropped.

Source and destination addresses

128 bits each, indicating the source and destination addresses.

As in IPv4, there are a number of address types that will be covered later in this chapter, but I would like to point out a couple of things here. First, the IPv6 values used by a particular host can change; this means that what you see in packet captures and in the host configurations may be different, especially if the interfaces have changed state. Second, if we examine the source address in Figure 8-24, it looks as though the address is 2001:401::1. This is the address after zero suppression is applied. The actual address can be seen in the hexadecimal pane below, in which the entire 128-bit address is displayed. Zero suppression will be covered later as well.

Noticeably absent from the header are the fields normally used to handle fragmentation. This is because fragmentation is no longer handled by the router. Instead, hosts will send the largest possible packet until receiving a "packet too big" ICMPv6 message from the router.

Hexadecimal Decode

Before leaving this packet, a closer examination of the hexadecimal in order to weld these fields and their definitions in place is a good idea:

- The very first hexadecimal character (6) is the version field.
- The next 28 bits (0 00 00 00 in hexadecimal) contain the values for the traffic class and flow label.
- These are followed by 16 bits (00 28 in hexadecimal) for the payload length. The upper panel provides the decoded base 10 value of 40. In this case, the encapsulated upper-layer protocol is the Internet Control Message Protocol v6 (ICMPv6), and the protocol value is 58 (3a in hexadecimal).
- The last field before the addressing is the hop count, which for this packet is 64, or 40 in hexadecimal.
- The source and destination fields are both 128 bits in length. In this case, the visible values in the upper decode window do not match those seen in the hexadecimal panel on the bottom. This is because Wireshark is using the shorthand method for indicating IPv6 addressing, in which long sequences of 0s can be suppressed. This is done using double colons (::) within the address. Both of the addresses are using this notation.

Extensions

Like IPv4, IPv6 has the ability to expand the header to include additional operations or capabilities. In Chapter 3, an example of this could be seen when specifying the path a packet might take or recording the route already taken. In IPv6, this extension is described by the "next header" field. A significant portion of RFC 2460 is dedicated to the inclusion of these additional headers. If they are to be added, they are inserted immediately prior to the upper-layer protocol and there can be more than one, as shown in Figure 8-25.

```
+----------------+--------------------+--------------------+------------------
|  IPv6 header   |  Routing header    |  Fragment header   | fragment of TCP
|                |                    |                    | header + data
| Next Header =  |  Next Header =     |  Next Header =     |
|   Routing      |    Fragment        |     TCP            |
+----------------+--------------------+--------------------+------------------
```

Figure 8-25. RFC 2460 header extensions

All of the extensions except for the destination options should appear only once. The additional headers are processed in the order specified by RFC 2460 (the order shown below) and, with the exception of the hop-by-hop extension, are not processed by nodes along the path. RFC 2460 defines four of these extensions:

Hop-by-hop

Describes discard options for the packet, based mostly on the type of destination address.

Destination

Provides optional information that may be examined by the destination node. As with the hop-by-hop options, RFC 2460 is primarily concerned with discard options.

Routing (type 0)

Indicates the routing order. This is similar to the IPv4 source routing option and describes the hops to take on the way to the destination or the hops to be recorded. This extension includes a routing type that indicates the variant. A special variant (0) was deprecated in RFC 5095 and further work on routing types was done in RFC 5871.

Fragmentation

Used by the source to send large packets. Recall that the IPv6 header does not have any fields associated with fragmentation. Normally a host will fragment packets per the discussion in Chapter 3. A router may also fragment packets in the event of an MTU change along the path. IPv6 specifies a minimum size of 1,280 bytes; any link that cannot support this will cause link-specific fragmentation and reassembly. In an IPv6 network, routers will not initiate fragmentation. Hosts will indicate fragmentation through the use of this header and the familiar identification, flags, and fragment offset fields. An example of IPv6 fragmentation is illustrated in Figure 8-26.

```
Ethernet II, Src: SmcNetwo_d1:e0:34 (00:13:f7:d1:e0:34), Dst: Cisco_00:32:
Internet Protocol Version 6, Src: 2001:401::cc94:d227:e449:f505 (2001:401:
⊞ 0110 .... = Version: 6
⊞ .... 0000 0000 .... .... .... .... .... = Traffic class: 0x00000000
  .... .... .... 0000 0000 0000 0000 0000 = Flowlabel: 0x00000000
  Payload length: 560
  Next header: IPv6 fragment (0x2c)
  Hop limit: 128
  Source: 2001:401::cc94:d227:e449:f505 (2001:401::cc94:d227:e449:f505)
  Destination: 2001:402::254 (2001:402::254)
⊟ Fragmentation Header
    Next header: ICMPv6 (0x3a)
    0000 0101 1010 1... = Offset: 181 (0x00b5)
    .... .... .... ...0 = More Fragment: No
    Identification: 0x00000010
⊞ [2 IPv6 Fragments (2008 bytes): #80(1448), #81(560)]
Internet Control Message Protocol v6
```

Figure 8-26. IPv6 fragmentation

Figure 8-26 displays a packet that was sent after the command `ping -l 2000 2001:402::254` was issued. This packet exceeds the MTU for the Ethernet network and so had to be fragmented, requiring two Ethernet frames to be generated. The source host changes the IPv6 header to include information about this fragmentation. As can be seen, the next header value is set to "IPv6 fragment," and the fragmentation header indicates that ICMP is encapsulated next. The fragment offset or position of the data is given along with the indication that this is the last fragment of the bunch.

Another two extensions are defined in other RFCs, and a full implementation of IPv6 would include these as well. Both of these extensions are part of a larger RFC 4301 context called "Security Architecture for the Internet Protocol." This architecture is based on IPSec for both IPv4 and IPv6. It also includes both the Authentication Header (AH) and Encapsulating Security Payload (ESP) descriptions:

Authentication Header (RFC 2402, obsoleted by RFCs 4302 and 4835)
> The AH provides data origin authentication and integrity for as much of the IPv6 header (and next-level protocol data) as possible. This option may be implemented alone or in tandem with encryption.

Encapsulating Security Payload (RFC 2406, obsoleted by RFCs 4303 and 4835)
> This extension provides for the encryption, and therefore the confidentiality, of the data encapsulated by the IPv6 packet. The encrypted tunnels can be provided between gateways or in the traditional client/server model. It is recommended that this be deployed with a strong integrity/authentication mechanism like AH.

Addressing

Now that we have worked through a topology example and examined the header, let's take a closer look at the addresses. IPv6 addressing does have some things in common with IPv4 addressing. For example, masks are still in use (as seen in the manual configuration dialog box for Windows 7 in Figure 8-15), and ideas similar to the unicast, multicast, and broadcast (not really) addresses are also still part of the picture, although with quite a twist. The biggest and most obvious difference is that IPv6 addresses are four times larger than those used in IPv4.

The 128 bits of an IPv6 address are organized into a standard format that breaks it up into 16-bit (2-byte) chunks. These chunks are separated by colons. Note that there are eight of them:

ABCD:ABCD:ABCD:ABCD:ABCD:ABCD:ABCD:ABCD

Each letter represents a hexadecimal value that is four bits long. With a little math, we get $4 \times 4 \times 8 = 128$. Unlike in IPv4, there is not a traditional class structure associated with an IPv6 addressing scheme, although the mask still serves to identify the network. Recall from the previous chapter that an IPv4 network and mask combination can be written in Classless Inter-Domain Routing (CIDR) format. For example, 192.168.1.0 255.255.255.0 will end up as 192.168.1.0/24. CIDR notation is used in IPv6 address with the understanding that /128 is the maximum value instead of /35.

The base structure is to split the address in half, with the prefix (network portion) and the suffix (host portion) both having 64 bits. This is the reason for the CIDR notation seen earlier. The addressing in the previous network example was 2001:401::1/64. Writing this out formally, we have the information in Table 8-1.

Table 8-1. Network and host portions

Network portion	Host portion
2001:0401:0000:0000	:0000:0000:0000:0001
FFFF:FFFF:FFFF:FFFF	:0000:0000:0000:0000

There is a global hierarchy associated with IPv6 addressing, and greater effort has been put into geographic assignments for the networks. The assignments will be covered in greater detail later in this chapter, so for right now we'll content ourselves with the hierarchical structure of the address. Generally, IPv6 addresses are aggregated and hierarchically structured to keep the aggregation. So, the 64-bit prefix is broken down as shown in Figure 8-27.

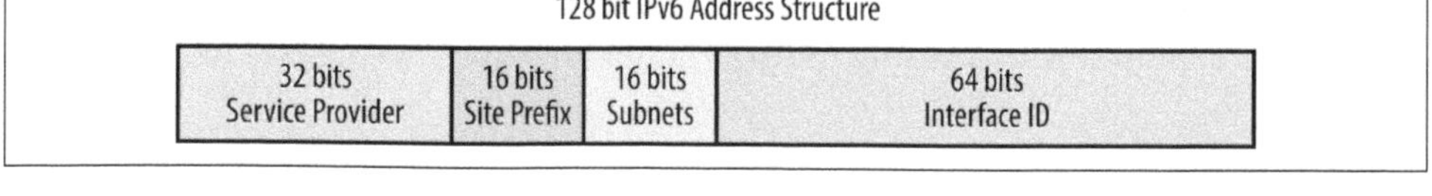

Figure 8-27. IPv6 address structure

Another way of looking at this is that a site will actually have 48 bits of address (32 + 16) and 16 bits of subnetting within the site. This structure forms the basis for our discussion, but there are quite a few variations. Other than the sheer numerical space indicated by the bits, this organization is not much different from what we have today in the sense that service providers control a good amount of the address space and the downstream customers receive chunks of that space. Subnets also work in similar fashion, with each one being a part of the larger site.

Global Assignments

From Chapter 3 we know that IPv4 addresses went through a series of architecture changes from classful to classless to global assignments. Along the way, the Regional Internet Registries (RIRs) were created to organize Internet addressing in their geographic areas. The Internet Assigned Numbers Authority (IANA) coordinates this on a global level. The structure was created not only for organizational reasons, but also to handle problems such as routing table growth on core equipment. IPv6 has also gone through some changes, even before global deployment. RFC 3177 provided the recommendations for addressing to end sites, and this was based on a /48 size for general cases and a /64 size for single subnets. But this "one size fits all" approach was considered too limited for the variation in end sites, so RFC 6177 now obsoletes 3177 and departs from this rigid structure.

Despite this more relaxed position and a reaffirmation of the feeling that sites should not be limited when trying to obtain IPv6 addresses, some concerns remain consistent. Clearly it is still important to manage the global IPv6 addressing scheme and contain routing table growth. The general assignments of the address space can be seen in Table 8-2. The entire list is available at the IANA website (*http://bit.ly/1oXa3RL*). Addresses not seen in the table are either reserved or unassigned.

Table 8-2. IPv6 global addressing

IPv6 prefix	Allocation
0000::/8	Reserved by IETF
2000::/3	Global unicast
FC00::/7	Unique local unicast (RFC 4193)
FE80::/10	Link-local unicast
FF00::/8	Multicast

The IANA site provides some clarifying notes on these values:

> The "unspecified address," the "loopback address," and the IPv6 Addresses with Embedded IPv4 Addresses are assigned out of the 0000::/8 address block.

> The "Well Known Prefix" 64:ff9b::/96 used in an algorithmic mapping between IPv4 to IPv6 addresses is defined out of the 0000::/8 address block, per [RFC6052].

The IPv6 Unicast space encompasses the entire IPv6 address range with the exception of FF00::/8. [RFC4291] IANA unicast address assignments are currently limited to the IPv6 unicast address range of 2000::/3. IANA assignments from this block are registered in the IANA registry: iana-ipv6-unicast-address-assignments.

An interesting tidbit about this process is that to date, we still do not have a great deal of experience deploying IPv6 on a large scale. In addition, per the address allocations listed on the IANA site, almost the entire world resides within the 2000::/3 block. This block is divided up among the five RIRs. A sample of these address allocations can be seen in Table 8-3.

Table 8-3. IPv6 global unicast assignments

Prefix	Designation	Date
2001:0000::/23	IANA	1999-07-01
2001:0200::/23	APNIC	1999-07-01
2001:0400::/23	ARIN	1999-07-01
2001:0600::/23	RIPE NCC	1999-07-01
2001:0800::/23	RIPE NCC	2002-05-02
2001:0A00::/23	RIPE NCC	2002-11-02
2001:0C00::/23	APNIC	2002-05-02
2001:0E00::/23	APNIC	2003-01-01
2001:1200::/23	LACNIC	2002-11-01
2610:0000::/23	ARIN	2005-11-17
2620:0000::/23	ARIN	2006-09-12
2800:0000::/12	LACNIC	2006-10-03
2A00:0000::/12	RIPE NCC	2006-10-03
2C00:0000::/12	AfriNIC	2006-10-03

Zero Suppression and Special Addressing

IPv6 addresses can be very long and can contain many 0s, not to mention that writing 128 bits of addressing can be a pain. For this reason, it is very handy to understand IPv6 *zero suppression*. Simply put, when an address section has leading 0s, it can often be truncated. For example, the address 1080:0000:0000:0000:0008:0800:200C:417A can be rewritten as 1080:0:0:0:8:800:200C:417A. In addition, when adjacent sections contain only 0s, these can be further reduced with a double colon. Rewriting again, we have 1080::8:800:200C:417A. This can make addresses a little more difficult to understand initially, but a lot faster to write.

In our basic network example, we were using addresses such as 2001:0401::1. The long form of this address would be 2001:0401:0000:0000:0000:0000:0000:0001. In fact, the system output shows that this address can be made even shorter: 2001:401::1. Not only has the double colon been used here, but in the second section (401) the leading 0 was removed.

Another similarity with IPv4 is that there are reserved or special addresses in an IPv6 network. In Figure 8-19, the host routing table is shown. The host routing table contains all of the addresses that a host must process, and many of these are reserved or special addresses. If this information is combined with the IPv6 configuration for the node (Figure 8-18), a complete picture of the addresses used within IPv6 develops. But before we tackle the individual addresses, let's discuss the term *link* or *on-link*. Historically, these terms were used to specify a device that was on the same local area network, although they weren't commonly heard in casual networking conversations. IPv6 uses these terms quite a bit, and modern operating systems have also begun to include them in the vernacular.

Table 8-4 summarizes the addressing in an IPv6 network, per the RFC. Don't panic if you can't understand all of the addressing in the table, as there will be examples and further discussion later in the chapter.

Table 8-4. IPv6 address types

Address type	Hexadecimal	Binary
Link-local unicast	FE80::/10	1111 1110 10 FE80 + 54 bits followed by 64-bit interface ID
Unique local unicast	FC00::/8, FD00::/8	1111 1100, 1111 1101
Site-local unicast	FEC0::/10	1111 1100
Global unicast	Global routing prefix (N bits) subnet ID (M bits) interface ID (128-N-M)	Note: N and M should not total more than 64 bits.
Anycast	Refers to an address assigned to several interfaces. Actual address is taken from the unicast address space.	
Multicast	FF00::/8	1111 1111
Unspecified	0:0:0:0:0:0:0:0 (::/128)	0000....0000 (128 zeros). This address is not assigned to nodes and is used in the same way as the IPv4 version, for nodes that have not yet received an IP address. This address should never appear as a destination address. IPv4 version: 0.0.0.0.
Loopback	0:0:0:0:0:0:0:1 (::1/128)	0000....0001. This address is also not assigned to physical interfaces and is used for testing. For example, it can be pinged to test connectivity on the node itself as an indication in the troubleshooting process. This address will not be seen on the network. IPv4 version: 127.0.0.

Unicast Addresses

A unicast address is an address assigned to a particular interface, and as shown in Table 8-4, there are a few flavors: link local, global, unique local, and site local.

Link-local unicast

All interfaces are required to have at least one link-local unicast address. This also means that an interface can have more than one link-local unicast address. Link-local addresses are used for automatic address configuration, for neighbor discovery, and when routers are absent. Routers do not forward packets with link-local source or destination addresses. This is because these addresses are to be used on the local area network only. Link-local unicast addresses begin with FE80. Figure 8-28 contains an example of link-local addressing being used in a conversation between a router and a host on the network. In this case, both the source and the destination are link-local addresses.

```
Ethernet II, Src: Cisco_00:32:40 (00:0f:90:00:32:40), Dst: HonHaiPr_12:1c:a9 (00:1f:e2:12:1c:a9)
Internet Protocol Version 6, Src: fe80::20f:90ff:fe00:3240 (fe80::20f:90ff:fe00:3240), Dst: fe80::f077:1f25:cf06:ec54
⊞ 0110 .... = version: 6
⊞ .... 1110 0000 .... .... .... .... .... = Traffic class: 0x000000e0
  .... .... .... 0000 0000 0000 0000 0000 = Flowlabel: 0x00000000
  Payload length: 32
  Next header: ICMPv6 (0x3a)
  Hop limit: 255
  Source: fe80::20f:90ff:fe00:3240 (fe80::20f:90ff:fe00:3240)
  [Source SA MAC: Cisco_00:32:40 (00:0f:90:00:32:40)]
  Destination: fe80::f077:1f25:cf06:ec54 (fe80::f077:1f25:cf06:ec54)
Internet Control Message Protocol v6
```

Figure 8-28. Link-local unicast packet

Unique local unicast

Unique local addresses are not intended to be routed on the global Internet, although they are supposed to be globally unique. The idea is that these addresses would be used inside a site, but they are not interchangeable with the site-local addresses. These addresses are not configured automatically as part of the process outlined in this chapter. This is borne out by the topologies that were built for this chapter. At no time were unique local addresses captured in the packets. They will be used only if manually deployed. RFC 4193 provides several guidelines for their use.

Global unicast

Routers may forward packets with certain unicast addresses. As a reminder, an interface will have a link-local unicast address, but may have other kinds of unicast addresses as well. In the earlier example, values such as 2001:401::1 and 2001:401::254 were statically configured and might be used to reach an interface from outside, which means that they are *global* unicast addresses. Global unicast addressing is depicted in Figure 8-29.

```
Ethernet II, Src: Cisco_00:32:40 (00:0f:90:00:32:40), Dst: HonHaiPr_12:1c:a9 (00:1f:e2:12:1c:a9)
Internet Protocol Version 6, Src: 2001:401::254 (2001:401::254), Dst: 2001:401::71d9:6565:84e8:daeb
⊞ 0110 .... = Version: 6
⊞ .... 0000 0000 .... .... .... .... .... = Traffic class: 0x00000000
   .... .... .... 0000 0000 0000 0000 0000 = Flowlabel: 0x00000000
   Payload length: 99
   Next header: ICMPv6 (0x3a)
   Hop limit: 64
   Source: 2001:401::254 (2001:401::254)
   Destination: 2001:401::71d9:6565:84e8:daeb (2001:401::71d9:6565:84e8:daeb)
Internet Control Message Protocol v6
```

Figure 8-29. Global unicast packet

Site-local unicast

Another idea associated with IPv6 addressing is *scope*. Scope describes the area in which an address might operate. For example, an address used solely on a local area network might be said to have *local* or *link-local* scope. Addresses that can be reached from anywhere would have *global* scope. Site-local is an address type that seems to have added to the confusion, being an address in between what might be used for a network or for global communication. In other words, it was to be aligned with the idea of a site. But this begs the question, "What constitutes a site?" If we throw multicast addressing into the mix, where does this leave site-local addresses? RFC 3879 officially deprecates the use of the site-local address type, although it does not prohibit its use. Site-local addresses begin with fec0, as shown in Figure 8-30.

```
Ethernet II, Src: HonHaiPr_12:1c:a9 (00:1f:e2:12:1c:a9), Dst: Cisco_00:32:40 (00:0f:90:00:32:40)
Internet Protocol Version 6, Src: 2001:401::c4ff:7d50:414a:116c (2001:401::c4ff:7d50:414a:116c), Dst: fec0:0:0:ffff::3
⊞ 0110 .... = Version: 6
⊞ .... 0000 0000 .... .... .... .... .... = Traffic class: 0x00000000
   .... .... .... 0000 0000 0000 0000 0000 = Flowlabel: 0x00000000
   Payload length: 51
   Next header: UDP (0x11)
   Hop limit: 64
   Source: 2001:401::c4ff:7d50:414a:116c (2001:401::c4ff:7d50:414a:116c)
   Destination: fec0:0:0:ffff::3 (fec0:0:0:ffff::3)
User Datagram Protocol, Src Port: 49283 (49283), Dst Port: domain (53)
Domain Name System (query)
```

Figure 8-30. Site-local unicast packet

Multicast Addresses

A *multicast address* is used to reach a collection of nodes or their interfaces. Multicast addresses handle most of the functions previously performed by the broadcast address. IPv6 has several reserved multicast addresses, and hosts can belong to several multicast groups. The first eight bits in a multicast address will always be set to 1, which results in the FF at the beginning of each address, but the next byte carries a little more information. Figure 8-31 shows the general format of the multicast address, from RFC 3513.

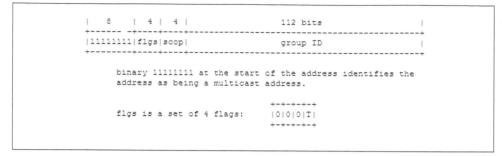

```
    |   8   |  4  |  4  |                 112 bits                    |
    +------ -+-----+-----+-----------------------------------------------+
    |11111111|flgs|scop|                 group ID                     |
    +--------+-----+-----+-----------------------------------------------+

            binary 11111111 at the start of the address identifies the
            address as being a multicast address.

                                    +-+-+-+-+
            flgs is a set of 4 flags:    |0|0|0|T|
                                    +-+-+-+-+
```

Figure 8-31. RFC 3513 multicast address general format

The T bit is set to 0 whenever the address is assigned or reserved. Nonreserved or transient addresses result in a 1. Examples of reserved addresses are shown in Table 8-5.

Table 8-5. IPv6 multicast addresses

Description	Address
All nodes addresses	FF01:0:0:0:0:0:0:1 (interface-local), FF02:0:0:0:0:0:0:1 (link-local)
All routers addresses	FF01:0:0:0:0:0:0:2 (interface-local), FF02:0:0:0:0:0:0:2 (link-local)
Solicited-node address	FF02:0:0:0:0:1:FFXX:XXXX (multicasting for a particular IPv6 interface)

But a more complete discussion of multicasting must return to the idea of scope. Recall that scope is an indication of the area over which the address might be used. Examples include link, site, and global. Bits 13–16 indicate this scope, and the values will range from 0–15, or 0–F in hexadecimal. Note that the differences seen in all nodes and all router addresses are in the scope. Per the RFC, transient multicast addresses are meaningful only within their scope. Common values are shown in Table 8-6.

Table 8-6. IPv6 multicast address scope

Scope value	Meaning
0	Reserved
1	Interface-local scope
2	Link-local scope
3	Reserved
4	Admin-local scope
5	Site-local scope
8	Organization-local scope
E	Global scope
F	Reserved

Values not included in the table are unassigned. While examining some of the packets seen on our small network, we can see that multicasting plays a big part in the communication. Figure 8-32 depicts a multicast frame with a link-local scope using the destination address of FF02::2.

```
Ethernet II, Src: HonHaiPr_12:1c:a9 (00:1f:e2:12:1c:a9), Dst: IPv6mcast_00:00:00:02 (33:33:00:00:00:02)
Internet Protocol Version 6, Src: fe80::f077:1f25:cf06:ec54 (fe80::f077:1f25:cf06:ec54), Dst: ff02::2 (ff02::2)
  0110 .... = version: 6
  .... 0000 0000 .... .... .... .... .... = Traffic class: 0x00000000
  .... .... .... 0000 0000 0000 0000 0000 = Flowlabel: 0x00000000
  Payload length: 16
  Next header: ICMPv6 (0x3a)
  Hop limit: 255
  Source: fe80::f077:1f25:cf06:ec54 (fe80::f077:1f25:cf06:ec54)
  Destination: ff02::2 (ff02::2)
Internet Control Message Protocol v6
```

Figure 8-32. Multicast all-routers address with a link-local scope

Anycast Address

This is a new address that, like the multicast address, is used to reach a collection of interfaces within the network. The idea is that a packet will be delivered to the closest interface (based on routing metrics) answering to that address. Upon examination, you cannot tell the difference between a unicast and an anycast frame; delivery and acceptance depend upon whether the interface has been configured to answer for that particular address. What makes a unicast address an anycast address is that it has been assigned to more than one interface, with these interfaces typically being on different nodes. Anycast addressing is also assumed to be of local (nonglobal) scope. There is a requirement for a router within a subnet to be aware of the anycast address for that subnet. This address is reserved and has the following format:

N bits (subnet prefix) 128 − N bits (00000000000)

So, the address would simply be the subnet followed by a string of 0s. The purpose of this address is to allow a node to communicate with any of the routers associated with the subnet.

Unspecified Address

In addition to the addresses already covered, there are a number of unique or unusual addresses that nodes must be prepared to process. The "unspecified" address is just such an address. Stated another way, unspecified actually means a lack of an address. In IPv4, this corresponds to an IP address of 0.0.0.0, which was used during initial configuration by a host communicating with or looking for a DHCP server. The IPv6 version of this is the double colon, but this is not to be confused with the double colon used in zero suppression. As an example, Figure 8-33 depicts a packet with an unspecified IPv6 address as the source. This one happens to be used in the neighbor solicitation process as the node learns about its own network. This indicates that the source host does not yet have an IPv6 address.

```
Ethernet II, Src: HonHaiPr_12:1c:a9 (00:1f:e2:12:1c:a9), Dst: IPv6mcast_ff:06:ec:54 (33:33:ff:06:ec:54)
Internet Protocol Version 6, Src: :: (::), Dst: ff02::1:ff06:ec54 (ff02::1:ff06:ec54)
⊞ 0110 .... = Version: 6
⊞ .... 0000 0000 .... .... .... .... .... = Traffic class: 0x00000000
    .... .... .... 0000 0000 0000 0000 0000 = Flowlabel: 0x00000000
  Payload length: 24
  Next header: ICMPv6 (0x3a)
  Hop limit: 255
  Source: :: (::)
  Destination: ff02::1:ff06:ec54 (ff02::1:ff06:ec54)
Internet Control Message Protocol v6
```

Figure 8-33. IPv6 unspecified address

The source address is highlighted and can be seen in the source field in the figure. You will not see this address used as a destination.

 This value also appears in the host routing table, much like the 0.0.0.0 value for IPv4. In both cases, the entry is meant to indicate a default route rather than an address used in a packet.

Required Addresses

So far, we have been discussing the different address types that might be used within an IPv6 network. In Chapter 3 we had a similar discussion regarding the addressing within an IPv4 network. But what is a host required to use? In other words, what addresses will be a regular part of the host routing table? The IPv4 addresses can be seen in Figure 8-34.

```
IPv4 Route Table
===========================================================================
Active Routes:
Network Destination        Netmask          Gateway       Interface  Metric
          0.0.0.0          0.0.0.0    192.168.1.254    192.168.1.2    276
        127.0.0.0        255.0.0.0          On-link        127.0.0.1    306
        127.0.0.1  255.255.255.255          On-link        127.0.0.1    306
  127.255.255.255  255.255.255.255          On-link        127.0.0.1    306
      192.168.1.0    255.255.255.0          On-link      192.168.1.2    276
      192.168.1.2  255.255.255.255          On-link      192.168.1.2    276
    192.168.1.255  255.255.255.255          On-link      192.168.1.2    276
        224.0.0.0        240.0.0.0          On-link        127.0.0.1    306
        224.0.0.0        240.0.0.0          On-link      192.168.1.2    276
  255.255.255.255  255.255.255.255          On-link        127.0.0.1    306
  255.255.255.255  255.255.255.255          On-link      192.168.1.2    276
===========================================================================
Persistent Routes:
  Network Address          Netmask  Gateway Address  Metric
          0.0.0.0          0.0.0.0    192.168.1.254  Default
===========================================================================
```

Figure 8-34. IPv4 host routing table

The corresponding values are contained in the IPv6 host routing table shown in Figure 8-19. Many of these serve a similar purpose for the IPv6 host. We saw from the early part of this chapter that the host routing table can change depending on conditions, although there is some commonality between the figures. Per RFC 3513, every host is required to recognize the following addresses as identifying themselves:

- Its required link-local address for each interface
- Any additional unicast and anycast addresses that have been configured for the node's interfaces (manually or automatically)
- The loopback address
- The all-nodes multicast addresses defined in Table 8-5.
- The solicited-node multicast address for each of its unicast and anycast addresses
- Multicast addresses of all other groups to which the node belongs

The RFC also has separate requirements for active routers. It is important to note that the node is required to understand these addresses, although some of them may not be implemented.

IPv4 and IPv6

IPv6 addresses can also contain IPv4 addresses. There are two cases in which this might be desired: tunneling and conversion. In both, the IPv4 address is carried in the low-order 32 bits, as depicted in Figure 8-35. The two bytes preceding these bits are an indicator as to the type. There are two values specified: all 0s and all 1s. All 1s corresponds to FFFF in hexadecimal and means that the address is converted rather than tunneled. A tunneling example is included later in this chapter.

```
|                   80 bits                | 16 |    32 bits       |
+-----------------------------------------+----+------------------+
|0000.....................................0000|0000|   IPv4 address    |
+-----------------------------------------+----+------------------+


|                   80 bits                | 16 |    32 bits       |
+-----------------------------------------+----+------------------+
|0000.....................................0000|FFFF|   IPv4 address    |
+-----------------------------------------+----+------------------+
```

Figure 8-35. IPv4 to IPv6 addressing

MAC Addressing

IPv4 presented us with unicast, broadcast, and multicast addresses, and these were used in conjunction with the Layer 2 counterparts. Similar rules apply in IPv6. The unicast addresses are straightforward, as there are no changes: unicast MAC addresses are used whenever the IPv6 addresses are unicast.

With broadcast and multicast frames, however, we see some significant differences, as shown in Figure 8-36. As we know, IPv6 does not use broadcast addresses, so the familiar MAC address of ff:ff:ff:ff:ff:ff is nowhere to be seen. The common IPv4 multicast addresses (frames having destination MAC addresses that begin with 01) are also not seen. In fact, the addresses that we now see in the Ethernet fields look very strange indeed.

```
⊟ Ethernet II, Src: Cisco_00:32:40 (00:0f:90:00:32:40), Dst: IPv6mcast_00:00:00:01 (33:33:00:00:00:01)
    ⊞ Destination: IPv6mcast_00:00:00:01 (33:33:00:00:00:01)
    ⊞ Source: Cisco_00:32:40 (00:0f:90:00:32:40)
      Type: IPv6 (0x86dd)
  ⊞ Internet Protocol version 6, Src: fe80::20f:90ff:fe00:3240 (fe80::20f:90ff:fe00:3240), Dst: ff02::1
  ⊞ Internet Control Message Protocol v6

0000  33 33 00 00 00 01 00 0f  90 00 32 40 86 dd 6e 00    33.....  ..2@..n.
0010  00 00 00 40 3a ff fe 80  00 00 00 00 00 00 02 0f    ...@:... ........
0020  90 ff fe 00 32 40 ff 02  00 00 00 00 00 00 00 00    ....2@.. ........
0030  00 00 00 00 00 00 01 86  00 74 03 40 00 07 08 00 00  ........  t.@.....
0040  00 00 00 00 00 00 01 01  00 0f 90 00 32 40 05 01    ........ ....2@..
0050  00 00 00 00 05 dc 03 04  40 c0 00 27 8d 00 00 09    ........ @..'....
0060  3a 80 00 00 00 00 20 01  04 01 00 00 00 00 00 00    :..... . ........
0070  00 00 00 00 00 00                                   ......
```

Figure 8-36. IPv6 MAC addressing

The multicast MAC address used in Figure 8-36 is 33:33:00:00:00:01. RFC 2464 specifies that the Layer 2 multicast address to be used with an IPv6 multicast packet "is transmitted to the Ethernet multicast address whose first two octets are the value 3333 hexadecimal and whose last four octets are the last four octets of destination."

Thus, multicast frames will be sent to addresses beginning with 33:33 and ending with the last four octets of the IPv6 address. This matches very closely what is happening at Layer 3. In Figure 8-37, the destination IPv6 address is FF02::1 and the MAC address also ends in 1. In the discovery process for the network, a number of IPv6 addresses beginning with FF are used. The list would include FF01, FF02, and FF0C. Figure 8-36 depicts another example of the addressing automatically chosen.

```
  Ethernet II, Src: HonHaiPr_12:1c:a9 (00:1f:e2:12:1c:a9), Dst: IPv6mcast_00:00:00:16 (33:33:00:00:00:16)
  ⊞ Destination: IPv6mcast_00:00:00:16 (33:33:00:00:00:16)
  ⊞ Source: HonHaiPr_12:1c:a9 (00:1f:e2:12:1c:a9)
    Type: IPv6 (0x86dd)
  Internet Protocol version 6, Src: fe80::f077:1f25:cf06:ec54 (fe80::f077:1f25:cf06:ec54), Dst: ff02::16
  Internet Control Message Protocol v6
```

Figure 8-37. IPv6 multicast MAC example

MAC Addresses and IPv6

Addresses used for the various interfaces can be tied to the MAC address or be dynamically generated. Interface identifiers must also be unique within the subnet. As we have seen so far, nodes use these addresses in different ways. For example, 2001:401::2 has a MAC address of 00-1f-e2-12-1c-a9. In the packet capture shown in Figure 8-30, the IPv6 address used for this node is 2001:0401::c4ff:7d50:414a:116c. This address is created as a result of autoconfiguration options. But running `ipconfig` to obtain the IP addresses for the same node reveals that there is some other funny stuff going on (see Figure 8-38).

```
Ethernet adapter Local Area Connection:

   Connection-specific DNS Suffix  . :
   IPv6 Address. . . . . . . . . . . : 2001:401::2
   IPv6 Address. . . . . . . . . . . : 2001:401::f077:1f25:cf06:ec54
   Temporary IPv6 Address. . . . . . : 2001:401::c4ff:7d5b:414a:116c
   Link-local IPv6 Address . . . . . : fe80::f077:1f25:cf06:ec54%10
   Default Gateway . . . . . . . . . : fe80::20f:90ff:fe00:3240%10
                                       2001:401::254
```

Figure 8-38. IPv6 addresses in use

An examination of the traffic coming from this same node also shows that it uses more than one address. Note that in Figure 8-39, the MAC address for the source has not changed.

```
Ethernet II, Src: HonHaiPr_12:1c:a9 (00:1f:e2:12:1c:a9), Dst: Cisco_00:32:40 (00:0f:90:00:32:40)
Internet Protocol version 6, Src: fe80::f077:1f25:cf06:ec54 (fe80::f077:1f25:cf06:ec54), Dst: fe80::20f:90ff:fe00:3240
 0110 .... = version: 6
 .... 0000 0000 .... .... .... .... = Traffic class: 0x00000000
 .... .... .... 0000 0000 0000 0000 0000 = Flowlabel: 0x00000000
   Payload length: 32
   Next header: ICMPv6 (0x3a)
   Hop limit: 255
   Source: fe80::f077:1f25:cf06:ec54 (fe80::f077:1f25:cf06:ec54)
   Destination: fe80::20f:90ff:fe00:3240 (fe80::20f:90ff:fe00:3240)
   [Destination SA MAC: Cisco_00:32:40 (00:0f:90:00:32:40)]
Internet Control Message Protocol v6
```

Figure 8-39. Same node, different address

Autoconfiguration and EUI-64

In an IPv4 network, IP addresses are either statically assigned or arrive via automated Dynamic Host Configuration Protocol (DHCP) messages. The standard deployment is DHCP. We use the Address Resolution Protocol (ARP) to discover the MAC addresses of neighbors that match particular IP addresses. ARP is built into the IPv4 protocol suite. Thus, a significant amount of the configuration and operation of an IPv4 network is automatic and invisible to the user. In the absence of DHCP or static addresses, what would happen? What if we couldn't use ARP? The Internet Engineering Task Force (IETF) Zero Configuration standard attempts to automatically provide an IP address and locate services that might be on the network. However, it isn't designed for large-scale use. While we have all seen 169.254.0.0-based addresses from time to time, we still cannot get much done after receiving one. And this still does not help replace the function of ARP. So without DHCP and ARP, IPv4 networks would have significant problems.

As mentioned in Chapter 4, ARP is not used in IPv6. Instead, IPv6 has several auto-configuration options, including discovery of nodes on the local area network and a mechanism to automatically generate an IPv6 address that can be used to communicate with local nodes. In this section, we will cover the mechanisms used to create an address. The neighbor discovery process will be discussed in the next section.

We know that addresses beginning with FE80 are called *link-local* and are used to communicate with directly connected neighbors or nodes on the network. One of the most common mechanisms used to generate an IPv6 address is the 64-bit Modified Extended Unique Identifier (Mod EUI-64) format. The idea is to take a 48-bit MAC address and convert it into a 128-bit IPv6 address, as follows:

1. Turn the MAC address into a 64-bit unique identifier for the node. This will be the host portion of the address:

   ```
   0000 0000 0000 0000 0000 0000 0000 0000 0000 0000 0000 0000 0000 0000 0000
   0000
   ```

2. We add the MAC address: 00:0F:90:00:32:40. But in the middle of the MAC address, the pattern FF FE is inserted:

   ```
   00 0F 90 FF FE 00 32 40
   ```

3. Converting to binary, we have:

   ```
   0000 0000 0000 1111 1001 0000 1111 1111 1111 1110 0000 0000 0011 0010 0100
   0000
   ```

4. The seventh bit in the sequence is called the "U" or universal bit. The value is flipped to ensure uniqueness:

   ```
   0000 0010 0000 1111 1001 0000 1111 1111 1111 1110 0000 0000 0011 0010 0100
   0000
   ```

5. Converting back to hexadecimal, we get:

   ```
   02 0F 90 FF FE 00 32 40
   ```

6. Finally, we prepend the link-local reserved value of FE80 and suppress the 0s:

   ```
   FE80::20F:90FF:FE00:3240
   ```

The example of an EUI-64-formatted address in Figure 8-40 is seen coming from the router in our topology. The address is highlighted. The dead giveaway regarding the format is the FF FE seen in the middle of the address.

```
Ethernet II, Src: Cisco_00:32:40 (00:0f:90:00:32:40), Dst: HonHaiPr_12:1c:a9 (00:1f:e2:12:1c:a9)
Internet Protocol Version 6, Src: fe80::20f:90ff:fe00:3240 (fe80::20f:90ff:fe00:3240), Dst: 2001:401::71d9:6565:84e8:daeb
⊞ 0110 .... = Version: 6
⊞ .... 1110 0000 .... .... .... .... = Traffic class: 0x000000e0
  .... .... .... 0000 0000 0000 0000 0000 = Flowlabel: 0x00000000
  Payload length: 32
  Next header: ICMPv6 (0x3a)
  Hop limit: 255
  Source: fe80::20f:90ff:fe00:3240 (fe80::20f:90ff:fe00:3240)
  [Source SA MAC: Cisco_00:32:40 (00:0f:90:00:32:40)]
  Destination: 2001:401::71d9:6565:84e8:daeb (2001:401::71d9:6565:84e8:daeb)
Internet Control Message Protocol v6
```

Figure 8-40. EUI-64-formatted address from the router

But using this link-local address presents a security problem for the node. Since this address can also be wedded to the global unicast address for the node, internal and external transmissions include the modified MAC address value for the node. Servers retaining information can then track usage, location, and content for this host. It is for this reason that nodes can also generate the random address values seen earlier in this chapter. These can be used for outbound transmissions. The random values are generated using a different algorithm entirely. From RFC 3041/4941:

> The very first time the system boots (i.e., out-of-the-box), a random value should be generated using techniques that help ensure the initial value is hard to guess [RANDOM]. Whenever a new interface identifier is generated, a value generated by the computation is saved in the history value for the next iteration of the algorithm.

> A randomized interface identifier is created as follows:

> 1. Take the history value from the previous iteration of this algorithm (or a random value if there is no previous value) and append to it the interface identifier generated as described in [ADDRARCH].

> 2. Compute the MD5 message digest [MD5] over the quantity created in the previous step.

> 3. Take the left-most 64-bits of the MD5 digest and set bit 6 (the left-most bit is numbered 0) to zero. This creates an interface identifier with the universal/local bit indicating local significance only. Save the generated identifier as the associated randomized interface identifier.

> 4. Take the rightmost 64-bits of the MD5 digest computed in step 2 and save them in stable storage as the history value to be used in the next iteration of the algorithm.

Recall that each host is required to have at least one link-local address per interface but can have several. It is now easier to understand the output from the ipconfig command, which depicts several addresses for the same node. What is interesting is that while valid nodes are now more difficult to track, so are the bad guys.

Autoconfiguration

Now that we have a better handle on addressing, let's remove the addresses from the hosts in the topology in order to better understand how an IPv6 network operates. The only statically configured addresses will be on the routers. This returns us to the beginning of the chapter and Figure 8-6. As mentioned earlier, IPv6 does not use ARP. So how do we solve the problem of address resolution? Remember that as part of basic network operation, hosts must be able to discover not only other computers on the same network, but the router or default gateway as well. We know from the earlier sections that the output from `ipconfig` and `route print` changed as the network was constructed. The question is, "Where did these addresses come from?"

IPv6 uses a series of messages to find these other nodes and the router. For network configuration, IPv6 makes much greater use of ICMP (ICMPv6) messaging than IPv4 did. The configuration messages include neighbor solicitation, neighbor advertisement, router solicitation, router advertisement, and redirects. These five constitute the discovery operation. When combined with other ICMPv6 operations and DHCPv6 (required when not statically configuring the IPv6 addresses), the network becomes fully functional. Many of these messages have been used as examples in previous sections and can be seen in the collection of packets in Figure 8-41.

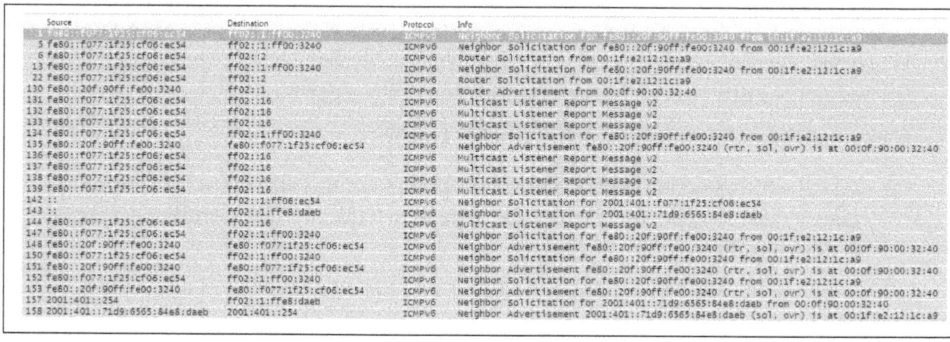

Figure 8-41. Autodiscovery packets

The addresses ending in 3240 and 254 are the other computer and the router, respectively. The next section describes some of the messages used to complete this operation.

Internet Control Message Protocol Version 6

ICMPv6, defined in RFC 4443, is very similar to its IPv4 cousin, though there are a couple of new message types. As in the previous version, there are two general message flavors: informational and error. The header for ICMPv6 is straightforward, containing fields for the type, code, and checksum (see Figure 8-42).

Figure 8-42. ICMPv6 general header

The fields can be described as follows:

Type
    8-bit field describing the kind of ICMPv6 message. Error messages have types 0–127 and informational messages use 128–255. Common types of ICMPv6 error messages include the following:

        1—Destination unreachable: Problems getting to host other than congestion
        2—Packet too big: Packet larger than path maximum transmission unit (MTU)
        3—Time exceeded: Hop count for packet is decremented to 0
        4—Parameter problem: Header or extensions are not recognized

    ICMPv6 informational message types include the following:

        128—Echo request: Responder function
        129—Echo reply: Responder function

Code
    8-bit field that corresponds to the type field. A type may have several associated codes.

Checksum
    Includes a check on the ICMP data and header.

As with ICMPv4, there are a couple of rules regarding ICMPv6. Since nodes can have several addresses, the ICMPv6 response message must come from the unicast address specified in the original message and not one of the other addresses associated with the interface. ICMPv6 error messages will attempt to include a portion of the message that caused the error to be generated. Messages that do not uniquely identify the host and ICMP error messages will not cause ICMPv6 messages to be generated.

The ICMPv6 messages used in the neighbor discovery process are actually part of RFC 2461. Their purposes are to do the following:

- Learn the Link Layer addresses of nodes that are close by
- Get rid of old information

- Discover routers willing to forward packets

As stated earlier, there are five messages included in the process: router solicitation, router advertisement, neighbor solicitation, neighbor advertisement, and redirect messages. These messages use the ICMPv6 format (RFC 4443), but the process and the new ICMPv6 message types are actually defined in RFC 4861. The two solicitation types (neighbor and router) are straightforward messages containing only the source Link Layer (MAC) address and the standard header. The only difference (other than the type) is that the neighbor solicitation is targeted at a particular link-local address. Both use multicast addressing. The advertisements are altogether different as they are trying to provide information that is useful to the other nodes on the network. An example of a neighbor advertisement is shown in Figure 8-43.

```
Ethernet II, Src: HonHaiPr_12:1c:a9 (00:1f:e2:12:1c:a9), Dst: Cisco_00:32:40 (00:0f:90:00:32:40)
Internet Protocol Version 6, Src: fe80::f077:1f25:cf06:ec54 (fe80::f077:1f25:cf06:ec54), Dst: fe80::20f:90ff:fe00:3240
Internet Control Message Protocol v6
  Type: Neighbor Advertisement (136)
  Code: 0
  Checksum: 0xc204 [correct]
⊟ Flags: 0x60000000
    0... .... .... .... .... .... .... .... = Router: Not set
    .1.. .... .... .... .... .... .... .... = Solicited: Set
    ..1. .... .... .... .... .... .... .... = Override: Set
    ...0 0000 0000 0000 0000 0000 0000 0000 = Reserved: 0
  Target Address: fe80::f077:1f25:cf06:ec54 (fe80::f077:1f25:cf06:ec54)
⊟ ICMPv6 Option (Target link-layer address : 00:1f:e2:12:1c:a9)
    Type: Target link-layer address (2)
    Length: 1 (8 bytes)
    Link-layer address: HonHaiPr_12:1c:a9 (00:1f:e2:12:1c:a9)
```

Figure 8-43. ICMPv6 neighbor advertisement

The advertisement messages include not only the addressing information, which is used by the IPv6 nodes to develop and understand the link-local topology, but a series of flags as well. The flags are defined as follows:

R (Router)
  Indicates that the sender is a router.

S (Solicited)
  Indicates whether a message was sent in response to a solicitation. It also indicates reachability.

O (Override)
  Indicates whether this information should be used in place of anything that might be cached.

The router advertisement is much more complex and provides quite a bit of information about the network. Some of the fields replace the options normally assigned by a DHCP server. A router advertisement is shown in Figure 8-44.

```
Internet Control Message Protocol v6
  Type: Router Advertisement (134)
  Code: 0
  Checksum: 0x7403 [correct]
  Cur hop limit: 64
⊞ Flags: 0x00
  Router lifetime (s): 1800
  Reachable time (ms): 0
  Retrans timer (ms): 0
⊟ ICMPv6 Option (Source link-layer address : 00:0f:90:00:32:40)
    Type: Source link-layer address (1)
    Length: 1 (8 bytes)
    Link-layer address: Cisco_00:32:40 (00:0f:90:00:32:40)
⊟ ICMPv6 Option (MTU : 1500)
    Type: MTU (5)
    Length: 1 (8 bytes)
    Reserved
    MTU: 1500
⊟ ICMPv6 Option (Prefix information : 2001:401::/64)
    Type: Prefix information (3)
    Length: 4 (32 bytes)
    Prefix Length: 64
⊞ Flag: 0xc0
    Valid Lifetime: 2592000
    Preferred Lifetime: 604800
    Reserved
    Prefix: 2001:401:: (2001:401::)
```

Figure 8-44. ICMPv6 router advertisement

The router advertisement includes several details about the network. The typical use of the flags field is to indicate the interaction with a DHCP server. The timers are defined as follows:

Router lifetime
> Time in seconds that the router can be considered useful as a default router.

Reachable time
> Time in milliseconds that the router can be considered reachable. A value of 0 indicates that the timer value has not been set. This is used as part of the neighbor unreachability test.

Retransmission time
> Time in milliseconds between the transmission of neighbor solicitation messages. This is also used in the detection of reachable neighbors.

The option for the maximum transmission unit (MTU) is tied to the Link Layer protocol. In this case, the network was built on Ethernet, which has a maximum data field size of 1,500 bytes.

> At times it is useful to be able to see the ARP table for a host or router. Since ARP is not part of IPv6, the related table would contain a list of neighbors. Within Windows 7, this list can be obtained with the netsh interface ipv6 show neighbors command.

Tunneling

If you have been looking through your IP stacks, routing tables, and the output of commands such as `ipconfig`, you may have noticed tunneling adapters or statements such as Teredo and 6to4. Since the core of the Internet and most company networks is still IPv4, sites that have deployed IPv6 natively often cannot talk to each other because the interconnecting routers do not use the same protocols. These adapters exist in order to allow the sites or endpoints to interconnect. The basic idea is that the IPv6 traffic (packets) will be encapsulated in IPv4 packets for transport across the IPv4 network. Once they reach the destination, the IPv4 packet header will be stripped off (detunneled), and the remaining IPv6 packet will be forwarded normally. This is by no means a new idea, and tunneling has many applications, such as in virtual private networks.

In the topology shown in Figure 8-45, two IPv6 networks are isolated from each other by an IPv4 network. The traffic on the two outside networks is restricted to IPv6, so the packets must be tunneled from one network to another. The typical method is to create tunnel interfaces on the routers and then direct the traffic over the tunnel interface. While tunneling is a bit beyond what we want to accomplish here, some of the Cisco configuration has been included here:

- `interface Tunnel0`
- `no ip address`
- `ipv6 enable`
- `tunnel source FastEthernet0/0`
- `tunnel destination 192.168.1.253`
- `tunnel mode ipv6ip`
- `ipv6 route 2001:402::/64 Tunnel0`

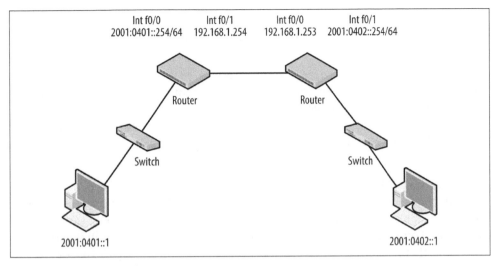

Int f0/0   Int f0/1   Int f0/0   Int f0/1
2001:0401::254/64   192.168.1.254   192.168.1.253   2001:0402::254/64

Router   Router

Switch   Switch

2001:0401::1   2001:0402::1

Figure 8-45. Tunneled topology

With these commands, the router is instructed to send traffic for the destination 2001:402::/64 over the tunnel and informed that the tunnel will be encapsulating IPv6 packets inside IPv4 packets. At the other end, another tunnel interface is created that performs the same operation but in the opposite direction. An example of this encapsulation is shown in Figure 8-46. This packet was generated as a result of a ping from 2001:401::1 to 2001:402::1 and was captured between the two routers.

```
Ethernet II, Src: Cisco_00:32:40 (00:0f:90:00:32:40), Dst: Cisco_3f:30:01 (00:11:21:3f:30:01)
Internet Protocol Version 4, Src: 192.168.1.254 (192.168.1.254), Dst: 192.168.1.253 (192.168.1.253)
Internet Protocol Version 6, Src: 2001:401::cc94:d227:e449:f505 (2001:401::cc94:d227:e449:f505), Dst: 2001:402::1
Internet Control Message Protocol v6
```

Figure 8-46. Tunneled IPv6 packet

From this capture, we can see that an ICMPv6 echo request was sent from 2001:401::1. This is an IPv6 node that simply sends the traffic to its default gateway. The router receives the packet and directs it to the tunnel interface, which is based in IPv4. An IPv4 header is applied as a wrapper, and the destination becomes the other end of the tunnel. Upon delivery to 192.168.1.253, the extra header is removed and the packet is forwarded to the initial IPv6 destination.

Current Status and IPv6 Day

Any discussion regarding IPv6 is typically filled with claims that its deployment is right around the corner, and groans from folks believing that since we have been talking about it for more than a decade, and because network address translation (NAT) has been so successful, it will arrive just in time for us to move to IPv8. The reality is probably somewhere in between. Certainly operating systems and equipment are offering more and more support for IPv6, but it is not likely that support for IPv4 will end in the next day or so.

Perhaps some guidance can be found in recent events. In the now famous memorandum from the White House Office of Budget and Management, US Chief Information Officer Vivek Kundra wrote that public-facing services and servers would be IPv6-compliant by the end of 2012 and that native IPv6 deployment would occur by the end of 2014. He also called for the immediate appointment of an IPv6 Transition Manager to oversee these efforts.

A few years ago, the Internet Society (*http://www.iana.org/assignments/ipv6-address-space/ipv6-address-space.xml*) (ISOC) organized World IPv6 Day as a method for testing IPv6 readiness. Many companies, including Google and Facebook, agreed to participate and on June 8, 2011, the first global trial of the protocol was run. Reports indicated that there were few major problems, and to quote from ISOC, "major websites around the world are well-positioned for the move to a global IPv6-enabled Internet."

In 2010, other tests were run in different countries. Each year there is another IPv6 launch of some kind, and its adoption is growing. To learn more, check out *http://www.worldipv6day.org/* or *http://www.worldipv6launch.org*.

To be complete, the ISOC site also states that IPv4 may never have to be turned off and that the IPv4 Internet will likely continue just as it has. I should also mention that in 2014 it was reported that ARIN was down to its last /8 address block. This marks the end of general IPv4 address availability in North America.

Summary

The move to IPv6 has been predicted for a couple of years. Some believed that it would happen in 2011 at the latest. The success of network address translation might have contributed to the delay. While NAT is a topic for another day, there is no doubt that it will continue to play a role in network topologies for some time to come. But based on releases from the White House and efforts such as World IPv6 Day, it is clear that IPv6 is going to become a bigger part of our lives, and maybe sooner than some of us think.

Operationally IPv6 and IPv4 have many things in common, such as routing, routing protocols, and ICMP. However, differences in the use of ICMP and addressing can make IPv6 somewhat daunting. This is not made easier by the collection of RFCs associated with the next-generation Internet.

In this chapter, we stepped through the construction of a small IPv6 network to demonstrate IPv6 addressing and similarities between the two protocols. After an in-depth discussion of addressing, the autoconfiguration process was examined. While IPv6 does have several mechanisms designed to aid a host in establishing connectivity, it does add some complexity. Rounding out the chapter was a discussion of tunneling as a major migration tool and the status of IPv6.

Additional Reading

- RFC 2460: "Internet Protocol, Version 6 (IPv6) Specification" (obsoletes 1883)
- RFC 3587: "IPv6 Global Unicast Address Format"
- RFC 3879: "Deprecating Site Local Addresses"
- RFC 4193: "Unique Local IPv6 Unicast Addresses"
- RFC 4219: "Things Multihoming in IPv6 (MULTI6) Developers Should Think About"
- RFC 4291: "IP Version 6 Addressing Architecture" (obsoletes 3513)
- RFC 4443: "Internet Control Message Protocol (ICMPv6) for the Internet Protocol Version 6 (IPv6) Specification" (obsoletes 2463, updates 2780)
- RFC 4861: "Neighbor Discovery for IP Version 6 (IPv6)" (obsoletes 2461)
- RFC 4941: "Privacy Extensions for Stateless Address Autoconfiguration in IPv6" (obsoletes 3041)
- RFC 5375: "IPv6 Unicast Address Assignment Considerations"
- RFC 6085: "Address Mapping of IPv6 Multicast Packets on Ethernet" (updates 2464)
- RFC 6177: "IPv6 Address Assignment to End Sites" (obsoletes 3177)

Review Questions

1. Match the following addresses to their type:

a. ::	A. Multicast
b. FE80	B. Global unicast
c. FF00	C. Unspecified
d. 2001:402::1	D. Link-local

2. How many bits are in an IPv6 address?
3. IPv6 does not use ARP. True or false?
4. IPv6 does not have a broadcast address. True or false?
5. Name five messages that are part of the neighbor discovery process.
6. Link-local addresses are globally routable. True or false?
7. IPv6 addresses do not use a network mask. True or false?

8. IPv6 Day pointed out some major flaws in ISP readiness. True or false?

9. MAC addresses behave the same way on an IPv6 network as they do on an IPv4 network. True or false?

10. When tunneling IPv6 packets, the IPv6 header is removed. True or false?

Review Answers

1. a) C, b) D, c) A, d) B

2. 128

3. True

4. True

5. Router solicitation/advertisement, neighbor solicitation/advertisement, redirect

6. False

7. False

8. False

9. False

10. False

Lab Activities

Activity 1—Build the Topology Shown

Materials: Router capable of IPv6, switches, computers, and Wireshark

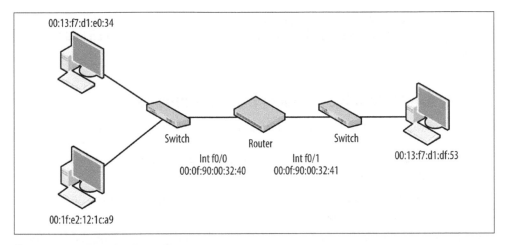

00:13:f7:d1:e0:34

Switch

Router

Switch

00:13:f7:d1:df:53

Int f0/0
00:0f:90:00:32:40

Int f0/1
00:0f:90:00:32:41

00:1f:e2:12:1c:a9

Figure 8-47. Activity 1 topology

1. Cable the network.
2. Ensure that the nodes have IPv6 enabled.
3. At each phase of construction, capture packets and examine the output from the `ipconfig` and `route print` commands. Can you follow the changes?

Activity 2—Configure the Router IPv6 Addresses

Materials: Router capable of IPv6, switches, computers, and Wireshark

1. Start captures on the end nodes.
2. As the routers are configured, examine the traffic generated. What ICPMv6 messages are displayed?
3. Examine the output from the `ipconfig` and `route print` commands. Can you follow the changes? Where did these entries come from?

Activity 3—Configure the Hosts with Global Unicast IPv6 Addresses

Materials: Router capable of IPv6, switches, computers, and Wireshark

1. Start a capture on each host. Does the traffic change with the static configuration?
2. Manually configure the IPv6 addresses on the hosts. Select addresses from the allocation for your region (Table 8-3) and use a mask of /64.

3. Examine the output from the `ipconfig` and `route print` commands. Explain the output from these commands in terms of the type of addresses seen and how they got there.

Activity 4—Explain the Neighbor Discovery Process

Materials: Router capable of IPv6, switches, computers, and Wireshark

1. Reexamine the packet captures from the previous activities. When and why did these packets occur?
2. If you are using a Windows machine, examine the output from the `netsh inter face ipv6 show neighbors` command.
3. Using this information, and the information from the host routing table, explain the IPv6 neighbor discovery process.

Activity 5—EUI-64

Materials: Router capable of IPv6, switches, computers, and Wireshark

1. Select a packet from your captures that has been converted to the EUI-64 format.
2. Starting from all 0s and using the process found in this chapter, complete the EUI-64 conversion process on paper using the MAC address for the node in the capture.
3. Did your calculated value match the one caught in the packet?

CHAPTER 9

Transmission Control Protocol

No matter what you do when connected to a network—for example, connecting to a web server or printer—the connection is governed by a small number of protocols. These protocols provide logical endpoints to which you might make requests, send replies, or send data. While there are many protocols that work together in order to transmit information from one location to another, the Transmission Control Protocol (TCP) and the User Datagram Protocol (UDP) are responsible for tethering the applications on either end of the connection together.

When an application is written, the developer determines whether it will be based on TCP or UDP. These two protocols govern a majority of the traffic running on networks today, though they do not handle it in the same way. For example, visiting a web page creates a TCP connection between the client computer and the web server. Operationally, this connection has a particular behavior. In contrast, a Voice over IP (VoIP) connection has a very different behavior, so UDP is used to encapsulate the data.

This chapter covers TCP in detail, including the packet flow between client and server machines and an explanation of the packet content. Since these connections are between clients (host computers) and a server, the client/server model will also be covered. As in the previous chapters, our discussion will center on topics found in standards or RFCs and actual network operation.

TCP was first described way back in 1981 in RFC 793. It has since been updated several times, with some of the most recent work regarding security threats. This chapter will also provide some guidance in that direction.

The Client/Server Model

Models, like the ones covered in Chapter 1, are not very exciting to read about, and the client/server model is no exception. However, since there are a number of terms in this chapter that come from this architecture, it is important to go over some of the details.

Figure 9-1 shows the basic client/server model. Loosely, *clients* are computers on a network. People sit at computers and use them for watching videos like those on You-Tube or trying to get work done, such as printing or storing files. Many of these activities can be accomplished only by communicating with another computer that does something for you—enter the *server*. Getting a little more technical, we might say that the client is software running on your computer, and the server is software running on another computer. Servers listen for connections, and clients make requests of the server. Often, the server is running on a server-class machine. *Server-class machines* are simply robust machines with lots of memory, lots of processing power, and high-speed network connections built with the idea that they will be answering requests for many clients. For example, you open up your favorite web client (browser) such as Firefox and connect to your favorite website, and presto—a client/server connection has been established. We will find that this connection can be uniquely identified through the addressing used for the transmission.

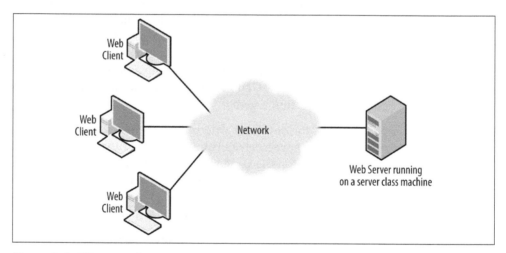

Figure 9-1. Clients and a server

If we look a little more closely at the client computer, we find that it is carrying out several tasks at the same time, and these tasks are associated with many destinations. This reinforces the idea that an individual client is not the computer but rather a program running on the computer, and that many clients can exist on one computer at the same time. When we connect to another computer because we want to watch a video or obtain a file, it is not the destination computer that we connect to, but a server program running on that computer. At any one time, a person using a computer might have a browser open and be working on email, printing, and messaging all at the same time. These are all different clients connected to different servers. It is not necessary that the user be actively engaged in these activities because once a connection is made, it is often retained until manually shut down or timed out. For example, when using

Facebook, you are still connected even when you are not updating your status. There are also many client programs running that have nothing to do with the person at the keyboard. Microsoft, Flash, and Java updaters are good examples of automated clients.

The programs running on a computer (for example, Outlook, the web browser, and the messaging and printing interfaces) are also called the mail, web (HTTP), messaging, and print clients, respectively. These clients establish connections with mail, web, messaging, and print servers. Each one of these servers can support connections from many different clients at the same time—the server-class machines they run on were built with enough horsepower (RAM, processors, network cards) to support simultaneous connections from hundreds or even thousands of end users. (It is not likely that Google runs its web servers on laptop computers.) This is the typical client/server network architecture, as illustrated in Figure 9-2.

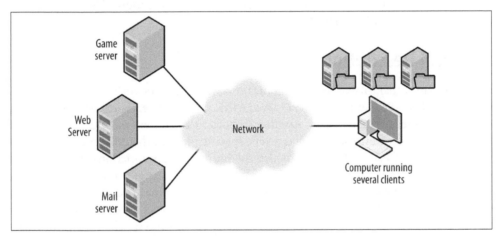

Figure 9-2. Many clients, one computer

The connection between the two ends can traverse many networks and is often referred to as a *logical connection*. Through the use of ports, TCP and UDP form the logical endpoints between the client and the server. No two Internet connections are the same, and they can be uniquely identified through the combination of four numbers: source port, destination port, source IP address, and destination IP address. Under normal conditions, all connections can be differentiated by at least one of these numbers.

A connection begins with the client forming a request to be sent to the server. The request originates from not only the client machine's IP address, but a randomly generated Layer 4 port number. The destination for the request is the server IP address and what is called a *well-known* port number. How these ports are chosen will be covered in greater detail later in the chapter. The exchange between the two machines is carried out over the logical connection using these four values. The combination of the source IP address and the source port constitutes a *socket* (Figure 9-3).

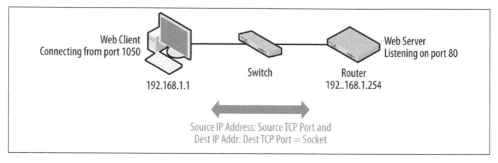

Figure 9-3. A TCP socket

The same is true for the destination IP address and the destination port. From the RFC, we know that "A pair of sockets uniquely identifies each connection." The packet shown depicts the addressing for a TCP connection.

Protocol Description

TCP governs a majority of the communication we see on networks today. It is standardized in RFC 793, dating from 1981. While this RFC has been updated several times, most of the ideas remain intact. Another important document is RFC 5681, entitled "TCP Congestion Control." TCP has a very specific place in the universe, operating at Layer 4 of the TCP/IP networking model. As one of its main functions, TCP differentiates between transmissions emanating from a single machine using different source ports. The basic problem is that on a network, TCP datagrams are encapsulated in IPv4 or IPv6 packets, which are in turn encapsulated in Ethernet or 802.11 frames. Two applications running on the same machine (such as email and web browsing) will both appear to originate from the same IP and MAC address. Responses to the two applications will go back to that single IP address. So how can we tell the difference between two transmissions destined for (or coming from) a single node or IP address?

We know that TCP was written to provide the connection point between logical processes via the ports or sockets (IP address and port combination) mentioned earlier. Thus, each time a particular application generates traffic, the data is encapsulated in a TCP (or UDP) packet first. This wrapper includes the source and destination ports. The TCP message is then encapsulated in an IP packet, which includes the source and destination IP addresses. Finally, we have the Ethernet or 802.11 frame, which encapsulates everything. This framing also provides the source and destination MAC addresses. Each one of these addresses is used in delivering the message to its final destination, with the port numbers providing the final stop. Examples of this encapsulation are shown in Figure 9-4.

```
Ethernet II, Src: Ibm_43:49:97 (00:11:25:43:49:97), Dst: Intel_16:76:09 (00:07:e9:16:76:09)
Internet Protocol Version 4, Src: 192.168.16.113 (192.168.16.113), Dst: 192.168.16.112 (192.168.16.112)
Transmission Control Protocol, Src Port: sip (5060), Dst Port: sip (5060), Seq: 1261, Ack: 1, Len: 198
Session Initiation Protocol
Ethernet II, Src: Avaya_ef:48:f8 (00:04:0d:ef:48:f8), Dst: GiantEle_05:cb:11 (00:09:6e:05:cb:11)
Internet Protocol Version 4, Src: 192.168.16.4 (192.168.16.4), Dst: 192.168.16.23 (192.168.16.23)
User Datagram Protocol, Src Port: clearvisn (2052), Dst Port: tsb2 (2742)
Real-Time Transport Protocol
```

Figure 9-4. TCP and UDP encapsulation examples

TCP is tied to the client/server architecture. Prior to sending data, TCP nodes go through a *handshake* process with the server. This establishes the starting point for the data exchange. As we will see in the next section, TCP is called *connection-oriented* because it controls the stages of the connection and keeps track of sequence numbers. TCP segments contain values indicating the amount of data transferred. They also inform the opposite end of the connection of how much data has been received. Transmissions between the client and server are bidirectional, so if we are going to ensure that all of the data is received, TCP must track both streams.

Reliable Communication

We often hear the terms *connection-oriented* and *reliable* associated with TCP. These terms are used so much that we might expect exhaustive coverage within the RFC—yet the first of these terms is used only once. *Reliable*, and its nemesis *unreliable*, have much heavier use within the same document. TCP is *connection-oriented* because it establishes a session via the socket. Recall that the socket is the collection of source and destination IP addresses and port numbers. While UDP does the same thing, it does not complete a handshake or keep track of values during the connection. TCP is *reliable* because the two ends of the connection work together in order to ensure that all of the data has been received. In the event of lost data or packets, TCP retransmits the missing bytes. TCP also supports graceful teardown of the connection. It's the sort of closure that we humans find soothing.

Another way to look at TCP is to compare it to other protocols operating on the same network. For example, Ethernet listens to the media before sending a frame. If the media is clear, the frame is sent. Without a collision, the sender assumes that the frame got away safely and arrived at its destination. IP isn't much better: the checksum is only for the header, and there is no provision for acknowledgment. Moving up to Layer 4, we see that UDP has a smaller header than TCP and is unconcerned with details such as sequence or acknowledgment numbers. One might say that these protocols are assuming that some other protocol or application will handle any problems that arise. This is the networking equivalent of opening the door and pushing the data out with a wave and a hearty "Good luck!" TCP blanches at that behavior, insisting that all of the bytes arrive safely by validating the streams via the sequence and acknowledgment numbers.

Protocol Structure

When an IP packet encapsulates a TCP datagram, the IP header will set the protocol identifier field to 6, as shown in Figure 9-5, which allows the receiver to begin to decode the next header.

```
Ethernet II, Src: WesternD_89:ba:fa (00:00:c0:89:ba:fa), Dst: Cisco_2c:0c:80 (00:11:21:2c:0c:80)
Internet Protocol Version 4, Src: 192.168.1.1 (192.168.1.1), Dst: 192.168.1.254 (192.168.1.254)
   Version: 4
   Header length: 20 bytes
 ⊞ Differentiated Services Field: 0x00 (DSCP 0x00: Default; ECN: 0x00: Not-ECT (Not ECN-Capable Transport))
   Total Length: 48
   Identification: 0x00d1 (209)
 ⊞ Flags: 0x02 (Don't Fragment)
   Fragment offset: 0
   Time to live: 128
   Protocol: TCP (6)
 ⊞ Header checksum: 0x75a7 [correct]
   Source: 192.168.1.1 (192.168.1.1)
   Destination: 192.168.1.254 (192.168.1.254)
   [Source GeoIP: Unknown]
   [Destination GeoIP: Unknown]
Transmission Control Protocol, Src Port: cma (1050), Dst Port: http (80), Seq: 0, Len: 0
```

Figure 9-5. IP header with a TCP protocol ID

Just like any protocol, TCP has a particular set of fields used to describe the features and functions of a particular message. The TCP header is 20 bytes in length (see the "header length" field), though this can be extended if options are used. As discussed previously, the main components are the source and destination ports, but since TCP is "connection-oriented" or "reliable" in terms of connections, it also keeps track of sequence and acknowledgment numbers. This information is highlighted in Figure 9-6, and we will go over an example in a few paragraphs. TCP also provides a number of flags that describe the current status of the connection.

```
Ethernet II, Src: WesternD_89:ba:fa (00:00:c0:89:ba:fa), Dst: Cisco_2c:0c:80 (00:11:21:2c:0c:80)
Internet Protocol Version 4, Src: 192.168.1.1 (192.168.1.1), Dst: 192.168.1.254 (192.168.1.254)
Transmission Control Protocol, Src Port: cma (1050), Dst Port: http (80), Seq: 1, Ack: 1, Len: 405
   Source port: cma (1050)
   Destination port: http (80)
   [Stream index: 0]
   Sequence number: 1      (relative sequence number)
   [Next sequence number: 406      (relative sequence number)]
   Acknowledgment number: 1      (relative ack number)
   Header length: 20 bytes
 ⊞ Flags: 0x018 (PSH, ACK)
   Window size value: 17520
   [Calculated window size: 17520]
   [Window size scaling factor: -2 (no window scaling used)]
 ⊞ Checksum: 0x78f9 [validation disabled]
 ⊞ [SEQ/ACK analysis]
Data (405 bytes)
```

Figure 9-6. TCP 20-byte header

The fields contained in a typical TCP packet are as follows:

Source port
16-bit field identifying the source port. Every TCP-based connection has a pair of Layer 4 endpoints called ports. This is the port number of the originator. These ports are typically random values above 1023.

Destination port
16-bit field identifying the destination port. This is the Layer 4 endpoint to which a client connects. This is commonly a well-known port, although it can be any value within the constraints of the field size.

 Servers often "listen" on what is known as a *well-known port*. These are ports reserved for servers. For example, File Transfer Protocol (FTP) servers listen for incoming connections on port 20. Web servers listen on port 80. Clients connect to these well-known ports, but a client's endpoint is identified by a random port called an *ethereal port*. The idea is that source port values will not conflict with the well-known ports.

Sequence number
32-bit field identifying the first byte or octet in the TCP data chunk, or *segment*. When the SYN flag is set, the sequence number is actually called the *initial sequence number* (ISN), and the first data value is set to ISN + 1. This is a standard state of affairs, and we will trace sequence numbers later in the chapter.

Acknowledgment number
32-bit field indicating to the other end of the connection the next expected sequence number. For example, if Node A sends 100 bytes of data to Node B, Node B responds with an acknowledgment number of 101. However, keep in mind that data can flow in both directions, so both A and B may send data with sequence numbers while at the same time recognizing receipt of data with the acknowledgment numbers in the same packets. What is also implied by these numbers is that the previous data was received. So, Node B is signaling not only that it is expecting byte 101, but also that the first 100 bytes were received without incident.

Data offset (header length)
4-bit field that like the Internet Protocol header length field, describes the size of the TCP header in 4-byte chunks. The header is usually 20–28 bytes in length, so this field will have a value of 5–7. The maximum size of the header is 60 bytes.

Reserved
6-bit field reserved (per the RFC) for future use. The field bits should all be set to 0. In actual practice, this field is not seen very often.

Control bit flags

TCP defines a series of operations based on the flags or how far the connection has progressed. The setup and teardown handshakes are two examples. The flags defined in the RFC are as follows:

SYN, ACK, FIN

These flags are set to indicate the status of a connection or in response to another flag. Their use is described further in "Basic Operation" on page 201.

URG

This flag indicates the presence of data that is "meaningful" and that the processing of "normal" data should wait. The value of the subsequent urgent pointer field refers to a sequence number referencing the urgent data. The example given in RFC 1122 is using this flag as a sort of interrupt mechanism for control information for an application. But this can be abused. For example, an attacker may set the URG flag in order to bypass a "normal" stream of data. For this reason, network devices implementing packet inspection may remove the urgent pointer. RFC 6093, written in 2011, therefore recommends that all new applications avoid the implementation of the urgent pointer. In actual practice, it is unusual to see this flag set or the urgent pointer used.

PSH

The push function is implemented in a send operation whenever an application wishes to force the transmission of data. Per the RFCs, the sender must set the PSH flag in the last message in a sequence. Without the PSH flag, a sender may buffer data in order to aggregate smaller segments into larger ones before transmission. At the receiver, small segments may be buffered before sending them to the application. Receipt of a TCP datagram with the PSH flag set forces the delivery or transmission of the data.

RST

This flag is set to force a reset of the connection. The effect of receiving a datagram with the RST flag set is to close the connection.

CWR, ECN-Echo, NONCE

RFC 3168 suggests the implementation of explicit congestion notification (ECN) within the IP header. The idea is that some of the code point bits can be repurposed in order to allow some indication that the network is experiencing congestion due to traffic load. To improve network conditions, ECN uses these flags to acknowledge the congestion condition: the receiver notifies the sender by setting the congestion experienced (CE) bit in the IP header, and senders set the CWR flag to indicate that the congestion window has been reduced. This results in a reduction in the amount of data flowing into the network.

The NONCE value is an assurance that if the IP header is rewritten, the one-bit NONCE written in the code-point bits is not lost. A larger discussion of these code points can be found in Chapter 3. Figure 9-7 shows the TCP header with the flags field expanded.

```
Ethernet II, Src: WesternD_89:ba:fa (00:00:c0:89:ba:fa), Dst: Cisco_2c:0c:80 (00:11:21:2c:0c:80)
Internet Protocol Version 4, Src: 192.168.1.1 (192.168.1.1), Dst: 192.168.1.254 (192.168.1.254)
Transmission Control Protocol, Src Port: cma (1050), Dst Port: http (80), Seq: 1, Ack: 1, Len: 405
    Source port: cma (1050)
    Destination port: http (80)
    [Stream index: 0]
    Sequence number: 1      (relative sequence number)
    [Next sequence number: 406      (relative sequence number)]
    Acknowledgment number: 1      (relative ack number)
    Header length: 20 bytes
  ⊟ Flags: 0x018 (PSH, ACK)
      000. .... .... = Reserved: Not set
      ...0 .... .... = Nonce: Not set
      .... 0... .... = Congestion Window Reduced (CWR): Not set
      .... .0.. .... = ECN-Echo: Not set
      .... ..0. .... = Urgent: Not set
      .... ...1 .... = Acknowledgment: Set
      .... .... 1... = Push: Set
      .... .... .0.. = Reset: Not set
      .... .... ..0. = Syn: Not set
      .... .... ...0 = Fin: Not set
    Window size value: 17520
    [Calculated window size: 17520]
    [Window size scaling factor: -2 (no window scaling used)]
  ⊞ Checksum: 0x78f9 [validation disabled]
  ⊞ [SEQ/ACK analysis]
    Data (405 bytes)
```

Figure 9-7. TCP 20-byte header with flags expanded

Window size value

16-bit field used by the sender of a TCP datagram to indicate the amount of data in bytes that it is willing to receive, beginning with the value seen in the acknowledgment field. In other words, it is the receiver's window size. Using this field, each client communicates a value that must be honored.

TCP nodes use a *sliding window* to handle flow control. That is, a sender is instructed to send only the amount specified in the window field of the arriving TCP datagram. Once its limit is reached with one or more packets, the sender closes the window, stopping the transmission. However, once the receiver acknowledges receipt via the acknowledgment field, the window opens back up, with the new size equal to the number of bytes acknowledged. An example will be shown later in the chapter.

Checksum

16-bit field containing, according to RFC 793, "the one's complement of the one's complement sum of all of the 16-bit words in the header and the text." For computing purposes, the checksum is set to zero and if there are an odd number of

16-bit words, a zero-padded word is added. To make things a little more confusing, per the RFC the checksum includes a portion of the IP header and any options that may be appended to the TCP header. This allows potentially corrupt segments to be flagged for possible discarding or retransmission.

Urgent pointer
16-bit field that indicates the sequence number of the byte after the urgent data, when the URG flag is set in the flags field.

Options
As in most "extendable" protocols, fields used for options go at the end of the TCP header. Options must be in multiples of eight bits for length. RFC 793 specifies two formats for the options if they are to be used: a single-byte "option kind" field, or this option kind byte followed by the length and option bytes. In RFC 793, the option kind field has three values (0, 1, 2) indicating end of option, no option, or the maximum segment size (MSS). An example of the maximum segment size option is shown in Figure 9-8.

```
Transmission Control Protocol, Src Port: http (80), Dst Port: cma (1050)
   Source port: http (80)
   Destination port: cma (1050)
   [Stream index: 0]
   Sequence number: 0      (relative sequence number)
   Acknowledgment number: 1      (relative ack number)
   Header length: 24 bytes
 ⊞ Flags: 0x012 (SYN, ACK)
   Window size value: 4128
   [Calculated window size: 4128]
 ⊞ Checksum: 0xbb89 [validation disabled]
 ⊟ Options: (4 bytes), Maximum segment size
   ⊟ Maximum segment size: 1460 bytes
        Kind: MSS size (2)
        Length: 4
        MSS Value: 1460
```

Figure 9-8. TCP options: MSS

Additional TCP options were added later, though, and even in the 1980s it was understood that larger values were required for the TCP sequence numbers tracking the bytes transferred. In 1988, RFC 1072, entitled "TCP Extensions for Long-Delay Paths," was published. This interesting RFC is a detailed discussion of the problems associated with the smaller 16-bit window size and recommends a window scaling factor. The scaling factor describes the number of bits by which the window size will shift, as illustrated in Figure 9-9. The packet shown in Figure 9-9 also contains a "selective ACK" option that allows the receiver to more efficiently track and recover missing data.

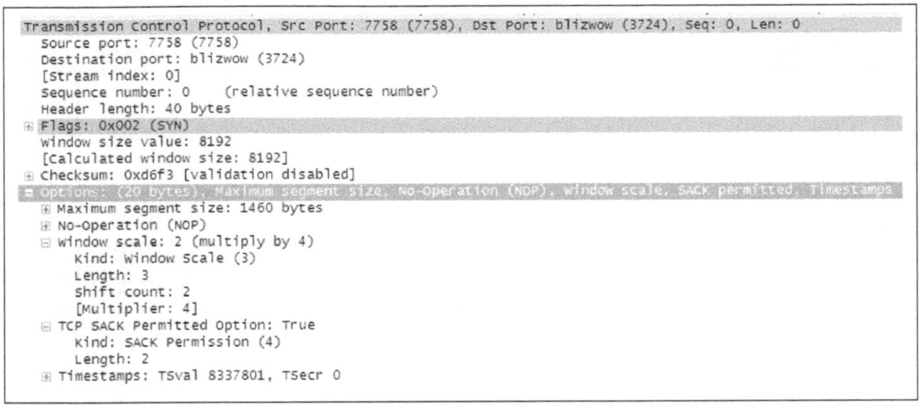

```
Transmission Control Protocol, Src Port: 7758 (7758), Dst Port: blizwow (3724), Seq: 0, Len: 0
   Source port: 7758 (7758)
   Destination port: blizwow (3724)
   [Stream index: 0]
   Sequence number: 0    (relative sequence number)
   Header length: 40 bytes
 ⊞ Flags: 0x002 (SYN)
   window size value: 8192
   [calculated window size: 8192]
 ⊞ Checksum: 0xd6f3 [validation disabled]
 ⊟ Options: (20 bytes), Maximum segment size, No-Operation (NOP), window scale, SACK permitted, Timestamps
   ⊞ Maximum segment size: 1460 bytes
   ⊞ No-Operation (NOP)
   ⊟ window scale: 2 (multiply by 4)
       Kind: window Scale (3)
       Length: 3
       shift count: 2
       [Multiplier: 4]
   ⊟ TCP SACK Permitted Option: True
       Kind: SACK Permission (4)
       Length: 2
   ⊞ Timestamps: TSval 8337801, TSecr 0
```

Figure 9-9. TCP options: window scaling

Perhaps the final word in extensions comes to us via RFC 6247, which moves many of the TCP options not in widespread use to "historical" status.

Padding
Variable-length field that ensures that the TCP header ends on a 32-bit boundary.

Ports

Before we go any further, it might be useful to spend a little more time with ports. We know that local area network frames are transmitted to/from MAC addresses. Similarly, IP packets are transmitted between IP addresses. Moving up to the Transport Layer (Layer 4) in our model, we now know that applications running on the various network nodes communicate from source ports to destination ports. The port is a software entity that tethers the transmission at the endpoint. Both the source and destination port numbers are given 16 bits of address space, for a range of 0–65535 (65536) in base 10 numbers. The following image from Chapter 1 (Figure 9-10) is a reminder of these addresses and protocols.

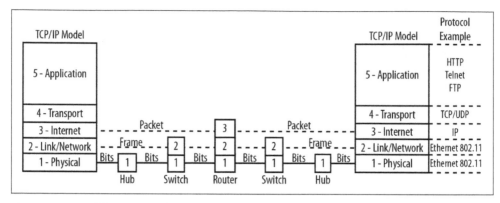

Figure 9-10. Addressing and connections

A machine running a server is said to be "listening" on a port. When a transmission comes to the server's IP address and attempts to connect on that port using a TCP packet with the SYN flag set, communication can commence. When the client attempts to connect to the server at the correct IP address but the incorrect port, the connection is either ignored or declined. Understanding this behavior is the basis for understanding port scanning.

Good practice dictates that servers of the same type listen on the same port. For example, all Simple Mail Transfer Protocol (SMTP) email servers listen on port 25, all web servers listen on port 80, and so on. In this way, clients can always find the desired service. These commonly used ports are referred to as the *well-known ports*, as their assignments were listed in RFC 790 and controlled by the Internet Assigned Numbers Authority (IANA). Well-known ports are also called *contact ports* because this is where the server is contacted. But this list kept growing, making the RFC listing cumbersome. The port list was subsequently moved to the IANA website (*http://www.iana.org*), but the RFC is still a good source of information for the port assignments (though today you should read RFC 1700 instead).

Per the RFC, well-known ports have been allocated values from 0–1023. Other processes avoid these values, at least on the server side. The next group of ports are called *registered ports*, and these were given the range of 1024–65535. These were intended to be used in "long-term" TCP connections, though "long-term" is not defined. There are names next to many of the port numbers, but they are not controlled or treated in the same fashion as the well-known ports. These can be assigned to any type of connection.

From an operational standpoint, a conversation is defined by two port numbers and two IP addresses. Servers are connected on a well-known port and clients dynamically select random ports.

After RFC 1700 was obsoleted by RFC 3232, IANA further clarified the port number assignments by referring the reader to RFC 6335. This RFC defines the following:

System Ports, also known as the Well Known Ports, from 0–1023 (assigned by IANA)

User Ports, also known as the Registered Ports, from 1024–49151 (assigned by IANA)

Dynamic Ports, also known as the Private or Ephemeral Ports, from 49152–65535 (never assigned)

As a side note, where possible, the TCP and UDP port number assignments are the same. Examples of well-known port assignments include the following:

```
chargen      19/tcp    Character Generator
chargen      19/udp    Character Generator
ftp-data     20/tcp    File Transfer [Default Data]
ftp-data     20/udp    File Transfer [Default Data]
ftp          21/tcp    File Transfer [Control]
ftp          21/udp    File Transfer [Control]
#            22/tcp    Unassigned
#            22/udp    Unassigned
telnet       23/tcp    Telnet
telnet       23/udp    Telnet
             24/tcp    any private mail system
             24/udp    any private mail system
smtp         25/tcp    Simple Mail Transfer
smtp         25/udp    Simple Mail Transfer
#            26/tcp    Unassigned
#            26/udp    Unassigned
nsw-fe       27/tcp    NSW User System FE
nsw-fe       27/udp    NSW User System FE
```

Basic Operation

Now that we have an understanding of port numbers and how they are used, let's take a look at an actual conversation. A typical TCP-based connection follows a very particular format called the *three-way handshake*. In the example shown in Figure 9-11, a network client connects to a router that also happens to be running a web server.

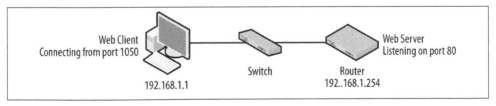

Figure 9-11. Small HTTP topology

When a client connects to the server, it sends a TCP datagram with the SYN flag set. The server responds with its own TCP datagram, setting the SYN and ACK flags. Finally, the client returns a TCP datagram with the ACK flag set. This handshake (shown in the TCP packet list) establishes the connection for both ends, and at this point the application-specific messages can be exchanged. For example, a client might send a Hypertext Transfer Protocol (HTTP) GET request to a web server. The packet list in Figure 9-12 depicts part of the conversation, beginning with the client handshake attempts as it connects to the HTTP server. Note that the handshake occurs regardless of the TCP connection's purpose.

No.	Source	Destination	Protocol	Info
2	192.168.1.1	192.168.1.254	TCP	cma > http [SYN] Seq=0 Win=16384 Len=0 MSS=1460 SACK_PERM=1
3	192.168.1.254	192.168.1.1	TCP	http > cma [SYN, ACK] Seq=0 Ack=1 Win=4128 Len=0 MSS=1460
4	192.168.1.1	192.168.1.254	TCP	cma > http [ACK] Seq=1 Ack=1 Win=17520 Len=0
5	192.168.1.1	192.168.1.254	TCP	cma > http [PSH, ACK] Seq=1 Ack=1 Win=17520 Len=405
6	192.168.1.254	192.168.1.1	TCP	http > cma [ACK] Seq=1 Ack=406 Win=3723 Len=560
7	192.168.1.254	192.168.1.1	TCP	http > cma [ACK] Seq=561 Ack=406 Win=3723 Len=560
8	192.168.1.1	192.168.1.254	TCP	cma > http [ACK] Seq=406 Ack=1121 Win=16400 Len=0
9	192.168.1.254	192.168.1.1	TCP	http > cma [ACK] Seq=1121 Ack=406 Win=3723 Len=560
10	192.168.1.254	192.168.1.1	TCP	http > cma [PSH, ACK] Seq=1681 Ack=406 Win=3723 Len=227

Figure 9-12. TCP HTTP packet list

If we look closely, we can pick out not only the source and destination IP addresses and TCP source and destination ports, but the flags and sequence and acknowledgment numbers as well. In our packet list, Wireshark has provided the names for the ports rather than the numeric values, so we will take a peek into some of the packets as we go. While the packet list is a handy way to look at what is happening, another useful technique is using a flow diagram like the one in Figure 9-13. A flow diagram assigns a vertical line to each node in the conversation and connects the nodes with the messages sent back and forth. Time advances as you move down the diagram. The three-way handshake used to start the transmission between the web client and the web server is indicated with the arrow at the top.

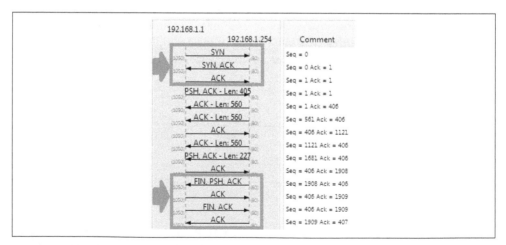

Figure 9-13. TCP flow diagram

The arrow at the bottom of the diagram points out the handshake that sends the connection into graceful termination. Along the way, the sequence and acknowledgment numbers advance as data flows between the two nodes. But remember that these are relative numbers, not actual. Table 9-1 provides a breakdown of both versions of the sequence and ACK numbers used in the conversation.

Table 9-1. TCP packet stream

Packet	Packet type	Direction	Sequence number	ACK number
2	TCP handshake: SYN	192.168.1.1 --> 192.168.1.254	0 (12c0dda0)	
3	TCP handshake: SYN, ACK	192.168.1.254 --> 192.168.1.1	0 (9053c2fd)	1 (12c0dda1)
4	TCP handshake: ACK	192.168.1.1 --> 192.168.1.254	1 (12c0dda1)	1 (9053c2fe)
5	HTTP GET: ACK, PSH	192.168.1.1 --> 192.168.1.254	1 (12c0dda1)	1 (9053c2fe)
6	TCP: ACK	1.254 --> 192.168.1.1	1 (9053c2fe)	406 (12c0df36)
7	TCP: ACK	192.168.1.254 --> 192.168.1.1	561 (9053c52e)	406 (12c0df36)
8	TCP: ACK	192.168.1.1 --> 192.168.1.254	406 (12c0df36)	1121 (9053c75e)

The first three packets in this transmission (2, 3, 4) are what is called the three-way handshake. Those familiar with TCP will sometimes refer to this as the SYN, SYN ACK, ACK exchange. The first SYN packet is shown in Figure 9-14. As can be seen, the source port is 1050 and the destination is 80 (HTTP).

```
Ethernet II, Src: WesternD_89:ba:fa (00:00:c0:89:ba:fa), Dst: Cisco_2c:0c:80 (00:11:21:2c:0c:80)
Internet Protocol Version 4, Src: 192.168.1.1 (192.168.1.1), Dst: 192.168.1.254 (192.168.1.254)
Transmission Control Protocol, Src Port: cma (1050), Dst Port: http (80), Seq: 0, Len: 0
  Source port: cma (1050)
  Destination port: http (80)
  [Stream index: 0]
  Sequence number: 0    (relative sequence number)
  Header length: 28 bytes
⊞ Flags: 0x002 (SYN)
  window size value: 16384
  [Calculated window size: 16384]
⊞ Checksum: 0xca04 [validation disabled]
⊞ Options: (8 bytes), Maximum segment size, No-Operation (NOP), No-Operation (NOP), SACK permitted
```

Figure 9-14. TCP SYN packet

As we can see, the transmission begins with the client (192.168.1.1) sending a connection request to the server (192.168.1.254).

Using the SYN flag, the two ends synchronize sequence numbers. In other words, they agree upon a starting place for counting. The actual value used can be seen in the packet hexadecimal values, and in this case we start with the following two-byte value: 12c0dda0. This has a base 10 value of 314,629,536. The Wireshark sequence number relative to this connection is 0 because Wireshark subtracts the original sequence number from each sequence and acknowledgment number value.

In this first packet, there is no acknowledgment number, since 192.168.1.1 has not received any data yet.

The server (192.168.1.254) responds with its own request to synchronize sequence numbers (SYN) while at the same time acknowledging the data sent by the client. So, the sequence number for the server is 9053c2fd in hexadecimal, or 2,421,408,509 in base 10. Again, the relative sequence number for this direction is 0. The ACK number for this packet is 12c0dda1, or 1. Remember that an acknowledgment indicates that data up to a certain point has been received, and the value used is the next expected byte.

The client returns a sequence number of 12c0dda1 (1) and an ACK of 9053c2fe (1). As a reminder, sequence numbers (and therefore acknowledgment numbers) in this part of the connection process simply increment and are not counters for data. Indeed, looking at the packets, we can see that they contain no data beyond the TCP header.

Once the handshake is completed, the connection can proceed. In this case, the client was connecting to a web server (destination port 80), so the next message seen is an HTTP GET request (packet 5) coming from 192.168.1.1. This is actually a much larger packet that sends a good amount of information to the server, mostly about the browser and encodings. This 405 bytes of data being sent from 1.1 to the router causes packet 6 to increase the ACK number. However, this packet also uses the PSH flag along with the now-familiar ACK. Since this came from the client, the sequence number (12c0dda1) and the acknowledgment number (9053c2fe) have not changed.

RFC 793 has the following to say about the PSH flag:

> Sometimes users need to be sure that all the data they have submitted to the TCP has been transmitted. For this purpose a push function is defined. To assure that data submitted to a TCP is actually transmitted, the sending user indicates that it should be pushed through to the receiving user. A push causes TCP to promptly forward and deliver data up to that point to the receiver.

It turns out that there are several times over the course of a connection that the PSH flag may be used. Some of the most common are at the beginning of the connection, to establish client parameters, and when the final piece of a segment is sent.

Packets 6 and 7 return the web page to 192.168.1.1, so the sequence number increases but the ACK number remains the same.

Packet 8 is the ACK from 192.168.1.1. It does not contain data, but the ACK number increases.

When the server receives the HTTP GET, several data packets are transmitted back to the client. These constitute the web page that the client desires. In these packets, we can really see the behavior of the sequence and acknowledgment numbers. From the IP header in packet 5, we can see that the entire datagram is 445 bytes. Subtracting 40 bytes for the IP header (20 bytes) and the TCP header (also 20 bytes), we know that the total data sent from the client was 405 bytes. Packet 6 returning from the server uses the same sequence number from its end (9053c2fe) since this is the first chunk of data. However, the acknowledgment number is 12c0df36 in hexadecimal, or 314,629,942 in base 10 numbers. Calculating the difference between the sequence numbers (314,629,942 − 314,629,536), we get 406, which is the next expected sequence number or byte of information.

As long as there are no incidents or accidents, the client and server will continue exchanging data, with the majority of it coming from the server. Client data will be in the form of requests such as for the actual page or other user actions. But most of those transactions will be part of HTTP. Once the client has the data, it may decide to terminate the connection. At this point, there will be a termination handshake, as shown in Figure 9-15.

No.	Source	Destination	Protocol	Info
21	192.168.1.1	192.168.1.254	TCP	optima-vnet > http [FIN, ACK] Seq=337 Ack=286 Win=17235 Len=0
22	192.168.1.254	192.168.1.1	TCP	http > optima-vnet [ACK] Seq=286 Ack=338 Win=3792 Len=0
23	192.168.1.254	192.168.1.1	TCP	http > optima-vnet [FIN, PSH, ACK] Seq=286 Ack=338 Win=3792 Len=0
24	192.168.1.1	192.168.1.254	TCP	optima-vnet > http [ACK] Seq=338 Ack=287 Win=17235 Len=0

Figure 9-15. TCP HTTP packets at teardown

The fact that the client and server are communicating in order to close the connection makes this a *graceful termination*. The two sides inform each other that the resources and sequence numbers are no longer required. As can be seen, the client acknowledges the last portion of the data and then signals the close with the FIN flag set. The server acknowledges and then signals its desire to sever the link. The client seals the deal with an ACK message. We can also see that the PSH flag is set in order to ensure that any data remnants are processed. In fact, TCP has to support two types of shutdown: the graceful handshake we see here and an *abort*, in which one or more RST packets are received.

TCP Sliding Window

The window size is a flow control mechanism that governs the amount of data that can be sent to or from a particular node. As RFC 793 states, the window size equals the "range of sequence numbers the sender of the window is currently prepared to accept." So, the receiver of the data tells the sender how much is acceptable. The concept of the sliding window, arguably the heart of TCP, refers to the ability of the window to expand and contract as data is acknowledged. Remember that as packet bytes are processed at the receiver, they are acknowledged with the returning packet. The acknowledgment number is the next *expected* byte.

At the sender, the window expands based on the number of bytes just acknowledged. The tricky part is that both ends of the connection pay attention to this value. If Node A indicates that it has a receive window of 17,520 bytes, Node B has a send window associated with that receive window. Compounding the issue is the fact that *both Node A and Node B can transmit data*. Thus, *each end of a connection may have a receive window and a send window*. We usually think of clients being on the receiving end of the data, and generally this is true—most of the data flows from the server to the client. However, some information must be passed to the server. This can be seen in the example used earlier in the chapter: the HTTP client sends an HTTP GET request, which contains data, and the client receives the web page, which also contains data. Figure 9-16 illustrates.

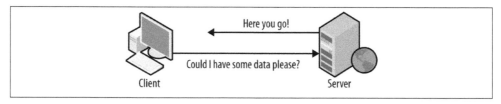

Figure 9-16. Data flow

Window Size and Performance

Window size can greatly affect the performance of a connection. Let us consider two things:

Window size
> If the window is large, a lot of data can be sent. As RFC 793 tells us, "Indicating a large window encourages transmissions." The means that the senders of data are more than willing to transmit lots of data into the network. But this also creates the possibility of congestion.

Rate of acknowledgment
> The rate at which the transmitted data can be acknowledged affects the window, because each ACK opens the sliding window back up. In practice, a large window size with rapid ACKs results in the window never actually closing.

In practice, with a reasonable window size and low packet loss, you'll probably never experience application performance issues. TCP also has the ability to adjust to network conditions by adjusting window size based on the acknowledgment rate. Figure 9-17 illustrates the sliding window approach.

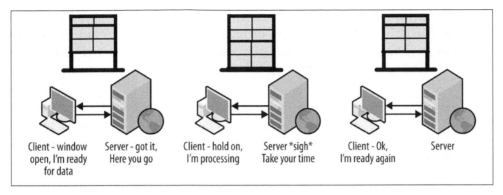

| Client - window open, I'm ready for data | Server - got it, Here you go | Client - hold on, I'm processing | Server *sigh* Take your time | Client - Ok, I'm ready again | Server |

Figure 9-17. Sliding window

To really understand the impact of window size, we have to understand that the original TCP design was for networks running on, by today's standards, slow connections. After all, it was published in 1981. The idea was that since end nodes could send more traffic than the network could handle, there had to be a mechanism to slow senders down.

These days, it is not uncommon to have large window sizes on local area networks because the connection speeds and processing capacity of the end nodes are so high. It would be unusual if the recipient of the data could not quickly process it and return a TCP datagram acknowledging that the data had arrived. In subsequent RFCs, this was recognized and the window scaling factors discussed earlier were introduced.

Sliding Window Experiment

To illustrate the behavior and effect of window size, let's take a look at a couple of examples. The first is the very same capture example used earlier in this chapter. At the end of the handshake, we can see that the window size advertised by the client is 17,520 bytes. This can be seen in packet 4 in the previous TCP HTTP packet list (Table 9-1). The receive window size describes how much data it is willing to accept. This means that the server (192.168.1.254) must receive acknowledgments from the receiver (192.168.1.1) in order to expand the window again, as shown in Figure 9-18. Expanding the window allows more data to be sent.

```
 5 192.168.1.1      CLIENT REQUEST       HTTP   GET / HTTP/1.1
 6 192.168.1.254  SERVER SENDS 560 BYTES  TCP   [TCP segment of a reassembled PDU]
 7 192.168.1.254  SERVER SENDS 560 BYTES  TCP   [TCP segment of a reassembled PDU]
 8 192.168.1.1       CLIENT ACK          TCP   cma > http [ACK] Seq=406 Ack=1121 win=16400 Len=0
 9 192.168.1.254  SERVER SENDS 560 BYTES  TCP   [TCP segment of a reassembled PDU]
10 192.168.1.254  SERVER SENDS 227 BYTES  TCP   [TCP segment of a reassembled PDU]
11 192.168.1.1       CLIENT ACK          TCP   cma > http [ACK] Seq=406 Ack=1908 win=17520 Len=0
```

Figure 9-18. Sliding window detail

But before we go on, let's remember some numbers. Ethernet frames have a maximum payload of 1,500 bytes. But subtract the standard 20-byte IP and TCP headers, and we are down to 1,460 bytes per TCP-based message—if we assume that there is no application header. Figure 9-19 illustrates the encapsulation overhead.

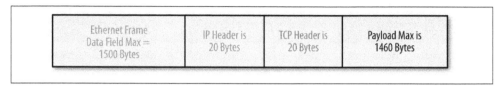

Figure 9-19. Encapsulation overhead

We should also remember that the TCP sequence number field is two bytes long. Thus, the sequence numbers can keep track of only 65,536 (0–65,535) bytes. This does not take RFC 1323 (on TCP performance) into consideration. A window size measured in the thousands of bytes means that the sender can transmit a bunch of Ethernet frames filled to the brim without worrying about the receiver at all—in effect, loading the network without any throttle on sender behavior. And, as evidenced by the previous example, this is not usually a problem.

However, if the window size is smaller, the window may collapse so that the sender has to stop sending while the receiver processes the data and generates an ACK.

100 Mbps Ethernet experiment

With a little laboratory experimentation, we can examine the effect of window size. Using a program called *iperf*, the window size can be driven down until the performance of the application is actually affected. As evidence, we will see the reduction in overall throughput. For this experiment, a small routed topology, shown in Figure 9-20, was constructed.

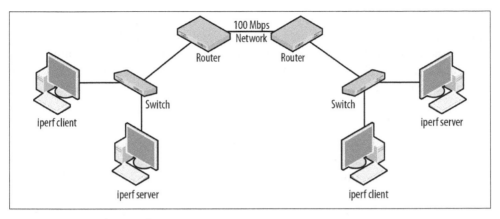

Figure 9-20. iperf network

Note that there are a couple of *iperf* servers and clients, in order to create some competition for the available bandwidth. Let's see what happens on a fast network if we change the amount of data that the servers are allowed to transmit before the windows close. In this case, three window sizes were compared: 1,000, 8,000, and 64,000 bytes. The numbers you see in Table 9-2 (and Table 9-3) are averages over several iterations.

Table 9-2. iperf data with 100 Mbps link

Window size (bytes)	Average time for the transfer (secs)	Data transferred (KB)
1,000	26.4	128
8,000	.2	128
64,000	.233	128

At the sender, small windows result in the window opening, sending a small chunk of data, and slamming shut. The data is processed, an ACK is received, and the window is opened again. If the source machine knows that the receiver is willing to accept only 1,000 bytes at a time, it will be limited to a single packet. Even if the sender is ready to go, it must wait for the receiver to give the OK. At 1,000 bytes, we can see that the transfer takes 26.4 seconds.

As we move to a window size of 8,000 bytes, the speed of the transfer dramatically increases because the data is allowed to flow unabated. The client and server can exchange as much data as they want without adversely affecting the network or other nodes on the same network. For application tuning, we might take note that above a certain threshold, increases in window size make very little difference to performance. This is an indication that we have reached the point where the link cannot support any more data or the client is keeping up with the sender.

It appears that with few exceptions, on fast networks, decreasing the TCP window size can have only a negative effect on performance. This begs the question, "Why would we ever want to reduce the size of the TCP window?" To answer this, we have to examine this performance in the context of several TCP flows, or at least data flows competing for the same bandwidth. With the switched network, there is little competition on the link for an individual host and even the aggregation points or uplinks typically have increased capacity. However, on a WAN link, the opposite is often the case.

T1 WAN experiment

The bandwidth on a WAN link is typically less than on the slowest internal link. For example, consider T1s at 1.544 Mbps serving a small network composed of 10/100/1000 Mbps Ethernet connections. In this case, one or two nodes may be able to fill the outbound connection, effectively choking off the other nodes. This is one situation where a reduced window size may help by limiting the amount of data that can be exchanged between endpoints on opposite sides of the T1.

For the next phase of the experiment, we simply change the link running between the two routers to a full-duplex T1 line, as shown in Figure 9-21. We still have a couple of servers that will compete for bandwidth, but now over a line with a capacity approximately 1.5% that of the previous topology.

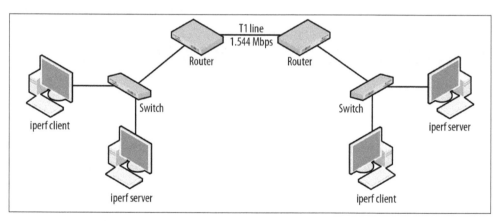

Figure 9-21. iperf network with T1

For the T1, as the window size increases from 1,000 to 8,000 bytes, the behavior mimics that seen on the 100 Mbps topology. However, as we move to the 12,000-byte window size, things take a turn for the worse, as seen in Table 9-3, with performance dropping. This size was used instead of 64,000 bytes because a T1 struggles with the larger size.

Table 9-3. iperf data with T1

Window size (bytes)	Average time for the transfer (secs)	Data transferred (KB)
1,000	26.2	128
8,000	.8	128
12,000	2.5	128

If we compare the results seen here to that of the prior experiment, we see that there are two main differences: the top window size is 12,000 bytes instead of 64,000, and the transfer time went down but then started creeping back up. As in all experiments, there are several variables to be considered, and in this experiment a small number of nodes share the entire bandwidth. Results can vary with the amount of data sent, number of nodes, speed of the network, network conditions, etc. Here are the key points:

Window size and WANs

Limiting TCP window size might be a method used to ensure that all of the nodes have an opportunity to transmit, especially given that the T1 rate is limited to 1.544 Mbps. When senders are prevented from filling the bandwidth of the lower-speed WAN connection, other streams of information are able to use the remaining link capacity. This is assured by the window closing on the transmitters that might be monopolizing the bandwidth.

As window size shrinks, your control over the data and the performance reliability go up, and the variability between tests goes down. This doesn't mean that you should go around shrinking the size of the TCP windows running on your network, as you may cause major throughput problems. But it does serve as an example of how unfettered applications can wreak havoc with your WAN bandwidth.

Average time for the transfer

The transfer time for the data was very stable while the window size was low—stable but long. This is because the window keeps closing. As we increase the window size, more data is able to flow into the network, making the transfer much more efficient. On a fast network, the window size can increase almost without bound (see the upcoming discussion of window scaling), because acknowledgments to data are not delayed by network capacity or node processing.

For the WAN link, once window size increases beyond the network's capability to handle the data, the performance reliability suffers greatly. In this case, between 8,000 and 12,000 bytes we find the turning point, with the transfer time increasing. Above 12,000 bytes, the network behavior was unpredictable.

The increased link speed and processing power of the end nodes on today's networks make it easy for the nodes to receive and process data. And this brings us to RFC 1323. As networks improve, there is less need to maintain these relatively small TCP window sizes. However, it is always a good idea to check in on your applications and how they are behaving.

Silly Window Syndrome

There have been a number of tweaks to the operation of TCP transmission windows. But poor implementations can still result in degraded session performance, especially when a large or continuous amount of data is to be sent. One such problem is *Silly Window Syndrome*, in which the sender transmits very small packets, as is the case with an application like Telnet. At the receiver, the window shrinks and grows by small increments, as does the sender's perception of the window. The problem is that these small window changes result in a consistent halting approach to transmitting data. This is true even when the sender and receiver have additional resources available. Strategies like the Nagle algorithm, use of PSH flags, and collecting small chunks of data together are often combined to improve TCP throughput and avoid Silly Window Syndrome.

TCP Performance and Congestion Control

As discussed earlier in this chapter, TCP is a protocol that concerns itself with sequence numbers and reception of every byte sent during a connection. This is different from other Transport Layer protocols. This "robustness" can create problems for TCP operation in certain situations. TCP was written more than 30 years ago, though, and much work has been done to address some of these issues. This section covers a couple of these important ideas and their RFCs:

Window scaling (RFC 1323)
  If one considers the problem introduced by either very fast links, very long distances, or a combination of the two, one might imagine a scenario in which the sender, being notified of the window size, might be able to exhaust the available sequence numbers before an ACK is received. In this case, the window would close, not because the receiver needed processing time or had filled its buffer, but because of bits in flight. Thus, TCP performance is not a function simply of link speed, but of link speed *and* delay. And because TCP tracks or controls sequence numbers, the protocol is insistent that all sequence numbers arrive. In other words, all transmitted bytes must be acknowledged.

  If bytes or sequence numbers are missing, they must be retransmitted. The retransmission is typically triggered upon expiration of a timer on the sender. This expiration tells the sender that a certain portion of the data has not been acknowledged and is therefore assumed lost. The connection is placed on hold while the missing data is retransmitted. Thus, packet loss can be catastrophic for TCP in terms of performance.

  Now imagine a series of lost packets—or a link failure on a pathway of extremely long links, such as in a satellite or transoceanic network—and the possibility of *wrapping* the sequence numbers (that is, using up all possible sequence numbers in one connection because the link is fast or long enough to exhaust the values). This was the reasoning behind adding window scaling factors, which allow the TCP window to increase beyond the sequence numbers offered by the window field.

RFC 1323 also discusses round-trip measurements using TCP timestamps. Called the Round Trip Time Measurement (RTTM), the sender inserts a timestamp that is reflected back in the receiver's ACK. This TCP extension provides reasonably accurate delay measurement, which can be important in understanding TCP performance with larger windows.

Congestion control (RFC 5681)

Two quotes capture the goals of this particular RFC. The first is from the RFC itself: "In some situations it may be beneficial for a TCP sender to be more conservative than the algorithms allow." The second is from Internet pioneer Jon Postel, who said, "Be liberal in what you accept and conservative in what you send." Recalling some of the ideas discussed in this chapter, we can imagine conditions where aggressive TCP senders may serve to add to congestion in the network. In fact, it is *likely* that TCP senders create the congestion in the network. That said, it may be helpful to add mechanisms by which TCP senders may act to reduce this congestion. RFC 5681 introduces four such techniques, along with new variables, such as the congestion window (CWND), for implementation. The advertised window and ACK are the "receiver-side" limits on transmission. The congestion windows is the "server-side" limit. The mechanisms for dealing with congestion include:

Slow start

In order to prevent a TCP sender from overwhelming the network with a large amount of data, senders initially transmit a small amount of data. After receiving feedback from the network, this rate may increase. The initial window (IW) size for the sender's congestion window is calculated based on network parameters such as the maximum transmission unit. The congestion window, or the amount of data that can be sent, has a certain value.

If the congestion window is smaller than the sender maximum segment size (SMSS), slow start is used. As ACKs that acknowledge receipt of new data arrive, the congestion window increases as a function of the number of ACKs and the SMSS. This continues until the congestion window exceeds the slow start threshold (SSTHRESH), or network performance begins to suffer. The SSTHRESH value is typically the maximum window size.

Congestion avoidance

As soon as the ACKs received cause the congestion window to exceed the slow start threshold, the sender transitions into the congestion avoidance strategy. Congestion avoidance measures the round-trip time (RTT) for the transmissions. The congestion window is again increased by the SMSS for every ACK of new data.

The idea of "new" data is important because it indicates that the stream of data flowing between the two endpoints is constant and consistent. However, delays will cause ACKs to refer to bytes that may have been transmitted by older packets, and this indicates congestion. The congestion window is then set to a value based on the *bits in flight*, or unacknowledged data.

Fast retransmit

Problems in the network path or packet loss may result in packets arriving at the receiver out of order or not at all. Thus, the sequence numbers will be out of order. To repair the potential problem, the receiver issues duplicate ACKs until the missing or out-of-order sequence numbers are recovered. The receiver is supposed to generate an immediate ACK upon repair of the missing data. In fast retransmit, the sender is allowed to respond directly to the duplicate ACKs from the receiver, selectively retransmitting the missing sequence numbers. This occurs after three consecutive duplicate ACKs.

Fast recovery

After missing sequence numbers are recovered or retransmitted, the transmission returns to its state immediately before the loss (as opposed to slow start).

Figure 9-22 depicts a TCP packet in which several of these options are utilized.

```
Transmission Control Protocol, Src Port: 7758 (7758), Dst Port: blizwow (3724), Seq: 0, Len: 0
  Source port: 7758 (7758)
  Destination port: blizwow (3724)
  [Stream index: 0]
  Sequence number: 0    (relative sequence number)
  Header length: 40 bytes
⊞ Flags: 0x002 (SYN)
  window size value: 8192
  [Calculated window size: 8192]
⊞ Checksum: 0xd6f3 [validation disabled]
⊟ Options: (20 bytes), Maximum segment size, No-Operation (NOP), window scale, SACK permitted, Timestamps
  ⊞ Maximum segment size: 1460 bytes
  ⊞ No-Operation (NOP)
  ⊟ window scale: 2 (multiply by 4)
      Kind: window Scale (3)
      Length: 3
      Shift count: 2
      [Multiplier: 4]
  ⊟ TCP SACK Permitted Option: True
      Kind: SACK Permission (4)
      Length: 2
  ⊞ Timestamps: TSval 8337801, TSecr 0
```

Figure 9-22. TCP packet with multiple options set

Port Scanning

Port scanning, or just plain scanning, is one of the catchiest phrases in the security field, yet it is often misused (or at the very least, misunderstood). Few of the folks on the trigger end of a scan have ever watched what happens on the network during said scan. The same can be said of the folks being scanned. But understanding what is happening and how it works can be very beneficial for defense. For example, knowing what a scan looks like can help the target in understanding not only that a scan is underway, but perhaps the actual goal of the scan. In addition, companies often use scans to perform their own vulnerability assessments, scanning themselves to help understand what might be at risk.

There are several types of scans. For the purposes of this chapter (and Chapter 10), we are chiefly concerned with *port scans*. Stated another way, these scans are directed at Layer 4 active ports. A port scan has the very specific purpose of discovering to what ports a network device might be listening. The reason for this is very straightforward; as discussed earlier in this chapter, connections are established on these "listening" ports. If attackers can connect to a particular port, it is possible that they may be able to accomplish some form of mischief.

Commonly accessed ports include HTTP (port 80) and FTP (ports 20 and 21). Many devices use a web interface for control or administration. A shocking number of administrators forget to change default parameters or stick with clear-text HTTP instead of HTTPS. Many FTP servers have an "anonymous" account. Operating systems also open specific ports. Scanning a Windows machine has different results than scanning a computer running Linux.

One way to more easily understand how this works is to think of a door-to-door salesman knocking on every door in a neighborhood to see who is home. Anyone answering can be sold something. In the same way, a thief might check to see what houses are occupied. Having a big dog keeps the salesman and the thief away, in the same way that closing ports to connections can keep the hackers out (Figure 9-23).

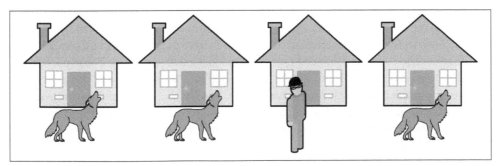

Figure 9-23. Houses and ports

Other scans that are sometimes lumped in with port scans include ARP requests, ping sweeps, and fingerprinting. An ARP scan is directed at a particular network, and the scanning machine sends a series of standard ARP requests to IP addresses that might be present. Any machine answering with an ARP response can now be targeted by more-intense scans. ping sweeps accomplish much the same thing but use ICMP echo requests and replies for the purpose. However, ICMP echoes do have one capability that ARP messages do not: they can be used to determine what kind of operating system is present on the target. Operating systems each have a different set of default behaviors, including the ports that might be open, services running, and traffic generated. In the case of ICMP, operating systems and devices answer the requests differently. Combined, these things can be used to determine a great deal about the target.

What does a port scan look like on the network? We will start from the premise that the attacker is very bold and is simply selecting a target and scan type. On the receiving end, we would see a series of TCP packets with the SYN flag set. As we know, TCP connections are established via the three-way handshake that begins with a TCP SYN packet. Without a SYN/ACK in response, the attacker assumes that the port is not available. For this experiment, a small network was set up consisting of a standard computer and an attacking machine. The topology is shown in Figure 9-24.

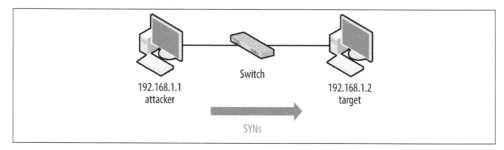

Figure 9-24. Attack topology

The attacking machine generates a series of TCP packets with the SYN flag set. These look like clients attempting to connect. The attacker is trying to discover what the target is willing to do or allow. Examples of these connection attempts can be seen in Figure 9-25. In this case, the attacker is using the source port of 36584 and sending SYN messages to the Wireshark labeled ports of blackjack, auth, and rtsp. These names correspond to ports 1025, 113, and 554, respectively. The attacker can send these messages to as many ports as desired. These can be sent rapidly to a series of ports in order, or randomly over a long period of time. This makes the scan more difficult to spot. The target may not even understand that an attack is underway. This approach is sometimes called *stealth scanning*.

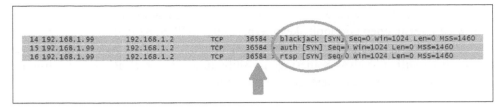

```
14 192.168.1.99      192.168.1.2        TCP    36584 > blackjack [SYN] Seq=0 Win=1024 Len=0 MSS=1460
15 192.168.1.99      192.168.1.2        TCP    36584 > auth [SYN] Seq=0 Win=1024 Len=0 MSS=1460
16 192.168.1.99      192.168.1.2        TCP    36584 > rtsp [SYN] Seq=0 Win=1024 Len=0 MSS=1460
```

Figure 9-25. Attacker SYNs

When presented with a TCP SYN packet, the receiver can either answer with a
SYN/ACK as if willing to start a connection; answer with an RST (reset) to close the
connection; or do nothing. Let's take a look at the exchange when the resets are used
(circled in Figure 9-26).

```
27 192.168.1.99      192.168.1.2        TCP    36584 > smtp [SYN] Seq=0 Win=1024 Len=0 MSS=1460
28 192.168.1.99      192.168.1.2        TCP    36584 > ssh [SYN] Seq=0 Win=1024 Len=0 MSS=1460
29 192.168.1.2       192.168.1.99       TCP    smtp > 36584 [RST, ACK] Seq=1 Ack=1 Win=0 Len=0
30 192.168.1.99      192.168.1.2        TCP    36584 > sunrpc [SYN] Seq=0 Win=1024 Len=0 MSS=1460
31 192.168.1.2       192.168.1.99       TCP    ssh > 36584 [RST, ACK] Seq=1 Ack=1 Win=0 Len=0
```

Figure 9-26. TCP SYN reset

The attacker (192.168.1.99) sends TCP packets with the SYN flag set to the ports for
SMTP (25) and SSH (22). The receiver's (192.168.1.2) response is to reset the ports,
closing the connection. There are a several key points here. First is that the topology
was set up for simplicity and control. Do not be fooled: attacks or scans like this may or
may not use the same networks we use. So, a scan can come from *anywhere*. Second,
the ports are not scanned in order. Finally, this scan was run quickly, and we can see
that another SYN was sent before the target could even respond to the others.

The results (Figure 9-27) show what was learned about the target machine.

```
Starting Nmap 6.25 ( http://nmap.org ) at 2013-07-17
17:48 Eastern Daylight Time
Nmap scan report for 192.168.1.2
Host is up (0.00s latency).
Not shown: 96 closed ports
PORT     STATE SERVICE
21/tcp   open  ftp
135/tcp  open  msrpc
139/tcp  open  netbios-ssn
445/tcp  open  microsoft-ds
MAC Address: 00:11:25:43:4C:5B (IBM)

Nmap done: 1 IP address (1 host up) scanned in 16.75
seconds
```

Figure 9-27. Quick scan results

From this output, we can see that ports 21, 135, 139, and 445 were found to be open. But what does an open port look like in terms of the TCP exchange? In Figure 9-28, we can see that the attacker sent a TCP SYN to the FTP port of 21. But this time, the receiver comes back with a SYN/ACK message possibly indicating an FTP server waiting for connections. Both of these messages are shown in Figure 9-28.

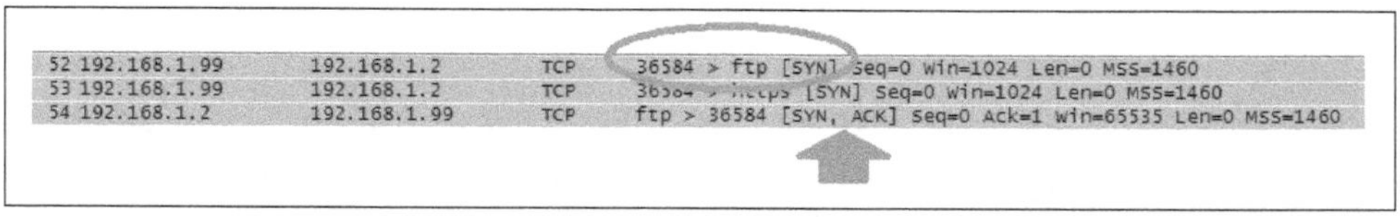

```
52 192.168.1.99      192.168.1.2      TCP    36584 > ftp [SYN] Seq=0 Win=1024 Len=0 MSS=1460
53 192.168.1.99      192.168.1.2      TCP    36584 > https [SYN] Seq=0 Win=1024 Len=0 MSS=1460
54 192.168.1.2       192.168.1.99     TCP    ftp > 36584 [SYN, ACK] Seq=0 Ack=1 Win=65535 Len=0 MSS=1460
```

Figure 9-28. FTP open port

The collection of open ports can tell us what type of operating system is running on the target. Another attack can then be run that is operating system–specific. When monitoring the network, seeing a collection of SYN packets, especially if the quantity is above established baselines, might indicate that an attack is imminent. Many administrators incorrectly view the port scan as the attack, but a port scan is usually part of the reconnaissance or information gathering as a prelude to something more damaging, such as system compromise. It is good to worry about port scans, especially if you see a lot of them. Anytime connection attempts are made on ports outside of those used by your servers, it should be a warning, and you should try to figure out the purpose of the port scan.

Summary

The Transmission Control Protocol (TCP) is one of the most widely used protocols in the networking world. With many applications migrating to the Internet and HTTP, its use seems to be expanding. This chapter covered the operation and structure of TCP, along with the flags used in the exchanges. Critical to the operation of TCP is the concept of the sliding window. This chapter included a discussion and tests revealing the nuts and bolts of this approach to the transmission of data. TCP is also one of the most researched and updated protocols, with many features added and improvements made after the publication in 1981 of the original RFC describing the protocol. This chapter addressed many of these updates, including window scaling and congestion control. Finally, as the protocol used to connect clients and servers, TCP is the vehicle for many attacks; the section on port scanning provided more information about this vector.

Additional Reading

TCP has several RFCs, many of which address a single aspect of the protocol or lump it in with the collection of communication protocols used on modern networks. When searching the Web for RFCs, it is a good idea to pick your topic and then use the keyword *tools*, which will give you the collection of RFCs associated with that topic. TCP-related RFCs include the following:

- RFC 793: "Transmission Control Protocol" (This is the one that started it all.)
- RFC 1122: "Requirements for Internet Hosts—Communication Layers"
- RFC 1323: "TCP Extensions for High Performance" (obsoletes 1072)
- RFC 3360: "Inappropriate TCP Resets Considered Harmful"
- RFC 3390: "Increasing TCP's Initial Window"
- RFC 5681: "TCP Congestion Control" (obsoletes 2581)
- RFC 6093: "On the Implementation of the TCP Urgent Mechanism"
- RFC 6528: "Defending against Sequence Number Attacks"

As well as Wireshark, I used a couple of other tools during the writing of this chapter:

- iperf (*http://iperf.fr/*)
- Nmap (*http://nmap.org/*)

Review Questions

1. The client/server model refers to software programs running on computers that are communicating with each other. True or false?
2. What are the four numbers used to uniquely identify an Internet connection?
3. TCP port numbers can be found at what layer of the TCP/IP model?
4. How many bytes are allocated to the sequence numbers and window size, respectively?
5. What flags are set in the messages that are part of the TCP connection handshake?
6. A TCP acknowledgment number is the next expected sequence number. True or false?
7. Describe the TCP sliding window mechanism.
8. Name the four congestion management techniques of TCP.
9. Higher-speed links contributed to the addition of what TCP modification?
10. In a port scan, how would an attacker discover that a port is open?

Review Answers

1. True

2. Source IP address, destination IP address, source port, destination port

3. 4

4. 2 and 4

5. SYN, SYN ACK, ACK

6. True

7. Slow start, congestion avoidance, fast retransmit, fast recovery

8. The TCP sliding window is a flow control mechanism used by the receiver to prevent the sender from transmitting too much data. As data is sent, the window begins to close. As the receiver acknowledges data, the window starts to open again.

9. Window scaling

10. Reception of a SYN/ACK in response to a SYN from the attacker.

Lab Activities

Activity 1—Establishing a TCP Connection

Materials: A computer with Internet access, Wireshark

1. Connect your computer to the network and start Wireshark.

2. Visit your favorite unencrypted network—for example, *www.google.com.*

3. Stop the Wireshark capture but do not close the program.

4. Type **tcp** in the filter bar for Wireshark and click Apply.

5. See if you can identify the startup handshake packets.

Activity 2—Tracking Sequence and Acknowledgment Numbers

Materials: A computer and the capture from the previous exercise

1. Using the same packet, take a look at the TCP messages that were transmitted between the source and destination.

2. Identify both the relative and absolute sequence and acknowledgment numbers used for the connection.

3. For the first five messages containing data, see if you can track the values used by the source and destination to keep track of the data transmitted.

Activity 3—Examining the TCP Flags

Materials: A computer and the capture from the first exercise

1. For the same set of packets, identify the flags that were used in the connection. For example, when was the PSH flag used? Why?

2. In your connection, were there any additional features from TCP in play? For example, was window scaling used?

Activity 4—Finding the Termination

Materials: A computer and the capture from the first exercise

1. For this set of packets, can you find the termination of the connection?

2. Was it graceful or reset?

3. What were the flags used?

Activity 5—What Can You See?

Materials: A computer and the capture from the first exercise

1. Since this is your own connection, you can take a look at the data contained within the TCP segments themselves. Going to a web page that is unsecured is not much different from reading a text file. Examine the content from the TCP messages. The encapsulated protocol will probably be HTTP.

2. Compare what you see in your browser to what you can read in the packets. Notice anything?

CHAPTER 10

User Datagram Protocol

The User Datagram Protocol (UDP) is the "other" Transport Layer protocol. In other words, if a connection is not using the Transmission Control Protocol (TCP) at Layer 4, it is using UDP. Layer 4 transmissions are often described as being either *connection-oriented* or *connectionless*. TCP, described in Chapter 9, is connection-oriented. As we know, TCP keeps track of every single byte of information sent and has several mechanisms for dealing with varying network conditions. UDP is connectionless.

What does it mean to be connectionless? As we will see later in this chapter, UDP is a relatively simple protocol, especially when compared to TCP. The header is small with little variation between packets, which also means that not much can be done to control or manage the data stream. But UDP does have a particular place in the universe: it provides encapsulation for real-time and unmonitored data.

While TCP connections are tightly controlled with rules for responses and sequence numbers that are tracked, UDP connections are not. Thus, anytime a series of messages or datagrams are required to flow between endpoints but strict control is not wanted or needed, UDP is the protocol of choice. Some very good examples of this include Voice over IP (encapsulated in the Real-time Transport Protocol), gaming, and network monitoring vehicles such as the Simple Network Management Protocol (SNMP). For protocols such as SNMP, UDP-based encapsulation makes sense because the messaging is often request/response based and the TCP handshake would add unnecessary overhead. The Domain Name System (DNS) and the Dynamic Host Configuration Protocol (DHCP) also use UDP because of the nature of these transactions. In addition, the data is not often time-sensitive or part of a larger stream. In the case of Voice over IP (VoIP), the data stream is real-time, meaning that the responsiveness of the connection is important. However, lost or delayed packets are not recovered because their delayed reception might actually reduce call quality.

This chapter will cover the operation and structure of the User Datagram Protocol and illustrate some common uses for this popular Layer 4 transport protocol. We will also discuss DHCP and DNS, both of which use UDP.

Protocol Description

Layer 4 is also known as the Transport Layer. This is true for both the TCP/IP and Open Systems Interconnection (OSI) networking models. Both TCP and UDP are transport protocols. UDP is defined in RFC 768, which dates from 1980. Per the RFC, it is assumed that IP will be the Layer 3 protocol. In addition, UDP is said to provide a "datagram mode" for interconnected computers. The datagram mode is also described as being "transaction oriented," and according to the RFC, "delivery and duplicate protection are not guaranteed." Transactions are often simple requests, followed by the responses—almost the complete opposite of TCP.

Though TCP and UDP do not have much in common, they do share the traits of the Transport Layer. Both protocols utilize the socket connection, which means that the logical endpoints of the connection are tied together via the source IP address, Layer 4 source port number, destination IP address, and Layer 4 destination port number. The port assignments for the various applications follow the same rules as the TCP assignments. For a larger discussion of both sockets and port numbers, take a peek at Chapter 9.

The RFC version of the header is shown in Figure 10-1. As you can see, it is quite simple.

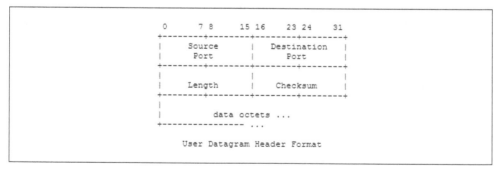

Figure 10-1. RFC UDP header

The fields for UDP are defined as follows:

Source port
> 16-bit field identifying the sender's port. Interestingly, the RFC calls this an optional field and states that when it is not used, the values will be set to all zeros. In practice, this would be very rare.

Destination port
> 16-bit field identifying the Layer 4 connection point at the destination or receiver.

Length

16-bit field indicating the byte length of the datagram, including the header. Per RFC 768, if UDP is used, the smallest possible value in this field is eight bytes.

Checksum

16-bit field containing the one's complement of the one's complement sum of the pseudo and UDP headers, and the data. The pseudo header includes a portion of the IP header and is shown in Figure 10-2.

```
     0       7 8     15 16     23 24    31
    +--------+--------+--------+--------+
    |             source address       |
    +--------+--------+--------+--------+
    |          destination address     |
    +--------+--------+--------+--------+
    |  zero  |protocol|   UDP length    |
    +--------+--------+--------+--------+
```

Figure 10-2. RFC pseudo header

Figure 10-3 shows an example UDP packet. The values for the source and destination port numbers are 2056 and 161, respectively. In this case, the destination port falls into the well-known range and is directed at the SNMP process. Wireshark is trying to help out by providing the name of the port, but the name is not actually included in the transmission. Unlike TCP, there have not been many modifications to UDP.

```
Ethernet II, Src: Ibm_43:49:97 (00:11:25:43:49:97), Dst: Cisco_35:1a:d0 (00:19:55:35:1a:d0)
Internet Protocol Version 4, Src: 192.168.1.1 (192.168.1.1), Dst: 192.168.1.254 (192.168.1.254)
User Datagram Protocol, Src Port: omnisky (2056), Dst Port: snmp (161)
   Source port: omnisky (2056)
   Destination port: snmp (161)
   Length: 50
 ⊞ Checksum: 0xa8ab [validation disabled]
Simple Network Management Protocol
```

Figure 10-3. UDP SNMP get request

SNMP is a good example of an application that does not require high priority and is not accessed by end users. It is often automated, with SNMP agents sending packets called *traps* to the network management system or server. The server can also make requests of SNMP agents installed on the network. In either case, the connection is a request-and-response exchange. SNMP agents and servers send messages requesting or providing information. The opposite end responds with the answer. The amount of data or packets exchanged may be very small, so the additional requirement of a handshake would be excessive. Thus, SNMP fits the description of a transmission that can use UDP.

As mentioned previously, another example of a system that uses UDP is Voice over IP. While many of the signaling protocols deployed in VoIP architectures are based on TCP, the voice and video data is encapsulated within UDP. Examples of the TCP signaling connections would include registering with the call server, the initial call setup, and the call termination. However, several other key transmissions are based on UDP, including DHCP and the Trivial File Transfer Protocol (TFTP), as shown in Figure 10-4. Notice the Wireshark filter.

```
Filter: udp                                          ▼ Expression... Clear Apply Save

No.    Time        Source          Destination        Protocol    Length Info
   21 23.724359  0.0.0.0          255.255.255.255    DHCP         590 DHCP Discover  - Transactio
   24 25.722341  172.30.1.254     172.30.1.11        DHCP         342 DHCP Offer     - Transactio
   27 27.224387  0.0.0.0          255.255.255.255    DHCP         590 DHCP Request   - Transactio
   28 27.225903  172.30.1.254     172.30.1.11        DHCP         353 DHCP ACK       - Transactio
   31 27.735978  172.30.1.99      172.30.1.255       UDP           82 Source port: 58709  Destin
   38 29.253349  172.30.1.11      172.30.1.99        TFTP          66 Read Request, File: 46xxup
   39 29.257614  172.30.1.99      172.30.1.11        TFTP         558 Data Packet, Block: 1
   40 29.260210  172.30.1.11      172.30.1.99        TFTP          60 Acknowledgement, Block: 1
   41 29.260537  172.30.1.99      172.30.1.11        TFTP         558 Data Packet, Block: 2
```

Figure 10-4. UDP protocol list

This list of packets was a collection from a VoIP phone starting up and receiving the parameters necessary to communicate on a data network. But what happens once a call is placed? Some voice data packets are shown in Figure 10-5. End user voices are sampled, and the samples are packetized and then sent across the network in Real-time Transport Protocol (RTP) packets while the conversation is going on.

```
Filter: udp                                          ▼ Expression... Clea

No.      Time        Source         Destination       Protocol
    32 12.167548  172.30.1.11     172.30.1.1        RTP
    33 12.181709  172.30.1.1      172.30.1.11       RTP
    34 12.187547  172.30.1.11     172.30.1.1        RTP
    35 12.201783  172.30.1.1      172.30.1.11       RTP
    36 12.207552  172.30.1.11     172.30.1.1        RTP
```

Figure 10-5. UDP RTP packet list

One RTP packet from this list is shown in Figure 10-6. In this case, we can see that the UDP port numbers are 10660 and 34008. For a VoIP connection, the port numbers to be used are negotiated during the call setup procedure.

```
Ethernet II, Src: AsustekC_d6:05:9b (00:11:d8:d6:05:9b), Dst: GiantEle_05:cb
Internet Protocol Version 4, Src: 172.30.1.1 (172.30.1.1), Dst: 172.30.1.11
User Datagram Protocol, Src Port: 10660 (10660), Dst Port: 34008 (34008)
   Source port: 10660 (10660)
   Destination port: 34008 (34008)
   Length: 180
 ⊞ Checksum: 0xd82a [validation disabled]
   Real-Time Transport Protocol
```

Figure 10-6. UDP RTP packet

Operation

UDP is a very straightforward sort of protocol. On an IPv4-based network, the IP datagram will indicate that the payload is UDP-based by inserting the value 17 in the protocol ID field, as seen in Figure 10-7.

```
Ethernet II, Src: AsustekC_d6:05:9b (00:11:d8:d6:05:9b), Dst: GiantEle_05:cb:11
Internet Protocol Version 4, Src: 172.30.1.1 (172.30.1.1), Dst: 172.30.1.11 (172
  Version: 4
  Header length: 20 bytes
⊞ Differentiated Services Field: 0xb8 (DSCP 0x2e: Expedited Forwarding; ECN: 0x0
  Total Length: 200
  Identification: 0x0000 (0)
⊞ Flags: 0x02 (Don't Fragment)
  Fragment offset: 0
  Time to live: 64
  Protocol: UDP (17)
⊞ Header checksum: 0xdf24 [correct]
  Source: 172.30.1.1 (172.30.1.1)
  Destination: 172.30.1.11 (172.30.1.11)
  [Source GeoIP: Unknown]
  [Destination GeoIP: Unknown]
User Datagram Protocol, Src Port: 100      st Port: 34008 (34008)
Real-Time Transport Protocol
```

Figure 10-7. IP packet encapsulating UDP

This value is a base 10 number. The hexadecimal value is 11. When the network is based on IPv6, the value is still 17.

As with TCP, a server written for UDP "listens" on a particular port. Client messages come in as part of a request or a response to the server on that port. But perhaps the best way to see the operation of UDP is to follow one of the most common service protocols in use today: the Dynamic Host Configuration Protocol (DHCP).

Dynamic Host Configuration Protocol

The place to start reading about DHCP is RFC 2131, although the message format is defined in RFC 951, "Bootstrap Protocol (BOOTP)." When you are using Wireshark and looking for DHCP, you use either the "udp" or the "bootp" filter.

DHCP uses UDP port 67 on the server side and port 68 for the client. DHCP is often described as the protocol used by hosts to get an IP address from a server. While this is true, it only scratches the surface of what DHCP can be used to do. From the RFC:

> DHCP is designed to supply DHCP clients with the configuration parameters defined in the Host Requirements RFCs. After obtaining parameters via DHCP, a DHCP client should be able to exchange packets with any other host in the Internet.

DHCP can be pretty powerful. In fact, there are about 30 parameters listed in RFC 2131 that can be exchanged via DHCP, and this RFC has been amended several times. When a client connects to an IP-based network, it must have an IP address in order to communicate with the rest of the world. But how does one get an IP address from an IP-based server on an IP-based network when one does not have an IP address? Tricky. The answer is *broadcast messaging*—using Layer 2 and 3 broadcast addresses in the frame and IP packet. Watch for the addressing as we move through the operation. There are several messages defined for DHCP, many of which can be seen in the DHCP startup capture in Figure 10-8.

```
0.0.0.0            255.255.255.255    DHCP    DHCP Request   - Transaction ID 0x6a36c7d1
10.140.100.254     255.255.255.255    DHCP    DHCP NAK       - Transaction ID 0x6a36c7d1
0.0.0.0            255.255.255.255    DHCP    DHCP Discover  - Transaction ID 0xa180b125
10.140.100.254     255.255.255.255    DHCP    DHCP Offer     - Transaction ID 0xa180b125
0.0.0.0            255.255.255.255    DHCP    DHCP Request   - Transaction ID 0xa180b125
10.140.100.254     255.255.255.255    DHCP    DHCP ACK       - Transaction ID 0xa180b125
10.140.100.2       255.255.255.255    DHCP    DHCP Inform    - Transaction ID 0x16ab7b2a
10.140.100.254     255.255.255.255    DHCP    DHCP ACK       - Transaction ID 0x16ab7b2a
```

Figure 10-8. DHCP startup messages

The message types are as follows:

DHCPDISCOVER

Used by the client to find a DHCP server. This message is a broadcast at Layer 2 (ff:ff:ff:ff:ff:ff) and Layer 3 (255.255.255.255). The source IP address used by the client in this case is 0.0.0.0, meaning "this host." The host also generates a random transaction ID in this first packet in order to help tie messages together.

DHCPOFFER

Upon receipt of a DISCOVER message, the server responds with the OFFER. As can be seen from the packet list in Figure 10-8, this message is also a broadcast, but the host sending the message accepts it as an OFFER because DHCP messages contain that transaction ID. Hosts can wait for several offers to come in. The DHCPOFFER packet from this list is expanded in Figure 10-9.

```
Ethernet II, Src: Cisco_0f:db:80 (00:13:c3:0f:db:80), Dst: Broadcast (ff:ff:ff:ff:ff:ff)
Internet Protocol Version 4, Src: 10.140.100.254 (10.140.100.254), Dst: 255.255.255.255
User Datagram Protocol, Src Port: bootps (67), Dst Port: bootpc (68)
Bootstrap Protocol
  Message type: Boot Reply (2)
  Hardware type: Ethernet
  Hardware address length: 6
  Hops: 0
  Transaction ID: 0xf3cfa508
  Seconds elapsed: 0
⊞ Bootp flags: 0x8000 (Broadcast)
  Client IP address: 0.0.0.0 (0.0.0.0)
  Your (client) IP address: 10.140.100.2 (10.140.100.2)
  Next server IP address: 10.200.200.17 (10.200.200.17)
  Relay agent IP address: 10.140.100.254 (10.140.100.254)
  Client MAC address: Intel_77:26:26 (00:0e:0c:77:26:26)
  Client hardware address padding: 00000000000000000000
  Server host name not given
  Boot file name: BStrap\X86pc\BStrap.0
  Magic cookie: DHCP
⊞ Option: (53) DHCP Message Type
⊞ Option: (1) Subnet Mask
⊞ Option: (58) Renewal Time value
```

Figure 10-9. DHCPOFFER

The options are used to provide the various network parameters. The number of possible options is quite large; for example, option 150 provides the TFTP server.

DHCPREQUEST

After the OFFER, the host sends a REQUEST indicating that it wishes to use the offered IP address (and other parameters) for its own. When making this request, the host identifies the server that made the OFFER by specifying the IP address and transaction ID in the message. At this point, the client is still using an IP address of 0.0.0.0.

A host may also use a REQUEST in order to ask for a particular IP address. In our example, this was the case: the host asked for the use of 10.140.100.11 as an IP address. The server declined with a DHCPNAK, instead offering 10.140.100.2. We see this behavior in hosts attempting to renew an address.

DHCPACK

This is a response from the server indicating that it will connect the accepted IP address with this particular client. Per the RFC, this is now *committed*.

DHCPNAK

This is a response indicating that the request from the client cannot be honored or is incorrect.

DHCPDECLINE

This is similar to the NAK, except in the other direction. The client informs the server that the address offered is unacceptable, possibly due to its being in use.

DHCPRELEASE

With this message, the client indicates to the server that the IP address is now relinquished. Committed IP addresses are given a lease time. At the end of the lease time, the clients must renew the addresses. In a RELEASE, the lease is no longer needed, and the server can assign the IP address to another node prior to the normal expiration of the lease time.

DHCPINFORM

This message is used to ask for particular configuration parameters.

The previous packet list depicts what happens when a host connects to the network and tries to obtain an IP address. If we examine this list a little more closely, we can see that the transaction IDs for all of the packets beginning with the DISCOVER and ending with the ACK are the same. The initial request (which was denied) and the INFORM exchange have different IDs. In the next series of packets (Figure 10-10), we see a similar operation, but for a different reason: release and renew. In troubleshooting connections or testing servers, it is common to manually release and subsequently renew an IP address for a particular client. This may also be necessary if the connection to the server times out. This can be done by disabling and re-enabling the connection. From the command line, we use the commands `ipconfig /release` and `ipconfig /renew`.

The first command causes a DHCPRELEASE message to be sent from the client to the server. The second causes the node to go through the request process again.

Source	Destination	Protocol	Info
10.140.100.2	10.200.200.3	DHCP	DHCP Release - Transaction ID 0x1022c8e3
0.0.0.0	255.255.255.255	DHCP	DHCP Discover - Transaction ID 0xf3cfa508
10.140.100.254	255.255.255.255	DHCP	DHCP Offer - Transaction ID 0xf3cfa508
0.0.0.0	255.255.255.255	DHCP	DHCP Request - Transaction ID 0xf3cfa508
10.140.100.254	255.255.255.255	DHCP	DHCP ACK - Transaction ID 0xf3cfa508

Figure 10-10. DHCP release and renew

It is common for both the client and the server to be aware of the IP address previously assigned to the host, as it is tied to the host MAC address. However, unless there is a reservation for the host (a reservation assigns a particular IP address to the host based on the MAC address), there is no guarantee that the same IP address will be obtained. Addresses given to hosts are temporary, and the length of this temporary assignment is called the *lease time*. In a dynamic environment, lease times can be short (less than an hour), but it is common for lease times to be measured in hours or even days.

Finally, the addressing used by DHCP is significant. If you read the chapters on Ethernet and IP, you know that these destination addresses are not forwarded beyond a router or gateway. This means that a DHCP server must be on the same local area network as the hosts that wish to use it. Besides, how would a server be able to find a host with a source address of 0.0.0.0 if it were not on the directly connected network? However, a technique called *DHCP relay* allows a router to forward traffic to a server on behalf of a client as long as it knows where the server can be found. An example of this can actually be seen in the DHCPOFFER shown earlier in this section, as the relay agent (10.140.100.254) is identified.

Domain Name System

As we have discussed many times in this book, traffic is forwarded and processed based on numeric values stored in tables or transmitted in packets and frames. But humans do not communicate in this way. We much prefer to use common names for web pages and give names to network devices to make them easier to remember. It is not uncommon to have a bunch of computers named after robots or mythical beasts. Thus, we must be able to convert between these names and the numeric IP addresses used by network devices. In the early days of the Internet, all of this information was stored in a single file called *hosts.txt*, which was distributed only to those needing the information. But the growth and changing nature of the Internet made this an untenable approach going forward. It was decided that the data would be stored in a large database, and to limit the load on the servers, the database would be distributed. This is the structure of the Domain Name System in use today. Whenever we access a service or site by name, the computer we are using must first make a DNS request in order to obtain the IP address actually used.

The Domain Name System is described in RFCs 1034 and 1035, though there are many companion documents. In general, the system comprises client software called a *re-solver* and the name-to–IP address mapping data stored on distributed servers. When a client makes a request or query via its resolver, it uses UDP port 53. Several servers may be involved in answering the request. Just as the IP address is part of the hierarchical IPv4 or IPv6 address space, the name is a part of the hierarchical *namespace* used by DNS. In a namespace, system administrators provide the information regarding their IP-to-name assignments. DNS provides the syntax for records and queries, as well as the methods used by servers to receive updates for the locally stored data. The idea encompassed by DNS is straightforward, but the system is composed of many components and lots of operational details.

Components

To gain a better understanding of DNS operation, familiarity with the following ideas will make things a little easier:

Namespace and resource records
> The namespace provides the tree-like structure for the system. Each node has a label such as *myhost*. Per the RFC, the domain name is "the list of the labels on the path from the node to the root of the tree," such as *myhost.mynet.com*. Domain names are read left to right, with the most specific portion on the left. If we have

the entire path back to the root, we call this *absolute* as opposed to *relative*. The subdomains of the root include such categories as *.mil*, *.com*, *.org*, and *.edu*.

Resource records contain the information about the nodes connected to the system. There are a couple of record types, such as address or mail. Queries from the resolvers specify the type of information desired.

Name servers

Name servers contain the information queried by the resolvers. Root servers are the final word in any request for information. Most name servers are not root servers; they typically contain a subset of the information comprising the namespace. Just as a router seeking a destination must occasionally ask its own default gateway for directions, name servers can forward queries to each other for answers they do not possess. A name server possessing all of the information for a particular part of the namespace tree is called an *authority*. RFC 1034 calls the section of the namespace tree for which a given name server has the authoritative information a *zone*.

Resolvers

Resolvers perform the lookups for the clients. In networking, it is common to describe the four numbers that should be given to the host in order to facilitate network communication: IP address, network mask, default gateway, and name server. Every host or resolver should be able to contact at least one name server.

The query and associated response shown in Figure 10-11 capture many of the components discussed in this section. The top circles indicate the UDP port used by DNS. We can see that the message on the left is the query and that the message on the right is the answer to this particular query. As in DHCP messaging, we use transaction IDs to organize the messages. That these two messages contain the same transaction ID allows us to follow the DNS exchange. The question asks for the IP address of the domain name *addons.mozilla.org*. The arrow on the right indicates the answer. A server may respond to a query in a number of ways: with locally stored information, by referring the client to another server "closer" to the destination, or by attempting to find the answer for the client. If the server refers the client to another server, the client resolver must query the new server. This is the DNS *iterative process*. If the server tries to answer the question for the client, the server becomes a resolver—this is called a *recursive lookup*.

```
Internet Protocol Version 4, Src: 128.238.84.152 (128.238.84.152)   Internet Protocol Version 4, Src: 128.238.32.22 (128.238.32.22), Dst: 128.238.84.152
User Datagram Protocol, Src Port: 53838 (53838), Dst Port: domain (53)   User Datagram Protocol, Src Port: domain (53), Dst Port: 53838 (53838)
Domain Name System (query)                                          Domain Name System (response)
  [Response In: 6180]                                                 [Request In: 6179]
  Transaction ID: 0x46cc                                             [Time: 0.001672000 seconds]
  Flags: 0x0100 Standard query                                       Transaction ID: 0x46cc
    0... .... .... .... = Response: Message is a query               Flags: 0x8180 Standard query response, No error
    .000 0... .... .... = Opcode: Standard query (0)                 Questions: 1
    .... ..0. .... .... = Truncated: Message is not truncated        Answer RRs: 2
    .... ...1 .... .... = Recursion desired: Do query recursively    Authority RRs: 4
    .... .... .0.. .... = Z: reserved (0)                            Additional RRs: 4
    .... .... ...0 .... = Non-authenticated data: unacceptable       Queries
  Questions: 1                                                         addons.mozilla.org: type A, class IN
  Answer RRs: 0                                                      Answers
  Authority RRs: 0                                                     addons.mozilla.org: type CNAME, class IN, cname addons.dynect.mozilla.net
  Additional RRs: 0                                                    addons.dynect.mozilla.net: type A, class IN, addr 63.245.216.132
  Queries                                                            Authoritative nameservers
    addons.mozilla.org: type A, class IN                             Additional records
      Name: addons.mozilla.org
      Type: A (Host address)
      Class: IN (0x0001)
```

Figure 10-11. DNS request and response

nslookup

When troubleshooting DNS problems, *nslookup* is a handy tool (an alternative, pre-ferred by many administrators, is dig). Built into most contemporary operating systems, nslookup can be used for a variety of queries, although the most common are forward (finding an IP address for a name) and reverse (finding a name for an IP address) lookups. nslookup is accessed via the command line in the same way that *ping* and *tracert/traceroute* are, and as with those programs, several options are available. The output of a request can be seen in Figure 10-12.

```
C:\>nslookup                              > 8.8.8.8
Default Server:  UnKnown                  Server:  UnKnown
Address:  10.120.1.1                      Address:  10.120.1.1

> www.rit.edu                             Name:    google-public-dns-a.google.com
Server:  UnKnown                          Address:  8.8.8.8
Address:  10.120.1.1
                                          > root
Non-authoritative answer:                 Default Server:  A.ROOT-SERVERS.NET
Name:    web01www01.rit.edu               Addresses:  2001:503:ba3e::2:30
Address:  129.21.1.40                                  198.41.0.4
Aliases:  www.rit.edu
                                          > 198.41.0.4
                                          Server:  A.ROOT-SERVERS.NET
                                          Addresses:  2001:503:ba3e::2:30
                                                      198.41.0.4
```

Figure 10-12. nslookup

On the left side of this image is the nslookup command followed by a forward lookup for *www.rit.edu*. The server (10.120.1.1) replies with the IP address of the name in question. On the right side are reverse lookups for a public Google server and one of the DNS root servers.

Updates for UDP

As you've probably noticed, UDP is not a complicated protocol, with its simple header and connectionless architecture. It does not have a setup procedure or sequence numbers. However, it has received some attention in the area of usage:

- RFC 3828 defines *lightweight UDP*, which in most aspects is very similar to standard UDP but removes the length field and replaces it with a *coverage checksum*. The reason for this is that in some cases, it might be desirable that damaged packets actually be delivered. Normally, an incorrect UDP checksum would cause these to be discarded. Video and voice systems can sometimes process damaged packets, extracting some portion of the real-time data. Discarding too many packets can cause an error-prone but usable connection to be severed entirely.

- This change in behavior would have to be supported by the lower-layer protocols as well. The idea is to let error tolerant-applications run their data through the network without hindrance. Thus, UDP Lite is sometimes referred to as *partial payload protection*. The UDP data is divided into two parts: sensitive and insensitive. *Sensitive* in this context means that the data would be adversely affected by error and therefore should be discarded should there be a problem with the standard UDP checksum. However, the *insensitive* data, indicated by the coverage checksum, will not be discarded. In this way, it is hoped that the applications with greater error budgets can operate without as much disruption from dropped packets.

- RFC 5405 provides developers with some hints for applications encapsulated in UDP. While TCP performance can be drastically affected by network conditions, to some extent it can also respond or adapt to changes in congestion or throughput. UDP cannot. For example, TCP has a specific behavior in the presence of delayed or lost packets, changing the rate at which data is sent. With the exception of the IP header Differentiated Services Code Point (DSCP) values used for provisioned quality of service, short headers, and simple message exchanges, there isn't much done to modify UDP connection behavior. The basic problem is that there is little to limit the rate at which UDP-encapsulated data is sent, and the sender(s) may outstrip the available bandwidth supply. The supposition is that it is up to the applications to control traffic sent into the network.

  As the requirements of individual applications can vary, RFC 5405 offers some things to consider when building unicast UDP applications—even to the point of suggesting alternative "fully featured" transport protocols such as the Datagram Congestion Control Protocol (DCCP) or Stream Control Transmission Protocol (SCTP). However, the primary idea presented in RFC 5405 is that UDP streams should deploy some form of congestion control and that it should be built into applications from the ground up.

Port Scanning

The chapter on TCP discussed port scanning in detail, but it is worth recalling that port scans can be run against UDP-based services as well. So, instead of looking for TCP

SYN messages, be on the lookout for excessive UDP connection attempts. An example of a UDP port scan can be seen in Figure 10-13.

```
Not shown: 992 closed ports
PORT      STATE         SERVICE        VERSION
123/udp   open          ntp            Microsoft NTP
| ntp-info:
|_  receive time stamp: 07/17/13 18:04:04
137/udp   open          netbios-ns     Microsoft Windows netbios-ssn
138/udp   open|filtered netbios-dgm
402/udp   open|filtered genie
445/udp   open|filtered microsoft-ds
500/udp   open|filtered isakmp
1900/udp  open|filtered upnp
4500/udp  open|filtered nat-t-ike
```

Figure 10-13. UDP scan

The behavior of a UDP scan is quite a bit different from that of a TCP scan. A UDP scan cannot take advantage of the handshake, so instead of a TCP RST, a closed port will result in an ICMP destination port unreachable message (Figure 10-14). Every port that is closed will result in this type of ICMP response.

```
No.  Source          Destination      Protocol  Info
  17 192.168.1.2     192.168.1.99     ICMP      Destination unreachable (Port unreachable)
  18 192.168.1.99    192.168.1.2      UDP       Source port: 61711  Destination port: 37813[Malfo
  19 192.168.1.2     192.168.1.99     ICMP      Destination unreachable (Port unreachable)

⊞ Frame 21: 70 bytes on wire (560 bits), 70 bytes captured (560 bits) on interface 0
⊞ Ethernet II, Src: Ibm_43:4c:5b (00:11:25:43:4c:5b), Dst: WistronI_1b:81:33 (3c:97:0e:1b:81:33)
⊞ Internet Protocol Version 4, Src: 192.168.1.2 (192.168.1.2), Dst: 192.168.1.99 (192.168.1.99)
⊟ Internet Control Message Protocol
    Type: 3 (Destination unreachable)
    Code: 3 (Port unreachable)
    Checksum: 0x80cc [correct]
  ⊞ Internet Protocol Version 4, Src: 192.168.1.99 (192.168.1.99), Dst: 192.168.1.2 (192.168.1.2)
  ⊞ User Datagram Protocol, Src Port: 61711 (61711), Dst Port: 37813 (37813)
```

Figure 10-14. Port unreachable

While UDP port scans might not be as common as TCP scans (servers typically listen for TCP connection attempts), that does not mean that we do not have to worry about them. Open UDP ports can reveal information about the systems, especially in the case of SNMP. Services may also require ports to be opened through the firewall, which may decrease your security. In addition, any scan against a system causes that machine to use resources in answering the incoming packets.

Summary

The User Datagram Protocol (UDP) is a Transport Layer protocol used by many common services and applications. Examples of these include the Domain Name System (DNS), the Dynamic Host Configuration Protocol (DHCP), Voice over IP (VoIP), and the Simple Network Management Protocol (SNMP). Like TCP, UDP establishes connections on Layer 4 ports. However, UDP does not have connection or teardown handshakes, acknowledgments, or flags for the various operations. This chapter covered the structure and operation of UDP along with an explanation of DHCP messaging and structure. A basic description of DNS and its operation was also provided.

Additional Reading

- RFC 768: "User Datagram Protocol"
- RFC 951: "Bootstrap Protocol (BOOTP)"
- RFC 1034: "Domain Names—Concepts and Facilities"
- RFC 1035: "Domain Names—Implementation and Specification"
- RFC 2131: "Dynamic Host Configuration Protocol"
- RFC 3828: "The Lightweight User Datagram Protocol (UDP-Lite)"
- RFC 5405: "Unicast UDP Usage Guidelines for Application Designers"
- RFC 6335: "Internet Assigned Numbers Authority (IANA) Procedures for the Management of the Service Name and Transport Protocol Port Number Registry"

Review Questions

1. At what layer does UDP operate?
2. In an IP header, how is the UDP packet identified?
3. UDP packets contain sequence numbers. True or false?
4. What word, beginning with the letter "c," is often used to describe UDP?
5. Name some of the applications or services identified in the chapter that use UDP for transport.
6. List the UDP fields.
7. The UDP checksum is a value calculated on the three main fields of the UDP header. True or false?
8. What is the maximum value of a UDP port?
9. List the numbers of the base DNS RFCs and the port number used by DNS.
10. Port scans are more common against TCP ports but can be directed at UDP targets. True or false?

Review Answers

1. Layer 4 (Transport)
2. A value of 17 in the protocol ID field
3. False
4. Connectionless
5. SNMP, RTP, TFTP, and DNS
6. Source port, destination port, UDP length, checksum
7. False
8. Based on the size of the field—65535.
9. 1034, 1035, 53
10. True

Lab Activities

Activity 1—DHCP

Materials: Computer with an operating network connection, Wireshark

1. Open up a command window and type the command **ipconfig**. This should show you your IP address along with your network parameters. We will be using variations on this command to force a DHCP exchange.
2. Start up Wireshark and begin a capture.
3. Issue the command ipconfig /release.
4. Issue the command ipconfig /renew.
5. In Wireshark, can you determine the packets generated as a result of these commands? Do you see the collection of DHCP messages outlined in this chapter? What UDP port numbers did you use?

Activity 2—DHCP Messages

Materials: Capture from the previous activity

1. Using the capture from the previous activity (and the "bootp" Wireshark filter), examine the flow of packets between the client and server.
2. Develop a flow diagram that describes how this exchange works.

3. Open the DHCPOFFER message. Can you find the network parameters that are in use by your node? How many options are being used?

Activity 3—UDP Header

Materials: Capture from Activity 1

1. Select one of the DHCP messages. Open the UDP header and examine the fields.
2. Compare the fields to the ones described in this chapter. What values do you have in your UPD header?
3. What is the value of the protocol ID field in the IP header?

Activity 4—DNS

Materials: Computer with an operating network connection, Wireshark

1. Start a capture using Wireshark.
2. Open up a browser and visit your favorite website.
3. Stop your capture and filter on DNS.
4. Find the DNS query made by your host and the subsequent answer. Can you see the IP address? Do the transaction IDs work? What happens if you put the IP address in the address bar of your browser?

Activity 5—nslookup

Materials: Computer with an operating network connection

1. Open up a command window.
2. Issue the command nslookup. What is the IP address of your name server?
3. Enter the address of your favorite web server (e.g., *A.B.com*).
4. What is the answer you received? Can you perform a reverse lookup?

About the Author

Bruce Hartpence is a faculty member in the Information Sciences and Technology (IST) Department in the Golisano College of Computing and Information Sciences (GCCIS) at Rochester Institute of Technology (RIT) in Rochester, New York. When he is not teaching classes, he can usually be found either building stuff in the lab or writing about networking.

His current projects include software defined networking, virtualization, and industrial training. For more information and updates, you can visit his website (*http://www.bruce hartpence.com*) or his YouTube channel (*http://www.youtube.com/brucehartpence*).

Colophon

The animal on the cover of *Packet Guide to Core Network Protocols*, first edition, is a helmetshrike.

The cover image is from *Cassell's Natural History*. The cover font is Adobe ITC Garamond. The text font is Linotype Birka; the heading font is Adobe Myriad Condensed; and the code font is LucasFont's TheSansMonoCondensed.

Have it your way.

Get even more for your money.

Join the O'Reilly Community, and register the O'Reilly books you own. It's free, and you'll get:

- $4.99 ebook upgrade offer
- 40% upgrade offer on O'Reilly print books
- Membership discounts on books and events
- Free lifetime updates to ebooks and videos
- Multiple ebook formats, DRM FREE
- Participation in the O'Reilly community
- Newsletters
- Account management
- 100% Satisfaction Guarantee

Signing up is easy:

1. Go to: oreilly.com/go/register
2. Create an O'Reilly login.
3. Provide your address.
4. Register your books.

Note: English-language books only

To order books online:
oreilly.com/store

For questions about products or an order:
orders@oreilly.com

To sign up to get topic-specific email announcements and/or news about upcoming books, conferences, special offers, and new technologies:
elists@oreilly.com

For technical questions about book content:
booktech@oreilly.com

To submit new book proposals to our editors:
proposals@oreilly.com

O'Reilly books are available in multiple DRM-free ebook formats. For more information:
oreilly.com/ebooks